WHY JEWS
SHOULD
NOT BE
LIBERALS

WHY JEWS
SHOULD
NOT BE
LIBERALS

Larry F. Sternberg

PELICAN PUBLISHING COMPANY
GRETNA 2006

First published by Pentland Press, Inc., 2001
First paperback edition, revised, published by arrangement with the author by
  Pelican Publishing Company, Inc., 2006

ISBN-13: 9781589803831
Library of Congress Control Number: 00-136680

Printed in the United States of America
Published by Pelican Publishing Company, Inc.
1000 Burmaster Street, Gretna, Louisiana 70053

*To my wife, Ellie, whose support encouraged me
to complete this writing*

Contents

Introduction

Why Jews Should Not Be Liberals was introduced to the public in mid-August 2001. Within one month, the world changed with the horrendous attacks on our nation via the World Trade and Pentagon homicides on 9/11/01. For the first time in our nation's two-hundred-plus-year history, aside from the brief incursion by our British friends in the War of 1812, we Americans experienced some fear that we were vulnerable in our homes from an external menace. This fear led to our president and Congress taking some precipitous actions. The Homeland Security Act passed, we changed our airport people and processes, as a nation we became more alert to potential dangers from enemies located within our borders, and we instituted an aggressive campaign to root out terrorists wherever they might be, culminating in our victorious military campaign to oust the ruthless Taliban group from Afghanistan.

Then beginning in mid-March 2003, we waged a brilliant military strike to remove the hated Saddam Hussein as dictator over the 24 million citizens of Iraq. The first phase of this lightning air and ground attack resulted in the capture of Baghdad in three weeks. What has followed is a more lengthy struggle to rid that nation of the remaining supporters of that vicious dictator, and to find the plans and programs related to Iraq's possession of weapons of mass destruction. It is no easy task to take a country the size of Iraq, living under the tyranny of Hussein for over twenty years, and turn it into a working democracy, but with our allies, notably Great Britain, we shall persevere until the task is completed. The capture of Hussein in December 2003 probably marked the beginning of the end of the terrorist resistance to our liberation of Iraq's people.

As our military casualties mounted during the struggle to free the Iraqi people, many of our citizens, plus those of other nations, began to question the wisdom of our war to depose the Iraqi dictator. It is only natural that we cringe as more of our brave soldiers, sailors, marines, and airmen suffer death and injury. Some people even began to liken our campaign in Iraq to the ill-fated one in Vietnam during the late 1960s and early 1970s. The fact that there is truly no comparison between these two wars, as far as numbers of casualties, opposition to our forces from the native population, and the reasons for our pursuing this war, seems to get lost in the criticisms being reported daily in our media.

Also forgotten most of the time is the fact that we are now engaged in a real war against a real enemy, and that to win that war we must pursue that enemy wherever it resides, and destroy it before it can wreak more damage against us. That enemy, which truly surfaced on 9/11/01, consisting of radical Muslim terrorists, does seek to destroy our way of life. Those countries that harbor and give aid to that enemy must in turn be made to change, by either military or other means. We need to remember that when we were fighting the evil of Communism, we did not hesitate to protect those nations that seemed to be in danger of being overcome by that worldwide menace. There was then no meaningful "anti-anti-Communist" movement here. Gradually more of our citizens will come to recognize that we are today fighting a similar or even, in some ways, a more dangerous enemy.

While the campaign in Iraq slowly progresses, it occurred to me in preparing this second edition that I should ask myself some questions about the theme of this book. Have the events of recent years affected the thinking and general political attitude of American Jews? Has there been any meaningful change in their perception of who are the true friends and enemies of the Jews? Is there any more substance to the argument that modern liberalism no longer reflects the traditions and principles of Judaism? At this point in time, my answers would have to be a mixture of yeses and nos.

If one judges by the rhetoric coming from the leaders of the Democratic party, Nancy Pelosi, Barbara Boxer, Howard Dean, Albert Gore, and their recent presidential candidate, John Kerry, one would have to conclude that if Jews are listening to these folks and are influenced by them, there has been no change. The Democratic party line has been to degrade and disparage the efforts of President Bush to remove Saddam Hussein as a menace to his own people, his neighbors, and eventually our own nation.

The concept of removing a great evil in this world, a belief that should be foremost in the hearts of most Americans, and in particular Jews, is somehow being omitted from the Democrats' analysis of our actions. They seem only to be interested in whether we were bowing to the wishes of the principle-less French and Germans, or the ineffective United Nations, in our drive to defeat our enemies. It should be noted that the one Jew who was a Democratic contender, Sen. Joseph Lieberman, did stay with his Jewish principles of removing evil by consistently supporting President Bush and our war to end Saddam's tyranny.

American Jews appeared to support our war to liberate Iraq in as mild a manner as possible. Slightly more than a majority, according to the polls, were strongly in favor of our initial military action. As the war progressed successfully, there was an upswing in this support, but as events turned murky in the rehabilitation of that country, predictably that support again drifted back to neutral or worse. True, Senator Lieberman remained a stalwart in his support of our president, and other Jewish senators, Boxer and Dianne Feinstein of California, reluctantly came aboard with their temporary support, which in Boxer's case soon faded as our casualties increased. In no way did their actions come close to the strong and unwavering support coming from our Christian allies, Tom DeLay, Gary Bauer, Newt Gingrich, and other prominent Republicans. (As an aside, I continue to hope that Senator Lieberman, an Orthodox Jew, will one day awaken to the fact that based on his religion and some of his policies, he now finds himself in the wrong party and that he would feel much more at home among the Republicans.)

Even though several pundits characterized this war against Iraq as one instigated by the "Jewish neo-conservatives" prominent in the

Republican administration, there seemed to be little recognition of this claim among the Reform and Conservative Jews. Their vision of the relationship between their politics and their Judaism remained cloudy. There were few if any voices among their ranks saying that this was a just war truly in keeping with the traditional Jewish principle of *Tikkun Olam,* repairing the world and ridding it of human evil.

If they were listening to the major networks and CNN and reading the *New York Times* or *Los Angeles Times,* they considered our victory in Iraq and our continuing successes in rooting out terrorism wherever we found it relatively unimportant events, compared to the liberals' main struggles for affirmative action, unlimited abortion, gay rights, gun control, and preserving the Arctic National Wildlife Refuge from drilling for oil. These latter issues were what was really critical to our national survival, according to the liberals, and the war against radical Muslim terrorists, who were our real enemy, was merely an unwanted sideshow.

Here and there were some faint stirrings of Jews who seemed to be getting the message. Democrats talked a good game but, as so well illustrated by President Clinton's eight years, accomplished little. Only when the rough-talking and acting-from-principle George W. Bush took office, and we were struck in our gut with the suicide planes, was action finally taken. Eventually some former left-leaning Jews caught on, as evidenced by an increasing number of particularly younger Jews slowly evolving and claiming they were switching parties. Whether this change will sustain itself through the next round of elections remains to be seen.

The acceptance of our Christian friends as true allies of Israel, and not as rivals competing for the religious affiliation of our children, also seems to be gaining ground. When Gary Bauer, a leading Christian spokesman, was given several standing ovations by the fairly representative Jewish group, the American Israel Public Affairs Committee (AIPAC), this seemed to signal the change that was occurring within at least some Jewish ranks. Monumental changes come slowly, but a beginning is always welcome when it seems to be headed in the right direction.

So where do we go from here? As far as the basic thrust of my book goes, there is little I would change in this new edition. True it is that the hoped-for federal surpluses have not as yet materialized, but my argument as to how those funds should be handled when they come to be remains sound. I could devote more time and space to describing the radical Muslim menace we face, but this subject is being written about with much greater detail and clarity than I could possibly provide. The struggle of Israel to secure its place among the nations of the world continues and again is being reported on daily. There is little I can add to this subject other than to point out that the strongest supporters of Israel in this country remain the Evangelical Christians, and not the politically liberal American Jews.

As to the reaction to the initial edition of my book, certainly the positive comments I have received from such notables as Dr. Milton Friedman, Dr. Laura Schlessinger, Gerardo Joffe, Rabbi Daniel Lapin, David Horowitz, Michael Medved, as well as rank-and-file Jews from all over the nation give me confidence that my message deserves attention from the vast number of American Jews, and non-Jews as well.

I hope that this second edition will generate new interest among the reading public and that the message contained herein will stimulate additional writings on this subject from authors more well known than me. Freedom is not free, and we American Jews must be ever mindful of the blessings we enjoy living in these free and wonderful and God-blessed United States of America.

WHY JEWS
SHOULD
NOT BE
LIBERALS

HOW IT ALL BEGAN . . .
A BRIEF OUTLINE

✡

Although the actual writing of this book began near the end of the twentieth century, and is not being completed until the twenty-first century is upon us, the thoughts it contains have actually been gestating for more than thirty years. Sometime after moving behind the "Orange Curtain" in Orange County, California, and becoming exposed to the then radically conservative views of that area, I became somewhat obsessed with the idea that the Jews of America must become political conservatives, and abandon their long-held politically liberal support. In order to accomplish this` Herculean feat, what was needed was to find politically conservative rabbis with whom I could associate and learn from and perhaps teach what I already had learned about the conservative philosophy. Thus began my quest for such rabbis.

To my great disappointment, I found only one at that time, Rabbi Judah Glasner of Los Angeles, an Orthodox rabbi with a small congregation in southeast Los Angeles, some fifty miles from our home. For several years, my wife and I, and occasionally our two preteen kids, made the pilgrimage on Friday nights to lend our support to the good rabbi, whose Orthodox services were conducted in Hebrew, a language we have never mastered. At that time I would discuss with the rabbi, my goal of converting American Jews to the conservative cause. He was always in full agreement and we tried through various methods to create such an intellectual and spiritual organization to achieve that goal. Alas, after a few years, the needs of supporting a family and pursuing a career, plus the rabbi's fragile health, resulted only in minimal results, and eventually abandoning that worthy cause. Still the desire to enlighten my fellow American Jews continued to beat within my heart. Today, with more leisure time at my disposal, and with perhaps some additional insight, this writing finally sees the light of day.

I approach this effort sporting no great credentials as either a biblical scholar or as one who has achieved great renown in the business and professional world. My professional career began as a certified public accountant back in the late 1950s, after spending three and a half years as a naval officer during the Korean War. Most of my business life was spent working as a financial officer for various small- to medium-size privately owned companies, two of which did succeed in going public during the 1980s. I have been fairly active politically, running for office twice without success on the Republican ticket.

However, I have devoted considerable time to the study of economics and political philosophy, and have evolved over the years from an "Eisenhower Republican" into what I would now describe as a "conservative voluntarist." I define this to mean one who believes that most beneficial results in this world come about through the voluntary actions of people acting in their own enlightened self-interest. On that point there is an interesting quotation from Samuel Gompers, a Jew, and the one who is generally credited to be the founder of the American Federation of Labor and the American union labor movement. Gompers, a cigar maker, said in 1920 at his last AFL convention, "I want to urge devotion to fundamentals of human liberty, the principles of voluntarism. No lasting gain has ever come from compulsion. If we seek to force, we but tear apart that which united, is invincible." Oh, for such leaders— union or management—who would advocate those sentiments today.

After moving to Orange County, California in the early 1960s, I became influenced by the publications of FEE, the Foundation for Economic Education, founded by a great political philosopher, Leonard Read. Since 1946, this organization has brought to the attention of the world the brilliant writings of Ludwig Von Mises, Henry Hazlitt, Frederich Von Hayek, Frederick Bastiat, and other expositors of free market, limited government, and private property principles. I have learned more from reading the various publications of FEE and attending their occasional seminars, than I have from any other source. I am somewhat surprised that many of my conservative friends are still not aware of this wonderful organization.

Thus, I am basically a literary amateur with a fairly solid foundation in free market economics, a rudimentary knowledge of Jewish law and tradition, but endowed with a burning desire to transmit a message to primarily American Jews, that their political and societal goals will best be achieved by abandoning the phony liberal gospel they have been indoctrinated with these past two generations. I also hope this writing will assist our Christian friends to understand why Jews have been so liberal these past two generations, and what it will take for them to change. The message I hope to transmit, using the words and thoughts of people far more learned than I, is that if one believes in his or her own Jewish religion, its traditions and laws, that politically, an American Jew must become a political conservative or libertarian or voluntarist, and not a liberal.

One problem I encountered as I began to write this book is that each day seemed to open new vistas for me to explore in order to render as complete a writing as possible. There is an enormous amount of reference material that could yield me new insights to reinforce my basic theme that American Jews should not be political liberals. From the Talmud to the Torah, to the assorted authors of magazine articles and prestigious books, there are pearls of wisdom and insight to study. Still, if I was ever going to complete this task, I needed to close off somewhere, without having researched much of the relevant material. Thus I plead my case that, for whatever it is worth, the words contained herein represent my best and latest thinking as of the date this book finally surfaces.

Before we get into defining what modern liberals believe and practice, a few words about conservatives and conservatism.

Sometimes people think of conservatives as folks who protest against any change and seek to maintain their own privileged position in life. It is true that conservatism seeks to retain what is best in our society and opposes radical changes made simply for the sake of change. The primary emphasis of conservatism, however, is on the freedom and rights of the individual, along with the duties and responsibilities that accompany those freedoms. As it is often said, the other side of the freedom coin is responsibility. In this country, to preserve those individual rights, American conservatism looks to the American Constitution as the ultimate defender and protector of those rights. From this flows the conservatives' emphasis on limiting the powers of government, because it recognizes that the balance between individual freedom and the powers of government is similar to a seesaw balanced over a fulcrum. When one side goes up, the other side must go down. If individual freedom is to remain up then government power must stay down.

In the early 1970s I became a member of Toastmasters, International and have remained active ever since. Toastmasters is a great organization, founded on principles of voluntary participation, a desire to improve one's communications skills, and a willingness to share ideas with your fellow members. I joined because this was one of the few forums open to me to express my politically conservative views, and where the audience had to sit and listen whether they agreed with me or not. I used to participate in speaking contests. In those days one could actually make a speech with a conservative political theme and sometimes win. In one of those contests that I did win, I wrote a definition of conservatism that still reflects my thinking of today.

I wrote that a conservative is usually a person with a deep faith in God, with a belief that our basic rights of life, liberty, and the pursuit of happiness are endowed by God, and that man cannot abridge these rights. The conservative believes that man is not blessed with all-powerful reasoning, and that solutions to most of our social problems can only be achieved on an individual basis. The conservative believes that man is both good and evil; that the real battle in life is fought between these

4

forces within each one of us. That winning this fight does not depend solely on winning on the materialistic level, but more on the individual spiritual level. Contrary to popular thinking, the conservative actually has more faith in man's capacity to do good than does the liberal, because he relies more upon man's innate sense of charity and his willingness to personally help the underdog. And finally, the conservative knows that the free enterprise system (capitalism) is the only system that gives to man the freedom to make the decisions that enable him to achieve his individual goals.

A more classic definition of conservatism that perhaps strikes closest to its roots is the one that follows by Russell Kirk, frequently described as the father of modern day conservatism. Kirk wrote in his memorable book *The Conservative Mind*, "The 20th Century conservative is concerned, first of all, for the regeneration of spirit and character—with the perennial problem of the inner order of the soul, the restoration of the ethical understanding, and the religious sanction upon which any life worth living is founded. This is conservatism at its highest."

I think it is noteworthy that Kirk's definition, and my own modest one, both stress the spiritual nature of conservatism, which comes so much closer to the Jewish tradition than does anything contained in modern liberal literature. Professor Michael Wyschogrod, a prominent Orthodox intellectual, spoke at a symposium sponsored by the journal *Judaism* in spring, 1964: "Judaism has never been radical in the economic or political sense of that word. It has been a religion of law against anarchy, of reverence for the past and love for its traditions and heritage. It has always had a very realistic appraisal of what lurks in man and the necessity for social and political bounds within which responsible freedom is exercised... It is the radicalism of the last century that has been the aberration in Jewish history."

There are undoubtedly many other definitions of conservatism that have been written, but let us content ourselves with these for the moment. Conservatives, simply put, have faith in the common sense of people to take actions that are in their own best interests and, given the appropriate information and education, they will do the right thing, both for themselves, their families, and their country, without having government force them to dance to the government's tune. We are all responsible for our own actions. We therefore are entitled to enjoy our victories and our pleasures and pay for our own mistakes and misfortunes. This is the essence of life, and government should be there only to serve as the honest referee to maintain and enforce the basic rules of honesty and decent conduct.

Conservatives believe that capitalism, the free market, is the most moral system yet devised for the conduct of daily life and that there can be no morality without responsibility. This is certainly not a new idea. George Washington, who would probably be considered as a conservative by today's definition, in his farewell address to the American people upon completing his second term of office as our first president, said, "Of all the dispositions and habits which lead to political prosperity, religion and morality are indispensable supports."

One of the problems that Jews, who tend to be impatient for immediate results, have with conservatism is that conservatism contains no quick answers to social problems. Conservatism is regarded as being negative because the primary thrust is to reduce government power and to rely on enlightened, self-interested individual action. Jews want to make an impact even when they abandon Jewish traditions, and thus liberals want to use the massive powers of government to try and achieve their goals quickly.

As I strive to relate today's important political issues to what I believe are traditional Jewish beliefs and values, and to emphasize the link between conservatism and Judaism, it is incumbent to describe what I have learned those Jewish beliefs and values are as defined by some Jewish scholars. Shubert Spero in *Morality, Halakha and the Jewish Tradition*, defines Judaism as "the religion, beliefs and practices of the Jewish people in their fully developed and traditional forms as found after the major Halakhic codification of the sixteenth century and before modern attempts of liberalization in the modern period." Spero goes on to state that Morality, with a capital "M," is the essence of Judaism and is a set of rules that prescribe the way people should behave and principles that are good or desirable for men.

There seems to be general agreement that the basic "constitution" of Judaism consists of the Torah, the Talmud, and the writings of the Prophets. Rabbi Daniel Lapin refers to the Bible as the "manufacturer's instruction manual" in his book *America's Real War*. Thus when one seeks to portray himself as a spokesman for the Jewish people to justify a particular position on the current political issues of the day, it makes sense that he or she should refer to those basic sources. I don't see today's Jewish liberals doing this. In fact, seldom if ever is the Bible quoted as a reference for a particular liberal position. They would be hard-pressed to find one to justify their recent endorsement of same sex marriage! The only Jewish group that seems to be consistently politically conservative in their writings is the Orthodox minority. As Seymour Martin Lipset and Earl Raab note in their 1994 book, *Jews And The New American Scene*, it is the Orthodox journalists that have "emphasized the complementarity of conservatism in religious matters and in politics."

Professor Seymour Siegel, writing in an article back in the late 1960s titled "Jewish Social Ethics—Liberal Or Conservative," compared Judaism and the conservative philosophy. Dr. Siegel identified Judaism as including: suspicion of centralization of power; high valuation of law, tradition, and restraint; reluctance to support abrupt alterations of social fabric; a realistic appraisal of human nature and its limitations; and necessity for restraint and discipline. Dr. Siegel concluded that Judaism with its attachment to the unchanging law of God, which towers over collectivism and totalitarianism, is a profoundly conservative tradition. It is generally agreed that the core values of Judaism are education, morality, and tradition, and it is these values that I believe American Jews should relate to in determining their political positions.

One of my goals in writing this book is to stimulate further discussion and writings on this subject. I certainly don't pretend to be the final authority on behalf of Judaism. But I hope that the leaders of Jewish life in America—the rabbis, the heads of the major Jewish institutions, Jews who are prominent in the media and the arts, and all politically active Jewish liberals—will begin to question whether they are being true to their faith when they make their political pronouncements on the issues of the day.

Now as to my caveats, this writing is not intended to define who is a Jew, or to reconcile the various Reform, Conservative, Reconstructionist, and Orthodox segments of today's American Judaism. Professor Ernest van den Haag, writing in his 1969 book, *The Jewish Mystique*, asks the question as to what makes a Jew? He answers that perhaps more than anything else, it is a man's feeling that, like it or not, he is Jewish and that is what makes him a Jew. If you are a Jew, you should know it; if you choose to ignore your heritage and birthright, you do so at your own peril. My hope is that Jews of all denominations will eventually work together for their common goals. I do believe, however, that the basic and unalterable principles of what it is to be a Jew are accepted by all of the various segments of Judaism. These are detailed in a later chapter.

This book is also not intended to be an all-encompassing history of Judaism in America, or to describe in detail the various immigration waves of Jews into America. There is an enormous library full of this detail. I refer to this movement at times only to help explain how we got ourselves into the political pickle we are in today.

Finally, as mentioned above, this writing cannot be an all-encompassing report and reference to the many various writers who have written in far more detail and knowledge about one or more of the subjects herein. In this respect I am merely a transmitter of some of their more relevant comments on the main subject matter of this book. On this concept of transmission, I am indebted to Herman Wouk's latest book, *The Will to Live On*, published in 2000, for his quotation from Confucius: "I am not an originator but a transmitter."

My main purpose is to present in one writing an analysis, an explanation, an argument, as to why the vast majority of American Jews have been for the past sixty-five years predominantly in favor of the liberal, Democratic Party and its policies, and why that stance is almost 100% contrary to Jewish law and tradition as I understand it. Perhaps most importantly, I hope to explain why it is finally time for American Jews to reverse their political stance, and why that reversal is so critical to the future of this country, and perhaps to the future of Judaism in America. I want this writing to be one that any Jew, regardless of his or her political persuasion, can pick up, read or scan, and then wonder if perhaps we American Jews have been following a false political philosophy as espoused by "unenlightened" Jewish leaders for lo, these many years. After all, our history is replete with episodes of following leaders who in the end proved to be false messiahs.

As we briefly defined conservatism, it is now appropriate to define what I mean as Democrat or liberal politics in today's atmosphere. The definition of a liberal has changed through the years. For much of the nineteenth and early twentieth centuries, it meant one who sought liberation from the tyranny of the czar or the rulers of a country. As late as the 1960s, Random House Dictionary defined a liberal as "one who is open-minded, tolerant, free from prejudice, generous, charitable, and advocating maximum individual freedom for all, as guaranteed by government." This definition is closest to what we now understand was that of a "classical liberal," but certainly does not define today's modern liberals.

Since then, definitions have changed. For at least these past two generations, to be a Democrat liberal means that you have great confidence in the powers of government, preferably at the federal level, to solve all of our social, economic, and at times personal problems. To put it in identifiable terms, we all know that Teddy Kennedy is a liberal. Whenever he takes a position on an issue, we can be confident it will be to support some form of government action or coercion to achieve his goals. In other words, he typifies the liberal position. Sometimes liberalism can also be compared to what the Supreme Court once said about pornography. There may not be a precise definition of same, but we all know it when we see it. Irving Kristol in *Two Cheers for Capitalism* wrote, "A liberal is one who says that it's all right for an 18-year old girl to perform in a pornographic movie as long as she gets paid the minimum wage."

We know that liberals believe people are all basically good, that if they do bad things, it is only because they were either abused as children, or that society has given them a bad break, and that some government grant of money or preference will solve their problems. People are really not accountable for their actions, say the liberals, there must be some outside force that creates the great disparity in income and achievement. Therefore we must mold and shape society to remedy the ills that have befallen all of those unfortunates that have not yet achieved the proper standard of living in these prosperous United States of America.

Liberals also believe that those of us who have achieved some success in our lives must then be called upon to sacrifice to aid those who have achieved less. And if we will not act according to their wishes, well then to use government power to force those actions is the only remaining course to take. Senator Daniel Patrick Moynihan of New York, a Democrat, wrote on 14 May 1969 in the *New York Post*, "Somehow liberals have been unable to acquire from birth what conservatives seem to be endowed with at birth; namely, a healthy skepticism of the powers of government to do good."

Judge Robert Bork makes the point in *Slouching Towards Gomorrah*, published in 1996, that modern liberalism stresses equality of outcomes rather than opportunities, otherwise known as radical egalitarianism. In order to achieve that goal, some have to be punished or held back, and some have to be pushed along. There's not much freedom there. Along with that principle, and somewhat in contradiction to it, is the evil twin of radical reduction of limits to personal gratification, or unlimited freedom, or if it feels good, just do it. Judge Bork goes on to write that these radical politics have become a substitute for religion to the detriment of our society.

Liberals either do not know what our Constitution says about limiting the powers granted to the federal government, or they simply choose to ignore what it says. Any and all problems are fair game for liberals to try and solve with new laws. Behind most of their philosophy lies the dirty little secret. Liberals believe they are smarter and wiser than most, that the average American citizen does not possess the brains or ability to make necessary decisions about his money or his life, and therefore, it is an absolute requirement for liberals to pass laws and implement them in such a way that citizens will receive what liberals know they should receive.

At the core of today's liberal philosophy is the concept that naked force should be used to accomplish whatever they believe to be in the best interests of those they seek to help. I cannot think of one liberal-sponsored program that seeks to reduce the coercive powers of government. Force is what is required to make people act (in their own best interests, of course). Whether it is higher taxes, or tighter regulations, or restrictions on how one can use one's property, liberals cannot resort to pure persuasion to win their arguments. No, the force of government must be used, regardless of whether that force is sanctioned by our Constitution. It is pure arrogance that drives liberals. Justice Louis Brandeis, our first Jewish Supreme Court justice wrote in 1928, "The greatest dangers to liberty lurk in insidious encroachment by men of zeal, well-meaning but without understanding."

There now has arisen what many people consider to be an additional defining characteristic of today's liberal philosophy. This is the concerted drive to remove God, or any mention of God, or exposure to any of God's commandments, from our daily lives. Whether it is to prevent the display of the Ten Commandments in public places, or the denial of a sports team to pray openly for their success, or to deny parents the option of sending their children to religious schools using some type of tax credit, or to prevent the teaching of creation in the public schools, or any one of another of many "anti-God" positions, liberals seem intent on completely secularizing our society.

Of course, there are still some leaders from the religious left that pass the liberal litmus test. Jesse Jackson, the National Council of Churches, and Al Sharpton are among the privileged folks who are permitted to use the holy name on behalf of liberal causes. Other than these chosen few, liberals seem to pronounce a plague on all others. Another notable exception has been Senator Lieberman, the Democrat VP nominee of the 2000 election, who frequently invoked God's name in blessing him with the VP spot. I'm sure that if liberals thought they could get the support from the American public to remove "under God" from the Pledge of Allegiance, they would. Obviously I have not given liberals enough credit for their perseverance on a subject, as witness the recent court challenge to the "under God" statement in the Pledge. It will be interesting to see if the Supreme Court, led by four liberals, will continue on its path to remove God from our daily lives. It might be more difficult to revise some of our cherished documents including the Declaration of Independence, Constitution, Lincoln's Gettysburg Address, the *Star Spangled Banner*, all of which contain references to God. To quote Judge Bork again, "Modern liberalism is hostile to religious conservatism of any denomination."

To sum up the main difference between today's liberals and conservatives, I will quote the pithy words of my own dear wife, Ellie. She defines a liberal as one who wants to do good with someone else's money; and a conservative as one who prefers that you do good with your own hard-earned money.

If one wishes to read no further, perhaps the essence of this writing for American Jews is this. If we want to help the poor and unfortunate, if we want to bring more justice and mercy into the world, if we truly want to brighten the lives of the millions that we do not know personally, then the way to do it is not the way of socialism, or modern-day liberalism. This Robin Hood variety philosophy is to take from the "rich" and give to the "poor." And if the civil rights of the "givers" are trampled in the process, and if the "takers" come to expect this largess as their rightful inheritance, so what? The end justifies the means, doesn't it? The problem is that this system simply does not work, never has, never will, and cannot achieve its stated purposes. Most importantly, it goes contrary to one of Judaism's basic tenets, that of justice, which means equal application of the laws without respect of persons. "Justice, justice, thou shalt follow that thou mayest live, and inherit the land which the Lord thy God giveth thee." (Deuteronomy 16:20)

Recent history in all of those nations who have practiced communism, socialism, or any other similar "-ism" validates this statement. All over the world, countries are abandoning their previous systems of controlled economy and are opting for some form of free market capitalism. Only in America, and particularly on the campuses of our leading universities, is the cause of socialism and communism still preached with authority and respect. The result is the continuing struggle between the forces of freedom and those who believe, in their infinite wisdom, that they hold all the answers to society's problems.

Thomas Jefferson wrote that there are two kinds of people. One type believes in the good judgment of people to make their own decisions. These decisions may not always be the wisest, but at least they will be good and honest decisions. The other is the kind that does not trust people to make their own decisions, but wants power centralized in Washington, so that those "enlightened" representatives can make the decisions that affect peoples' lives. Jefferson wrote this two hundred years ago. Yet his wisdom was recently verified by no less than President William Jefferson Clinton, who, when defending one of his proposals, was quoted as saying that he was against returning part of the budget surplus to the people, "because they would not make the right decisions as to how they spend those refunds." Is there anything that so demonstrates what Jefferson wrote? Liberals have that arrogance today and American Jews, knowingly or not, follow along and seem to accept that same belief.

But the Jewish tradition is to help people to help themselves; to train men and women to earn a living on their own instead of being on the public dole; to think for themselves; and to make their own decisions in life. All of history reveals that the only valid and lasting system for uplifting peoples' lives is the free market system, or as it is popularly known, capitalism. Whatever we can do to strengthen this blessed free market system, to make it easier for men and women to go into business for their own selfish purposes, and thus provide jobs for others, that is the theme that we American Jews should be advocating.

Is it not somewhat ironic that the answer Jews seek for *Tikkun Olam*, repairing the world, at least as it relates to the economics involved, may be summarized in one sentence? STRENGTHEN **AND** EXPAND THE FREE MARKET SYSTEM, GIVE IT **SUFFICIENT** TIME, WITH THE APPROPRIATE RULES AND GUIDELINES, ENLIST THE GOVERNMENT AS THE REFEREE TO ENFORCE THOSE RULES, AND WONDERFUL RESULTS **HAPPEN**. This is not a hope, or a promise, or a projection. This is real! The greatest example is our own United States of America. In just over two hundred years as a nation, this free market system has galvanized this nation into becoming the greatest economic power the world has ever known. We are the envy of the entire world. We have to spend billions, erect strong fences, and use our border patrols and armed forces, to keep others from coming here because the promise of freedom of opportunity is a beacon to the world. America, with all of its warts and inequities, remains the lodestar for the world's oppressed peoples.

Yet I hold out no real hope that American Jews are going to quickly shed their liberal philosophies, as they are currently understood. The primary reasons for the ongoing Jewish liberal doctrine is the belief that only by being liberal can one sympathize with and help the underdog, spread the wealth, and do good for as many people as can be reached.

A secondary reason is a lingering distrust of Republicans and conservatives as being anti-Semitic, a notion that is easily disproved today. One would hope that Jews would use their common sense to abandon those views. Professor van den Haag addresses this point, "Although well endowed with it, Jews are no more dominated by their intelligence than other people; they often use it to rationalize their emotions." It seems the late professor has correctly identified the power of emotion in controlling Jewish political beliefs. In spite of the dismal record of the Democrats in promoting their New Deal, Fair Deal, and Great Society programs, too many American Jews still view the Democratic Party as the one that is closest to fulfilling *Tikkun Olam*, repairing the world.

This doctrine is so emotionally ingrained within American Jews that change will be difficult. I do not propose that we Jews change our goals. Instead, what I hope to demonstrate is that the best way politically to accomplish these worthy goals is to change political affiliation from liberal Democrat to either conservative Republican or even Libertarian. Nationally syndicated talk-show host Larry Elder, who happens to be a conservative black American, describes himself as a "Republictarian." If there were such a group, this might be the most accurate designation for conservative Jews to choose. For now, though, we will have to work within the existing political parties.

JUDAISM AND CONSERVATISM

As I prepared the additional chapters and notes for this second edition of *Why Jews Should Not Be Liberals,* I gave some thought to perhaps changing the title to *Why Jews Should Be Political Conservatives!* An argument can be made that this title is more on the positive side and may not alienate those potential readers who instinctively recoil when their liberalism is challenged. Certainly the other side of the position that Jews should not be liberals is that they should "convert" to becoming conservatives, libertarians, or, to use the term I learned from Larry Elder, nationally syndicated talk-show host, "Republictarians."

However, when I reviewed the main theme of my book, that liberalism is a philosophy that is antithetical to Judaism, I realized it was not necessary to change the title. I thus decided not to. I still believed, though, that some additional writing was required to show the close relationship between being a Jew and being a political conservative. Therein lies the reason for this added chapter.

In order to show the unity between Judaism and conservatism, let us begin by listing the basics of what it is to be a Jew, as detailed by Rabbi Wayne Dosick in his book *Living Judaism: The Complete Guide to Jewish Belief, Tradition, and Practice.* There are undoubtedly other definitions that could be used, but Rabbi Dosick's summary seems to be the most appropriate one to compare with what I believe are the basic tenets of political conservatism.

As Rabbi Dosick describes, the basic beliefs of a Jew are:

1. Belief in the One and only One God.
2. Each person is given free will.

3. Each person follows or disobeys God's Commandments through personal choice.
4. Each person is responsible for his or her own actions, and there are consequences for moral or immoral behavior.
5. Ethical law comes from God, who is both Author and Authority.

Now follows the linkage between these basic concepts of Judaism and the principles of today's political conservatism.

Belief in the One and only One God. Conservatism is also based on a belief in a higher power, which is critical in denying that role to the state. As our founders wrote in the Declaration of Independence, all men are "endowed by their Creator with certain unalienable Rights . . . and that to secure these rights, Governments are instituted among Men." In that declaration, our founders proclaimed that the state, or government, does not have first hold on the minds and consciences of the people, but rather that our Creator (God) is preeminent. Today's conservatives are fighting on several fronts to retain the fundamental truths listed in the declaration, in the face of the assault on those principles from liberal judges and their supporters.

This same concept is so basic to Judaism, it is doubtful that there can be any differences even among the various shades of modern Judaism. As to conservative thinking, it is fundamental to this philosophy that there is a Supreme Being of some type, and that no matter what it is called, it does reign supreme in our lives. Yes, there are conservatives who claim to be atheists. I have a long-time friend who considers himself one. But that same friend, in times of trouble and sadness, does ask for the sympathy and blessings of some higher power and certainly does not plead for the blessings of the state.

In contrast, one of the real tragedies of modern liberalism is the liberals' apparent campaign to remove the devotion and allegiance that most Americans have to their own higher power. The entire drive to eliminate any reference to God in the schools, the athletic fields, and even the Pledge of Allegiance may become the final nail in the coffin of liberalism. Most Americans, as distinguished from today's Europeans, are still God-fearing or, as I like to say, God-blessing people. The attempt to remove God from their lives is having a negative effect and will continue to influence the votes and sympathies of many Americans for years to come.

However, American Jews remain reluctant to recognize that this "remove God" drive is another example that liberalism is no longer closely linked to Judaism, while conservatism is. If we Jews do nothing else but think deeply on this link between Judaism, belief in the One Supreme God, and which political philosophy most closely supports that belief, there would be meaningful changes in the political thinking of American Jews.

Each person is given free will. This stresses that we are not born slaves of some dominant state, but each of us is given free will by our Creator. That free will, which is inbred, may be used to live a good life or a mostly negative one. This also means that we are all born with certain natural abilities, and what we accomplish is due more to our individual exertions than some preordained conclusion. Modern liberals frequently focus on the poor among us, whom they assume will always stay poor. However, the record shows that, in this country, over 80% of the poor eventually climb the ladder to a fair state of prosperity. This is strong evidence that, with hard work and a little luck, we are all capable of determining our own fates in life.

Neither Judaism nor conservatism presumes that there is, or should be, some governmental power that determines what one's fate will be or what type of life each of us should live. If we are not given the power to make our own choices in life, then there cannot be the triumphs or failures that provide the real "highs and lows" of our lives. Without those individual swings, our lives would be much less interesting and worthwhile.

So many Americans have overcome the adversities of poverty and and risen to prominence and success in their chosen fields that one would think no further proof is needed to verify this point. Recent attempts by liberals to revive the discredited class-warfare theme are falling flat. In contrast, conservatives stress what can be accomplished through one's individual efforts, which is also an enduring principle of Judaism.

Each person follows or disobeys God's Commandments through personal choice. This rule builds on the one above. Judaism and conservatism both believe that each of us is free to choose the "high road" or any other road. We are not controlled by some outside force, although many of us will have tougher and higher obstacles to overcome in order to attain our desired goals. The notion that we must await some magical law or sweeping manifesto to overcome the barriers to achieving our goals is alien to Judaism and conservatism. Both philosophies stress that we, individually, have been given the power and the ability to choose to either follow some or all of God's Commandments or to ignore any or all of them.

Judaism believes that God gave us a good and sensible road map to follow in order to live a decent life. Most visible in that road map are the Ten Commandments. The relationship of conservatives to those basic Commandments is evident, in the emphasis they place on dealing honestly with your fellows and not stealing (as in cheating), murdering, or bearing false witness. These are all necessary components of our free-market economy, which conservatives champion. Conservatives do not believe that it is morally permissible to do whatever it takes to close a deal, if those actions are contrary to the basic Commandments.

The fundamental premise of conservatism is to limit the powers of government to the absolute minimum, thus leaving to our citizens the maximum amount of personal freedom to pursue their own goals in life. What must follow then is that each person has the freedom to choose which path to follow. The choice is his and no one should have the power to restrict the choices available to him. Just as *freedom* is the highest value prized by Jews, *freedom* was the guiding principle of our founders. Since conservatism looks to the Declaration of Independence and the Constitution for its foundation, it follows that the freedom so highly valued by Jews in their bible is the same freedom that forms the foundation of conservatism.

President Bush, in his January 2005 inaugural address, spoke eloquently in several passages about freedom: "There is only one force of history that can break the reign of hatred and resentment, and expose the pretensions of tyrants, and reward the hopes of the decent and tolerant and that is the force of human freedom. . . . The best hope for peace in our world is the expansion of freedom in all the world. . . . America's vital interests and our deepest beliefs are now one. From the day of our founding, we have proclaimed that every man and woman on this earth has rights and dignity and matchless value because they bear the image of the maker of heaven and Earth. . . . Advancing these ideals is the mission that created our nation." Thus our president, although not considered to be an uncompromising conservative, still exalts the value of *freedom,* which is at the heart of what modern conservatism and Judaism each espouse.

Each person is responsible for his or her own actions, and there are consequences for moral or immoral behavior. This principle perhaps marks the deepest difference between conservatism and modern liberalism. The tragedy of liberalism is that, somewhere along the way, its thinkers and leaders strayed from this basic concept and slipped into the false doctrine that we are not responsible for our own actions.

Modern liberalism preaches that if life is difficult, or if one is unhappy or engaged in criminal behavior, then somehow it is the fault of society, which must be reformed in order to balance out the negative results. No longer is the individual to be held accountable for his illegal or immoral or just bad behavior. This refusal by liberalism to hold the individual responsible for his actions is so contrary to Judaism and to conservatism that the difference stands out with blinding illumination.

Throughout the Torah and the Talmud, Judaism stresses the fact that each of us is responsible for our own actions, that we are to live moral and decent lives, and that we have been given the guidelines and rules for living a good life. Conservatism, with its emphasis on adhering to the rules as set down by our founders in the Declaration of Independence and Constitution, is consistent with Judaism by proclaiming that the freedom given to us will hopefully be used in a positive manner to bring about a better life for all. At the same time, if the wrong choices are made, both Judaism and conservatism are not reluctant to use the force of government to punish those who break the law and who bring harm to their fellow citizens.

The bottom line with both Judaism and conservatism is that eventually we reap what we sow. When we Jews stray and pursue false idols like money, power, status, or self, as Norman Podhoretz wrote in his exhaustive book *The Prophets: Who They Were, What They Are,* we are degrading what should be our overriding faith in the One and Holy God. If we make the right choices, we can live lives that are both pleasant and worthwhile, and in most cases the outcome is dependent upon our trust, faith, and reliance on some higher power.

Ethical law comes from God, who is both Author and Authority. This statement forms the heart of Judaism. Our religion stresses that the laws by which we should live come from God. It is our eternal struggle to live by those rules. Every time we have ignored them, it has led to our dispersal and unhappiness. Conservatism is also based on God's rules. In order to have a functioning government and an economy that works for the benefit of all, certain rules must be followed. The Commandments that thou shall not steal (or cheat), or bear false witness (lie), or murder, or worship false gods are at the heart of our free-market system, which is one of the building blocks of conservatism.

Conservatism places substantial importance on the spiritual side of man, that he will do what is right, because the entire system of free enterprise is based upon people living up to their word in their business dealings. Learned economists have cited the Commandment of "thou shall not steal" as perhaps the most important rule that has led to our successful system of free markets and free enterprise.

Liberals' current actions to blur the distinction between right and wrong, moral and immoral, and to encourage relativism in our thinking only trivialize the doctrine that there is a set of Eternal Laws, given to us by God, which we are to follow. We need to remember that, as Jews, we are directed to follow God's laws as best as we can and that it is foolhardy for us to adopt a political philosophy that is alien to that thinking.

The 2004 election seemed to bring into clearer focus that the majority of American voters are also rethinking the importance of morality and traditional values. Is it possible that the trend of recent years towards an increase in immorality, as displayed on our screens and television sets, may now be ripe for a reversal? Can it be that our major religions will once again become aflame with righteousness? When the Frenchman Alexis de Tocqueville visited this country in the 1830s, he wrote that it was only when he visited the churches of America and found them aflame with preaching justice and morality that he discovered the principle thrusting this nation onto the path of greatness. He wrote that America is great because America is good. When it ceases to be good, it will cease to be great. History does at times repeat itself. Hopefully American Jews will be a leading force in bringing about that revival.

So there we have it: Judaism and conservatism, twins in philosophy and, anticipating the future, twins in political thinking and action.

WHY AMERICAN JEWS
ARE STILL LIBERALS

There is no group, other than black Americans, that has so consistently voted Democrat in both local and national elections these past two generations as have American Jews. In the most recent presidential election of 2000, 79-80% of voting Jews voted for Democrat, Al Gore. This voting is in contrast to every other segment of America that eventually attains success in the financial and social worlds. All of the other segments, whatever their national origin, culture, color, or occupation, at least divide their voting in reasonable percentages. Not so the Jews. In the 1998 Congressional elections, it is estimated that 80-85% of voting Jews voted Democrat, and this was in the face of a soon to be impeached Democrat president. American Jews voted for FDR in the 1930s-40s, in the 80-90% range, and although this percentage has varied through the years, declining to perhaps 60% Democrat during the Reagan years, the graph again shows an upward trend.

The question is why? What is there about liberal Democratic policies that so attract Jews in America? What is it about the past sixty-five years that has so influenced American Jews politically to make them vote as almost a monolithic block? Throughout their history it appears that Jews and Judaism have never presented a united front. There have always been conflicts and differences of opinion. Witness today's Israel. Why cannot Jews here at least split their vote fifty-fifty, similar to the current division in Israel between the parties aligned to Likud and those aligned to Labor?

Why is it important to the future of this nation that Jews change their political bias? Why is it perhaps important to the future of Judaism in America for this political change to occur? Hopefully answers to these questions will emerge from the following pages.

Finally, how can this change be brought about? I have no illusions that this change will come quickly, but I believe a start must be made somewhere, and I am hopeful this writing will contribute to that beginning.

If one were to list the principle reasons for this liberal political attitude of American Jews, it might include the following (I am indebted to Nathaniel Weyl's *The Jew In American Politics* for several of these points), which will be discussed in greater detail in the pages to follow.

1. Jews in America, having attained a superior financial status on the average, feel some guilt for their prosperous state. To assuage that guilty feeling, it becomes natural for them to support any policy that "helps the poor and less fortunate."

2. Jews in America are still fearful of latent anti-Semitism, as represented in their minds by the Religious Right. Since this group appears to be predominantly conservative politically, they must be opposed.

3. Jews in America, becoming more secular and distant from their Orthodox origins, have substituted government assistance for their Jewish charitable institutions.

4. Jews in America desire to be thought of as not that different from their Christian fellow Americans, and thus are easy prey for all of those "feel good" programs which promise to solve the nation's problems.

5. Jews in America are concerned that if they express too independent a thought, such as school choice or welfare elimination, they will be categorized with those who are "hard hearted," a category Jews abhor.

6. Jews in America, in spite of their extensive scholarship and academic achievements, still do not really understand the workings of the free market or the miraculous results this free market has accomplished in this country.

7. Jews in America still believe that government contains certain miraculous powers, which if used correctly can bring about the nirvana right here at home. As Rabbi Daniel Lapin wrote recently in his book, *America's Real War*, there is something within the Jewish make-up that demands action to bring about desired results. Since the liberals believe that only by using the force of government can these results be swiftly achieved, Jews flock to this philosophy, while ignoring the results that invariably are the opposite of those that were intended.

8. Jews in America, although somewhat of an elite group, are still fearful of standing out too much from the crowd. Thus they ignore their Jewish belief of individual freedom, and what their thousands of years struggle has been about. This was not always the case. Prior to the FDR regime, American Jews were fairly evenly divided between the Republican and Democratic parties. It has only been since FDR that Jews have gravitated en-masse to the Democratic Party.

9. Jews in America have continued to select leaders of the major Jewish organizations who are confirmed liberals. These leaders present this liberal image to the country at large as the natural Jewish position with the corresponding following by the rank and file, with no real Jewish opposition other than a few Jewish public figures. The fact that today's liberals resemble the socialists of past days somehow escapes their thinking. Unfortunately the majority of the rabbis, Reform and Conservative, tend to support those leaders. Only the Orthodox rabbis, a much smaller number, hold out for traditional Jewish values.

10. Jews in America simply don't recognize who their true friends are, continue to be emotional about their politics to the detriment of not using their intellectual analysis, and thus remain political sheep to their liberal sheepdogs.

11. Finally, Jews in America conveniently ignore the history of their people, which has been an everlasting search and struggle for individual freedom. Throughout their history, Jews have sought only to be left alone to live their lives as they chose and to worship as they believed. For thousands of years, they were denied this freedom, wandering from land to land until by the grace of God they landed in this free land of America. Jews must always guard this freedom from the oppression of government with all the strength they possess. As secular liberalism, with its corresponding growth of government, has attained more power in America, for no other reason Jews should reject today's liberal philosophy and gravitate to the conservative or libertarian principles.

This last point, perhaps more important than any other, is the one that appears to be most overlooked as to why Jews in America should be violently opposed to any political party which advocates increased powers to government. That is because the age-old struggle by Jews worldwide has been to live their lives in freedom, without control by a government, no matter what form it took. Since the days of Abraham, who took his flocks and his families to find a land of freedom, Jews have only wanted to be left alone to live and worship as they chose. Only in America, for over three hundred years, have Jews been accepted as full citizens with all the rights and freedoms as possessed by other citizens. Only in America have Jews been able to make their way without any government sponsored controls or discrimination. Therefore, Jews must be almost paranoid in their opposition to any meaningful increase in government powers. It has been largely the Democratic Party that has expanded the powers of the federal government, beginning mainly with the administration of Franklin Delano Roosevelt in 1933. (It is somewhat ironic that FDR's original campaign platform promised to reduce federal spending by 25%. He soon abandoned this after winning the election.)

Because Jews have lived better here than anywhere else, and because the growth of government power has slowly but surely grown these past two generations, it is difficult to readily grasp how our freedoms have been eroded, but eroded they have been. When 40% of our income is now usurped by government, when we can no longer use our properties as we choose, when reference books containing regulations grow to consume our libraries, as we slowly sink beneath the morass of ever expanding we-know-what-is-good-for-you legislation, we must now realize what has happened to us and who is doing it to us.

As Jews, we of all people should and must rally against this growth of government control, and now finally, we Jews must change our attitudes and politics. The point is seldom if ever made by our Jewish leaders that every new law passed with its accompanying bureaucratic regulations, results in a diminution of our individual freedom to act as we choose. The taxes we pay, the multitude of rules and regulations that govern our everyday lives, all of this impinges upon our freedom to act, and this freedom is perhaps the most precious value that we must preserve for ourselves and our future generations.

There is one additional thought on the importance to this country of Jews changing their political leanings. If we Jews, the so-called "chosen people," destined to lead the world to the one God, and to bring ethical monotheism to all, are to fulfill that God-given duty, then certainly when it comes to leading the United States back to its moral and spiritual roots, we must take that lead. If one accepts the fact that this is a God-blessed country, which I do, and that we have been given the opportunity to create a just and righteous society here, then we Jews should be leading the charge. Instead, we seem to be followers of the politically correct philosophy of the day, which has been liberal for the past two generations, and has accompanied or perhaps been responsible for our steadily decreasing state of morality. It is now time to assume our rightful place in adhering to our own traditions and laws as they interact with modern politics.

There is another reason for the need of a political turnaround for American Jews. In his most recent book, *The Will to Live On*, Herman Wouk poses the question, "What is it going to take for American Jewry to return more to the roots of our religion and for Jews to become more observant?" He cites the current distribution of American Jews as being overwhelmingly Reform and Conservative, with only 8% Orthodox. Is it to be only the remnant, the Orthodox, who will carry on the basics of Judaism in America, he asks? Wouk's hope, as I read it, is that through a resurgence of Jewish education, a revival of learning among Jewish organizational leadership of Jewish history, plus an acknowledgment of our inherited ethical identity, American Jewry will somehow sustain itself amidst the strain of assimilation. He seems to acknowledge that it is unlikely that the modern American Jew will take up the study of Torah and Talmud on a regular basis, but he still hopes for this.

My hope is that perhaps in some minuscule way, this writing can help bring about that religious change. By recognizing and becoming convinced of the link between Judaism and political conservatism, there might also occur a renewed enthusiasm for learning more about our Jewish history and traditions, which can eventually lead more of us to wanting to live our lives as observant Jews. If this political change should happen, it would then follow that more Jews will abandon the secular liberal philosophy that has served as such a poor substitute for our own rich Jewish religion. Jews will simply have to recognize that the liberal politics many of them have followed these past two generations are not in our Jewish tradition and may have led to increased assimilation. During the 1999 impeachment trial of President Clinton, I searched vainly for any Jewish political leader to condemn the immoral behavior of this man who was entrusted with representing the highest office in the land. There were several Jewish Democrats who were members of the House of Representatives committee exploring the impeachment question. All of them refused to vote for impeachment or even condemn the president's conduct. A half-hearted condemnation came from Senator

Joseph Lieberman of Connecticut, an Orthodox Jew, in a speech on the Senate floor. But the good senator then seemed to clam up on the subject, and in the end voted to acquit Clinton of his perjury and obstruction of justice. That seemed to be the closest any Jewish leader came to speaking out. Apparently political power was so important that Jewish principles of morality took a back seat. Where was the outrage? Where was the Jewish "spin" on this behavior? What would have been the reaction of these Jews if the perpetrator had been a Republican?

"Morality is the essence of Judaism," writes Shubert Spero. It is the set of rules that prescribe the way people should behave, and these rules apply to the conduct of all human beings. There is no distinction made for rich or poor, or Democrats or Republicans. Morality applies to all humans. It is this blindness of our Jewish leaders to the defects and flaws of the leaders of the Democratic Party that is so disappointing. There is also a noticeable lack by these leaders of attempting to relate modern liberalism to any part of Jewish law and tradition. Perhaps this writing will challenge them to do that. It is this vacuum of moral concern which illustrates the dilemma we face in changing the politics of American Jews.

WEALTH, GUILT, AND ITS POLITICAL EFFECTS

✡

A 1995 listing in *Forbes* of the 112 billionaires in America showed that eighteen, 16% of the total, were Jewish (versus an overall 3% of the total population). Most could be considered big givers to Jewish causes. Undoubtedly all of them gave heavily to various charitable causes, but it was interesting that there were several that did not regard Jewish causes as high priorities. We cannot guess what is in the minds of these financial heavyweights, but it appears that being a Jew in America, and having achieved such financial heights, does not automatically turn one into a great supporter of Jewish causes or of Judaism itself. Elliott Abrams writes in his 1997 book, *Faith or Fear*, that giving by philanthropic Jews to Jewish causes has declined from 70% to just 28% of their total giving.

The fact that Jews are so over-weighted in the billionaire category, with five times more representation than the population as a whole, has what relevance as we seek to determine the place guilt plays in today's Jewish liberalism? Perhaps none, except that we do not see these Jewish billionaires, or any other billionaires, pledging the bulk of their fortunes to eliminating poverty in this land. Yet many of those folks are liberals. They happily support a multitude of liberal programs, and if they don't work, so what? At least their hearts are in the right place.

Perhaps this has something to do with that latent feeling of guilt, of having achieved wealth, either due to being Jewish, with its heritage of shrewdness in business and intellectual prowess, or just being lucky, while at the same time seeing so much relative poverty here. After all, these past two generations have had the benefit of the progress their parents and grandparents made after coming mostly penniless to America.

Although it may have been tough in the beginning, we have been blessed with the remarkable growth of the American economy since the Great Depression, plus the freedom to create business opportunities for ourselves with relatively little government interference. And so as Jews have increased their material wealth enormously these past sixty-five years, we may still feel that tinge of guilt for having so much compared to others around us. We question if we truly deserve our current wealth, status, and position. This questioning may influence our thinking and turn us to supporting any and all programs designed to help the poor and less fortunate.

Another reason for this feeling of guilt may stem from the notion that we as American Jews are not doing all we should be doing to help Israel remain a free and independent country. Sure we give a lot of money, and sure, some of us actually visit Israel from time to time, and sure a few of us actually go to live there, but there remains a feeling that the Jews in Israel are really fighting our battle against discrimination. Most American Jews do not want to give up their fairly prosperous life here in exchange for a tougher existence over there. So perhaps as a balance to this feeling, we comfort ourselves with the thought that we are helping the poor and downtrodden here in our adopted country with our massive government programs, and that helps to pay our dues.

In America, Jews have been accepted as citizens and as political equals from the very beginning of this nation. As Paul Johnson writes in his *History of the Jews*, it almost came to pass that Hebrew became the accepted language in the new America. The Old Testament was as avidly read by our founders as the New Testament. Thus sheltered by this feeling of "belonging" which had been such a rare feeling throughout our historical wanderings, Jews have truly prospered here in America as nowhere else.

Yet, the feeling persists: Are we doing everything we should be doing to bring about that status of well-being to all around us? *Tikkun Olam*, to repair the world, and make it right for everyone, is still one of our guiding principles. How can we use our wealth and our privileged status to bring this condition into reality?

Certainly we cannot do it alone. As the report on the Jewish billionaires shows, even they cannot make that much of a dent in problems of poverty. So where do we look for possible solutions? What power is there that has the capacity to move mountains, to achieve miracles quickly, to marshal the resources of an entire people to achieve their desired aims? As the liberals preach, it is Government with a capital "G." Thus for the past sixty-five years, since the coming of FDR, Jews in America have supported with great passion the various government programs designed to end poverty in America. The results, after spending five trillion dollars, leave much to be desired. As Charles Murray wrote in his book, *Losing Ground,* "We tried to provide more for the poor and produced more poor instead. We tried to remove the barriers to escape poverty, and inadvertently built a trap."

There are as many people below the poverty level as when the entire monstrous campaign began. But no matter, supporting these programs gives Jews that good feeling that they are truly benefactors of the poor, and that eventually, given enough time and money, these programs will succeed. Not perhaps in our lifetimes, but certainly within our children's, our grandchildren's, or later. Liberals don't seem to remember that the road to hell is paved with good intentions.

The question must be asked however, is all of this in harmony with Jewish law and Jewish tradition? If it is, great! If it is not, then show me how it is not and just perhaps we can change some thinking. Later on in this writing we hope to show that these programs and the philosophy behind them are in fact contrary to Jewish law and tradition.

As to whether Jews should feel guilty about their success in America, the answer is why should they? Jews have not profited by government programs. Most of their success has been of the bootstrap variety. Yet there beats within the core of many Jews a feeling that if they have it so good, it is not quite fair for others not to share the same blessings. Since we were oppressed for so many centuries, we empathize with the poor in America as perhaps no other group does. If this can be called "guilt," so be it. What does our Jewish tradition say about this?

Judaism is a religion of optimism, so writes Rabbi David de Sola Pool in his 1957 book, *Why I Am A Jew?* One of Judaism's basic creeds is to bring about the golden age, the Messianic era, when all will accept the one God. This belief requires that we can remake the world through positive action. We must enjoy life and try to improve it. We are to do this by exercising our free will to defeat the temptations of sin, suppress the evil inclination, and choose the good and the moral way of life. With his inborn goodness, man must be the architect of his own life. So where does guilt enter into all of this? Apparently it doesn't!

Perhaps it is the deep feeling that we in America, the descendants of those courageous Jews who left their homelands to come to America, are so much more fortunate than those left behind that we really don't deserve all of our blessings, and that we have not earned what we have compared to our aunts and uncles and brothers and sisters who did not make it here. When we read of the Holocaust, see and listen to the stories of the survivors, perhaps we are correct in feeling a little guilt in our good fortune. But should that then lead us to advocate and support the use of the coercive power of government to try and solve the problems of the poor and less fortunate here in America, a position that is contrary to the fundamental teachings of Judaism that believes that to become, we must overcome? It was the very concentration of government power in Germany that made it possible for Hitler to do what he did.

It is ironic that so many of our Jewish leaders are vociferous and adamant about the need to keep government out of any religious choice or the establishment, heaven forbid, of a government-sponsored religion, and rightly so. But when it comes to using that same dangerous government power to achieve their social purposes, suddenly government takes on a whole new benevolent image. This may come as a shock to those Jewish leaders, but that same benevolent government is fully capable of jailing you and yours if you don't pay your taxes, if you violate the endangered species laws, or if you should be so unlucky as to have water on your property and inadvertently dry it up and violate the wetlands laws. Government is naked power and its reach must be severely limited.

The rise to prominence and prosperity in America of most Jews has been without the benefit of massive government assistance. In fact, it can be argued that the very absence of such programs forced our ancestors and us to pursue our careers pretty much on our own. Not that we lacked help from our families, friends, religious supporters and, in my own case, the GI Bill of Rights after World War II. But by and large we did it on our own. We were able to accomplish whatever we have accomplished because the system of free enterprise in America permits anyone to achieve what he or she truly wants to achieve without a coercive government or state-sponsored religion denying us the ability and freedom to take the necessary actions to accomplish our goals. And equally important, our religion did not single us out either for favors or government-sponsored discrimination.

Milton Friedman, the outstanding Jewish economist, was quoted in the *Libertarian Party News*, June 1999, as saying, "The great virtue of a free market system is that it does not care what color people are; it does not care what their religion is; it only cares whether they can produce something you want to buy. It is the most effective system we have discovered to enable people who hate one another to deal with one another and help one another."

As a further benefit to American Jews, as Rabbi Lapin wrote in his book, *America's Real War*, it has been through the grace of the Christian leaders of this country, going back to our founding fathers with their benevolent feeling toward the Jews as enshrined in our Constitution, that enabled Jews to assume their full place as citizens in this new land, the same as all others. How different this was from our fate as Jews in Europe.

The fact remains that in spite of this position of economic well-being in America, Jews continue to be political liberals, marching in lockstep, with our black brothers who are on the other end of the economic ladder, in a seemingly unbreakable link of overwhelming Democratic support. Logic would dictate that Jews would be backing positions that would in some degree differ from those of the black community, who seek more and more government assistance and favoritism. If there is one word that most Jews abhor, it is "quotas." Yet when it comes to affirmative action, both on the job and in the educational system, Jews seemingly forget the problems we have had in the past with this hated word, and throw ourselves into the struggle to support quotas for other minorities. Again, is this our guilt overcoming our better instincts?

The irony of our support of affirmative action, more accurately described as "race preference" is that there is increasing proof that all of the favoritism and quotas for minorities do more harm than good for those same minorities. Black writers such as Thomas Sowell, Shelby Steele, Walter Williams, and others continue to decry these efforts to reward students and workers simply because of the color of their skin. In most cases the forcing of minority students into the top universities through quotas, results in an increased dropout rate. Only through individual effort and study can true progress be made, they say.

Let us now take guilt as a reason for Jews to be liberals and relegate it to the ashcan of false and obsolete theories. Jews in America have no more reason to feel guilty about their success here than do the multitudes of our newest citizens who came here from elsewhere. Does one think that the Vietnamese feel guilty about their amazing progress here these past thirty years? Or do the Latinos streaming up here from Central and South America and Mexico feel guilty as they begin to climb the ladder of progress from such lowly beginnings? On the contrary, they are proud of their progress here, as they should be.

Ernest van den Haag makes the point that although Jews want to be wealthy, they cannot seem to forget the fact that they were poor for so many hundreds of years. Although now their average incomes in America are far above the average, they still tend to identify with oppression and poverty. Living in America and in freedom for several generations, American Jews still tend to identify themselves with the underdog and take on their causes regardless of merit. This is another example of emotions dominating the intellect, and again illustrates the point that the past should not retain a stranglehold on the present or the future.

Isn't it time for American Jews to finally, and perhaps reluctantly, accept the fact that this free market republic of ours has been at the root of their success here, that they need feel no guilt about their current status, and that they do not have to remain liberals in order to escape that guilty feeling? I think that time is now.

ANTI-SEMITISM AND
THE RELIGIOUS RIGHT

When one talks to liberal Jews, mention the names of Joe McCarthy, Pat Robertson, and Jerry Falwell and their knee-jerk reaction is usually that this entire group is a bunch of anti-Semites. Most Jews don't bother to read what these guys really are saying or have said. They simply take it on faith that because their Jewish leaders and organizations have assigned them this label, it must be true. This knee-jerk reaction to conservative Christians is not new, and it avoids having to really think more about it.

One case in particular illustrates this point. In 1964, a book was written by Arnold Forster and Benjamin Epstein, two officials of the Anti-Defamation League (ADL), called *Danger on the Right*. The book attempted to describe those organizations believed to be a danger to Jews, and to assassinate the character of the leaders of those groups. The book is full of half-truths and their attack on one organization, the Christian Anti-Communism Crusade (CACC), was so full of lies and distortions, these authors should have been sued for libel.

It so happens that the founder and leader of the CACC, Dr. Fred Schwarz, was known personally by this writer for many years. Dr. Schwarz, of partial Jewish heritage from his father, was raised as a Christian. When his family immigrated to Australia, he became a physician. There he created a successful practice. In 1953, alarmed by the progress of communism throughout the world, Dr. Schwarz came to the United States to educate Americans about the dangers of communism. He came to this country, because he believed that only the United States was strong enough to eventually defeat the growing forces of communism. (He was right. Liberals still find it difficult to give President Reagan the credit for this.)

My wife and I began listening to Dr. Schwarz in the late 1950s. We probably have heard him speak both in person and on TV scores of times. We have read his monthly newsletter all of these years. We also corresponded with him, pointing out our Jewish heritage, which pleased him. The point here is that in all of Dr. Schwarz's speeches and writings, never was there the slightest trace of anti-Semitism. On the contrary, as a true Christian, Dr. Schwarz always spoke lovingly of the Jewish people. Yet in their book, Forster and Epstein attempted to brand the doctor as a charlatan who preached anticommunism only for the money he could raise and spend for his personal enrichment. They accused him of dabbling in politics, which would have voided CACC's tax-exempt status, and they helped to trigger an IRS examination of CACC. This examination, plus subsequent ones, found nothing in CACC's records to warrant its declassification as a tax-exempt organization. Was an apology ever forthcoming from those authors for their unproven charges against Dr. Schwarz? No, instead they were hailed as loyal Jews who had helped to expose those evil Christians who were trying to convert and subvert us poor, defenseless Jews.

In his book, *Beating the Unbeatable Foe*, Dr. Schwarz quotes a column written by William F. Buckley in the 5 June 1962 edition of *National Review*. Buckley makes the point that the ADL was founded to fight defamation, and since Dr. Schwarz had been widely defamed, then the ADL should be defending Dr. Schwarz instead of participating in spreading defamatory rumors. During his visit to New York in 1962, Dr. Schwarz offered to meet with Forster, who refused, apparently not wanting to find out that there was not a trace of anti-Semitism in Dr. Schwarz. Dr. Schwarz is now semi-retired, living again in Australia, but still communicating the truth about the evils of communism.

Joe McCarthy, another dark and evil figure for the Jews, never had the smell of anti-Semitism attached to him either. His two main assistants, Roy Cohn and Gerald Schine, were both Jews. McCarthy may have had many faults, but as Nathaniel Weyl wrote in his authoritative book, published in 1968, *The Jew in American Politics*, McCarthy was never anti-Semitic in any of his speeches, writings, or personal behavior. With all of his personal faults and his questionable value as a true anti-Communist, McCarthy was never a big government advocate. He never targeted the Jews in any way and cannot be regarded as a problem for American Jews.

Today's boogiemen—Pat Robertson, Jerry Falwell, et al—seem to have one thing in common. They tend to be evangelical Christians whose basic doctrine is that the Jews are God's chosen people and that the second coming of the Christian Messiah must be preceded by an in-gathering of the Jews in Israel. Thus, in spite of occasional lapses in some of their public statements, such as Robertson's comment that Jews are following the wrong track to the promised land, and Falwell's quote that the Antichrist must be a Jew because Jesus was a Jew, both Christian leaders are firmly committed to Israel and the well-being of Jews everywhere. The nationally syndicated radio talk show host, and prominent author and lecturer on Jewish themes, Dennis Prager said he made a deal with Jerry Falwell several years ago. Prager proposed that if Falwell would continue to give his full support to Israel, then if Jesus Christ should eventually reappear, at that time Prager and all Jews would then recognize Jesus as the true Messiah, and we would admit our mistake. What a deal, and Falwell agreed to it.

One Christian preacher that I know, Frank Eiklor, leader of the group Shalom International, devotes his life to trying to enlighten his fellow Christians as to the need to make amends for their previous persecution of Jews. Eiklor, formerly a self-described Jew-hater, now writes and speaks extensively on how the Jews are truly God's chosen people and that those who persecute Jews will themselves be cursed. Eiklor has a tough road to travel. Christians tend to resent his message because he is calling on them to repent for their past sins against the Jews and to change their current thinking and behavior. On the other side, some Jews tend to distrust him because they think he may be trying to soften them up for the final conversion. Neither worry is appropriate in my opinion. Eiklor simply has a calling to do what he is doing because he believes it is his destiny to do what he does. It is interesting that whenever some tragedy befalls the Jewish people in California, as happened in the recent shooting at a Jewish Community Center in San Fernando Valley, Eiklor was there with a check for the center to help repair the damage.

Beyond the individual personalities, if one probes deeper into the basic principles that drive the Religious Right, one finds absolutely no advocacy for increasing government power to achieve their religious goals. There is no call for establishing Christianity as the official American religion, to which all must pay obeisance. (There is really no need for that as America is unofficially already a Christian nation by overwhelming numbers.) The main point is that so long as there is freedom from a government-imposed religion, as mandated by the First Amendment to the Constitution, Jews can live safely in their homes, worshipping or not as they choose. The only issue of the Religious Right that touches on government control is the call for a Constitutional amendment to outlaw abortion, but this is not directed against Jews in particular. More on the abortion question later.

Liberals today sometimes quote Thomas Jefferson and his call for a "wall of separation" between Church and State, a thought expressed in one of Jefferson's 20,000 letters, as an argument for their position on eliminating religion from our public life. It is clear from all of Jefferson's writings, most importantly the Declaration of Independence, that he had no thought of eliminating God and the belief in a higher power, from our political life. Rather he was vehemently against forcing citizens to support any form of organized church or religion.

One of the three accomplishments Jefferson requested to appear on his tombstone is that he wrote the Virginia Statute for Religious Freedom. (The other two were that he authored the Declaration of Independence and founded the University of Virginia.) The Virginia Statute proclaimed that Almighty God had created the mind free, and that to compel a man to furnish contributions of money to support any church is wrong. Further that all men should be free to profess their opinions in matters of religion and that opinion in no way should affect their civil capacities. It was the power of government to force people to support a particular church or religion that Jefferson vigorously opposed.

It is also interesting to note that when the Virginia Statute was proposed in 1786, a great majority rejected an amendment declaring, "Coercion is a departure from the plan of Jesus Christ." Jefferson and his supporters meant that the protection from this coercion should extend to all people, Jews, Gentiles, Christians, Muslims, Hindus, and infidels of every denomination, and not just to believers in Jesus Christ. Isn't it ironic that Jewish liberals should try and use Jefferson as a source for their position that religion has no place in politics, when Jefferson was a champion of the rights of all people to freely express their religious beliefs?

As a footnote on Thomas Jefferson, his estate at Monticello, Virginia, had fallen into disrepair after his death in 1826. It was Commodore Uriah Levy, a Jewish officer in the United States Navy, who purchased Monticello and began to restore it. After he died, and after the United States government failed to continue to maintain the estate, his nephew, Jefferson Levy, took over and continued the restoration until the estate was finally sold in 1890 to a foundation that still owns and preserves it. One could almost divine that there was some ethereal link between Thomas Jefferson, believed to have been a Deist, and the American Jewish people.

The argument over whether the Ten Commandments can be posted in schools and courts, or whether a nondenominational prayer can be said at public events, is so off the mark that it is a wonder that thoughtful Jews can support the liberal position on these issues. This nation was founded on the basis of religion and I am hopeful Congress and the courts will reverse the misinterpretation of the First Amendment by the liberals. It is sad to see the ACLU take such a leadership position on opposing these somewhat fringe items and yet be silent on supporting the right of parents to spend their own tax dollars to pay the tuition for the school of their choice for their children's education.

Jews cannot exist in a vacuum. They need to live with and get along with their Christian neighbors. To repeat, and it can never be overemphasized, the real enemy of Jews throughout their 4,000 year history has been a dictatorial government. The Religious Right almost without exception seeks to persuade, proselytize, and convert completely through voluntary actions. So what is there to fear from these good people? As Jews, nothing. If our main concern is that Jews for Jesus, and similar groups, will convert our kids, I've got news for you. Our intermarriage rate among secular Jews is now over 50%, and this unfortunate happening is not the result of the activities of any of these groups, Robertson, Falwell, the Southern Baptists, or any other non-Jewish group. We must look within for the reasons for this phenomenon.

We tend to ignore the fact that when our kids attend Jewish day schools, K-8, and even better when they stay through Jewish high schools, the rate of intermarriage shrinks to single digits. Yet our Jewish liberal leaders fight school choice, or some type of voucher system with a vengeance. In 1993 in California, a voucher system was beat back with $20,000,000 of teachers' union money, spearheaded of course by their Jewish leadership. The Jewish vote tended to follow the teachers' hysterical warnings about the coming elimination of the public school system if the measure passed. This was another example of American Jews looking through the wrong end of the telescope, and seeing boogiemen, when they should be looking at the broad picture of encouraging Jewish day schools by making it financially easier for Jewish parents to educate their kids there.

On the November 2000 ballot in California another voucher proposal appeared which would give a $4,000 voucher to parents to assist them in sending their children to any school of their choice. The California Teachers Unions and their liberal associates again opposed this measure with all of the strength and money they could assemble. Even though the minority parents according to recent polls, appeared to support the measure in great numbers, the proposal was soundly defeated by a two to one majority. No doubt California's Jews again followed the unions and the leading Democratic politicians to the detriment of their own interests. Eventually I hope and believe common sense will prevail, and some form of tax or tuition credit will be enacted. This will stimulate competition for the poorest performing public schools to the benefit primarily of the children attending today's inner city schools.

Another feature of Jews' fear of the Religious Right could be traced back to World War II, and the scourge of Hitler. Prior to 1941, America by a dominant majority, some say 90%, was opposed to getting involved in the conflict. Paul Johnson writes that in 1942, polls showed that Americans regarded Jews as the third biggest threat to the United States after the Japanese and the Germans. There was more anti-Semitism in this country during World War II than at any time in our history. Some of the leaders of the anti-war movement were isolationists who spoke out against getting involved in another European war; many were Republicans.

The news that Hitler was killing Jews was not widely known at that time. After that news surfaced, and in spite of Roosevelt's lack of action, American Jews tended to equate political conservatives of the day with a passive attitude towards Hitler. Only later did it develop that Roosevelt, the modern Jewish messiah to some Jews, had turned his back on helping the persecuted Jews of Europe. Having captured 90% of the Jewish vote in his various campaigns, Roosevelt believed that his first priority was to win the war, regardless of how many Jews were being slaughtered in Europe. So the railroad tracks leading to the concentration camps remained intact and the shores of America were closed to Jewish refugees until late in the war. If either of those decisions had been reversed, probably thousands of innocent Jews would have been saved. Roosevelt was another example of Jews following the wrong champion.

Still the stigma against the conservatives of that day persists to the present.

Ironically, today's conservatives are almost universally allied with Israel in preserving that country's borders and existence. It is the liberals today who are the ones pressuring Israel into a risky detente with the PLO. No other country in the world would take on the surrender of vital territories for the "promise of peace." Yet the Jews of America, the liberal ones, continue to distrust the conservatives who remain consistent in their support of a strong Israel. In fact, it is the conservatives in America, who are trying with little success, to enlighten the Jews of Israel that the Arab countries cannot be trusted until they renounce their goal of eliminating Israel. So, let us ask the question again: Should American Jews' fear of the Religious Right be a legitimate reason for Jews' liberal vote? I don't think so!

In his 1997 book, *Faith or Fear*, author Elliott Abrams recounts the recent history of both Catholics and Protestants in their changed view of Jews and Judaism. All of the major religions have renounced their previously held theory that it was the Jews who were responsible for the death of Jesus Christ, and that Judaism had become a "dead" religion after the Temple's destruction in 70 AD. As far back as 1965, in its declaration "Nostra Aetate," the Catholic Church stressed the church's origin in and its close relationship to Judaism. Jews remain very dear to God, it stated. In early 2000, Pope John Paul II made an historic speech in which he apologized for his Church's sins against the Jewish people throughout history. This is significant because it went far beyond what this same pope said in 1979 when he visited the death camp at Auschwitz and spoke then only about the horrors of that evil place. No mention was made then about the lack of Catholic concern during the time those atrocities were taking place. Thus there have been major movements in recent years to erase the long held stigma against the Jewish people.

In spite of these recent fortunate expressions, when I reread the brief history of anti-Semitism, as published by the Anne Frank Foundation in

1989, I cannot help but wonder if these positive changes are for real and will be permanent. When I was growing up in Chicago in the 1930s, I did not go out of my way to proclaim my Judaism. There was enough of the influence of Hitler around plus the general dislike of Jews among the Catholic toughs in the neighborhood that it was frequently the better part of valor to simply clam up when the subject was discussed. So I can understand somewhat why American Jews today may still be concerned about the remaining traces of this vile sentiment that may still be in existence.

There is no question that the 2,000-year history of hatred of the Jews for having killed and then rejecting their "God," is difficult to comprehend today in our enlightened twenty-first century. Still the central point that comes through to me is that although first the Christian Church, and then Martin Luther in the sixteenth century continued to preach their philosophy of hatred, it was only when they convinced the reigning monarchs to take action that Jews felt the full wrath of their anti-Semitism. It was only when the Christian Church was given the power of the State that they then could carry out their inquisitions. It was only when the State itself, as under Hitler and Stalin, began their death cycles, that Jews became the victims. The truth remains that it is the power of a centralized government that remains the real threat to Jews.

In 1974, American Lutherans acknowledged Martin Luther's anti-Jewish writings, admitting that they were beyond any defense, they regretted them, and did not support them. Most Protestant churches have changed their attitude toward attempting to convert Jews and in acknowledging the existence of Judaism. Still some liberal fears have not diminished; now they have targeted the politically conservative Christian Right, the evangelicals, as the enemy in spite of what the facts appear to be.

A 1994 American Jewish Committee survey found that American Jews perceive Republicans and conservatives as being more anti-Semitic than Democrats and liberals. This same report found little connection between anti-Semitism and non-extremist political or partisan orientation. This word has apparently not been given much publicity by our Jewish leaders. They prefer to remain comfortable with their boogiemen of the Religious Right and conservatives. To liberal Jews, it appears the only acceptable form of discrimination is their antagonism toward religious Christians. "Don't bother me with the facts" seems to be their attitude.

Alan Dershowitz in his 1991 book, *Chutzpah*, sees a sinister campaign underway by the Christian Right to establish Christianity as the official religion of America. This will inevitably lead, thinks Dershowitz, to Judaism becoming a second-class religion, and that somehow what will follow is the selection of Christianity as the true or preferred or dominant one. Dershowitz wonders why "some on the Jewish religious right also join the Christian religious right in favoring restrictions on a woman's right to choose abortion, in opposing gay rights, in favoring the death penalty, and in demanding censorship of sexually explicit material."

He goes on to write that perhaps support for the Lubavitch (Orthodox) movement reflects a sense that secular Jews are not authentic. It is difficult to find any link between the positions he favors with any Jewish laws or traditions. He can only conclude that the alleged right-wing agenda of "breaking down the wall of separation between religion and government is dangerous to the status of Jews in America. It is bad for Jews, and it is bad for America." What is surprising is that this noted legal scholar apparently does not believe what the First Amendment says: "Congress shall make no law respecting an establishment of religion, or prohibiting the free exercise thereof." Nothing is stated about favoring one religion over another or establishing an official "American religion." If the Religious Right were going to try and do what Dershowitz is afraid they are trying to do, then certainly an amendment to our Constitution would be required. There has never been nor, I believe, will there ever be such a movement for an amendment to establish an official State religion in this country.

Walter Williams, the great political economist and writer, wrote in a 1999 *Orange County Register* column, "The Holocaust's true lesson is that there is no greater potential for evil than powerful centralized government. This century alone, not counting war, 170 million people have been murdered by their own government. Neither we in the United States nor Jews in Israel have learned the lesson of the Holocaust."

As a final note on this subject, an article by Daniel Pipes in the May 1999 issue of *Commentary*, makes a strong case that it is the Muslim world that is the chief enemy of Jews worldwide, and particularly in these United States. Mr. Pipes details the various violent episodes perpetrated by Muslims in our recent history, including the bombing of the World Trade Center in 1993, up to 1997's shooting on top of the Empire State Building which killed seven tourists. Now with the horrific attacks on our country of 9/11/01, perpetrated by radical Muslim terrorists, Jews should finally be convinced as to who their enemies really are. Let us not forget the myth that was soon circulated in various Arab quarters that somehow Jews were behind those attacks because the number of Jews killed in the World Trade Center collapse was fewer than projected. It is particularly unfortunate that throughout much of the Muslim world, Jews are still often portrayed as a people that does not deserve to live, let alone have its own nation of Israel. There is little doubt that anti-Semitism from Christians is almost everywhere on the decline, whereas that miserable philosophy is on the rise in the Muslim world. We don't hear much about this from our Jewish leaders in the United States, but we constantly are warned about the dangers from the Religious Right. When are we Jews going to wake up?

JEWISH CHARITY,
A LIBERAL EXCLUSIVE?

✡

Deep within the Jewish religion and tradition, and deep within the hearts and minds of most Jews, both observant and secular, lies the belief that charity—helping those less fortunate—is of the highest calling. It may not have made the Ten Commandments, but it is still a weighty obligation for Jews. Although the Hebrew language has no direct word for charity, the closest is generally considered to be *Tsedekah*. The basic meaning of this word is "justice," but still it probably is the most commonly used word by Jews to describe the act of giving.

The Biblical roots for charity within Judaism probably go back to kind acts committed by our patriarchs, to Abraham welcoming the strangers into his tent, and the commandment that one should leave the corners of the field to be harvested by the poor who do not have enough to eat. "And when ye reap the harvest of your land, thou shalt not wholly reap the corner of thy field, neither shalt thou gather the gleaning of thy harvest. And thou shalt not glean thy vineyard, neither shalt thou gather the fallen fruit of thy vineyard; thou shalt leave them for the poor and for the stranger; I am the Lord your God." (Leviticus 19:9-10) Dr. Meir Tamari in his book, *With All Your Possessions*, adds an interesting caveat from the Talmud on this point that first the poor themselves had to harvest the corners before they were entitled to consume that food. This was done to encourage the poor to work for what they got, and to prevent the attitude of being entitled. Undoubtedly there are many other roots to charity to be found in the Torah, the Talmud, and other writings, but for our purposes, we can accept the notion that charity is of vital importance to most American Jews.

By definition, charity is an act of kindness from one person to another with no expectation of reward for that action. Moses Maimonides (1135-1204) was generally considered to be one of the greatest Rabbinate scholars and philosophers. He developed eight principles of charity, the greatest of which was helping another to become an independent, self-financing person. The next greatest one was to be an anonymous giver so the recipient would not know whom the giver was. And so on down the line of charity, to the least one, where whatever was given was almost pulled away from the giver under some kind of moral threat. When European Jews first came to America, the practice of establishing "poor boxes" in every home was prevalent, as was the lending of funds, generally through the local temple, to those who needed them either for sustenance or to start up a business.

In today's America, giving by Jews to their favorite causes is legendary. Israel would probably not exist today without the generosity of American Jews, nor would many other worthwhile organizations. A December 1998 article in *Moment* magazine describes how a few of the prodigious Jewish contributors are now targeting much of their giving to certain specified Jewish causes. Steven Spielberg, for example, is dedicating much of his giving to establishing an historical record of the Holocaust through interviews with thousands of survivors via his Righteous Persons Foundation. Michael Steinhardt and Charles Bronfman have launched the Birthright Project whose purpose is to give every Jew in the world between ages fifteen and twenty-six, a first-time ten-day trip to Israel as a free gift from the Jewish people. Steinhardt and Morton Mandel are teaming up to help Jewish teachers become more effective and to be better paid. Other Jewish billionaires, however, do not focus their giving on Jewish causes. Regardless of whether these rare individuals give to Jewish causes or to other worthwhile institutions, there is a limited number in this category, so most charity must come from other sources.

Until modern times, this giving was always from individuals or foundations established by those individuals. When income taxes became larger, charitable giving took on an added glow; it was tax-deductible for both Jews and non-Jews alike. Somehow though, the notion grew that for Jews to exercise their charitable instincts, they had to be liberals, and even worse, that conservatives were less charitable than were liberals.

Here is one possible explanation. As American Jews drifted away from the roots of their religion and became more secular, they did not lose their charitable tradition. Instead, they wanted to see more accomplished in helping the poor than their own giving seemed to accomplish. As Rabbi Lapin has written, Jews are ambitious and want more and faster action whenever possible to achieve their goals. When the welfare laws first came into existence on a very modest basis, many Jews seized upon these laws as necessary supplements to their own giving. Now there were greater funds available to accomplish their avowed goals. Few stopped to think through where and how these funds were coming from and how they were to be disbursed. Where before Jews did not question the notion that giving was a personal act, which made the giver feel better and did not shame the recipient, now the impersonal government stepped into the middle as the "honest broker." Now funds were extracted from the givers through taxes on their income or property and the recipients no longer had any personal ties whatever to the givers.

Eventually, as the income tax rates climbed and politicians vied for the title of being the most generous, charity became a political issue rather than a personal one. Those in the political world that could dream up the most extravagant programs to enlarge this so-called "charitable" action were generally those who would get reelected. Who were the creative people who were most imaginative, the most able to sell their new programs to help the poor? Why it was none other than our own homegrown liberals in the Democratic Party, led by the esteemed FDR, on through the magnificent, strong-arm leadership of Lyndon Johnson, with his Great Society programs.

The "selfish, non-caring conservatives" were soon left far behind in this game of how many new ways can we use our tax monies to help the poor. And who were the folk generally at the head of the charitable givers? Of course, it was our charitable Jews. Like lemmings being led over the cliff to their demise, American Jews led by their always charitable leaders, gravitated to that party which promised the most help to the less fortunate. Wasn't it wonderful? Now we could feed our basic Jewish instincts of charity and most of it didn't even have to come from our own pockets. And what we gave was tax deductible! (Remember that the personal tax rates before Ronald Reagan's presidency were as high as 70%.)

Oh sure, we Jews still continued to give at prodigious rates, but now the burden would be shared by everyone. Even if "everyone" did not want to have this forced giving thrust upon him or her, we knew what was best for all concerned. Thus was born the notion that only by joining the Democratic Party, only by proudly being called liberals, only then were American Jews fulfilling their ancient calling of *Tsedekah*, helping the poor. The fact that in America it was because our free market system of capitalism provided sufficient excess funds to permit this tax structure to come about, and because Americans became the most proficient tax collectors and taxpayers the world has ever known, somehow escaped much analysis. We Jews simply knew this was the way to go!

As the old saying goes, if something appears too good, it usually is. After an entire generation of forced giving through our taxes, we find almost as many Americans below the poverty level as when the Great Society programs were launched back in the 1960s. Finally in the late part of the twentieth century, over the strong opposition of Congressional liberals, our federal welfare programs were being reformed. Only now are we facing up to the challenge and trying to accomplish the worthwhile goal of helping people through more voluntary efforts. Will American Jews now begin to recognize that they have been following a false God in their support of these non-voluntary programs? It still may be too early to assume that, but we can at least recap why Jews should not use the concept of charity to justify their belief that only by being liberals could they satisfy their Jewish tradition of charity.

Charity is personal; to make it non-personal through enforced government programs negates the entire concept of charity. While it is true that in Jewish tradition, communal philanthropy was an obligation to help the poor, the actual giving came primarily from individual Jews. Conservatives are no different from liberals in wanting to give a helping hand to those who need it. So why should Jews believe that only by being liberal can they be truly Jewish? Dr. Tamari writes that there was nothing in the Jewish charitable system that resembled the redistribution tendencies of the welfare state.

Julius Rosenwald perhaps heads the list of American Jewish conservatives who were great givers. Cofounder of Sears Roebuck, Rosenwald was a staunch conservative, a close friend and supporter of Herbert Hoover in 1932, as were many of his Jewish friends. Rosenwald became one of the great contributors to the education of black children. From 1917 to his death in 1932, Rosenwald was personally responsible through gifts and other fundraising for the building of over 5,000 schools in the South, which educated over 600,000 black children.

Currently, Theodore Forstmann, a politically conservative Jew, is contributing many millions of dollars to the establishment of scholarships to permit poor children to attend schools of their choice, and not be forced to attend inferior schools. Jewish liberals have no monopoly on being great givers, but it is sad to see so many great givers believe that they must be liberals to carry out that noteworthy action. In today's roaring twenty-first century economy there are many new computer-driven Jewish billionaires who are not liberals and who are making enormous charitable contributions to their favorite organizations. One of these, Mr. Henry Samueli, cofounder of the booming company Broadcom, is giving away some of his millions as if there were no tomorrow. More power to him!

What seems to be overlooked, or not even considered, is that it is our free market system, which is based on voluntary cooperation between people, that is the basis and the raison d'être for the wealth and good fortune of all Americans, including Jews. To cast aside this truth, or even worse, never to consider it, is a conundrum that needs to be overcome. If a Steven Spielberg wants to give away huge portions of his personal fortune, more power to him. But please, let us not accept the notion that only by supporting liberal Democrats and their particular programs can he fulfill his charitable instincts. If the liberals truly had their political way in America, Spielberg and other billionaires would probably have most of their excess earnings taxed away, for the "good of the poor."

One of today's prominent debates is whether to eliminate the "death" or estate tax. The liberals defend it because only 2% of estates are subject to it. If Jews would analyze who comprises the bulk of that 2%, and realize that Jews are a big part of that number, perhaps they would rethink their opposition to the elimination of this class-envy tax. It is the old story of biting the hand that feeds you.

If it is the free market system that provided the framework for making a lot of money, and if it is the conservatives who have been the champions of strengthening and maintaining the relative purity of that wonderful system through limiting the powers of government, then for Heaven's sake, recognize that truism, and don't march in lockstep with those who play on your sentiments that only by being a liberal can you be a truly charitable human being.

The bottom line to all of this is that the oft given reason from rabbis to famous personalities to the average person in the street that only by being a liberal will we be truly generous to those less fortunate is a myth. It is time for American Jews and their leaders to pierce the fabric of what is truly charity and acknowledge that neither political party has a monopoly on this feature of our society. Even better would be their acknowledgment when all is said and done that it is the conservative philosophy of maximum individual liberty, limited government, and reduced taxes that provide the bedrock for the continued prosperity of American Jews, which in turn enables them to perform their acts of individual giving.

One final thought on this issue. The late, great Los Angeles Rabbi, Edgar Magnin once wrote, "There are two expressions for charity in Hebrew. One is *'tsedakah'* which means justice, and implies that whatever we do for others is a divine command, since all we have comes from God and we must share it. The other expression is a little closer to the English word charity. It is *'gemiluth hasadim,'* best translated as 'acts of kindness.' It has to do with attitudes, feelings, gentility, sensitivity. The emphasis is on attitude, feelings, with no mention of coercion." Rabbi Magnin emphasized that "one's attitude when giving is what makes it charity."

One can conclude from the rabbi's profound observation that coercive government programs merely harden the hearts of the givers and strip away any kindly feelings they may have had for the takers. The takers soon begin to believe that this forced welfare has become their God-given right and they form organizations to preserve that "right." This is what our welfare programs have produced and it is time for American Jews to recognize this fact. The results of revising and reducing the welfare programs are now coming in. The welfare rolls have been reduced by 50% nationwide, due mainly to the more restrictive rules, plus a strong economy. To try and satisfy our charitable instincts through supporting mandatory government programs is not only ineffective, but is also not in the Jewish tradition.

On reflection then, is it not the liberal philosophy of today that is out of step with Jewish tradition? When will the Jewish leaders and the rabbis of America step up to the plate, and acknowledge that the liberal Democratic Party has no monopoly on providing good things for the less fortunate? When will I hear at a High Holiday sermon that we must bless our free market system in America for providing us with the excess capital that is now ours to give away, instead of hearing that we are less than worthy Jews if we now vote for some restricting of government aid to illegal immigrants? I won't hold my breath.

CHARITY OR JUSTICE...
WHAT IS MORE JEWISH?
✡

The fact that charity is so strongly embedded within Judaism and is used by so many American Jews as the main reason to remain political liberals requires further analysis and discussion. Is it only by being liberals that Jews can satisfy their charitable yearnings? Do liberals really have more heart and goodness than conservatives, even if they have the same goals? Is charity such a dominant strain within Judaism that it alone should dictate our politics? Or does Judaism primarily demand "justice" for all, with "charity" being only a subset of the more inclusive term "justice"?

If "justice" is the dominant theme of Judaism, then perhaps Jews who remain liberals mainly to honor the "charity" tradition are misreading Jewish tradition. I understand that here I step into the complex world of biblical and Jewish scholarship. Since I do not pretend to be a biblical scholar, I feel free to tackle this question while acknowledging my innocence on the subject. At the same time I hope that this chapter works to buttress my argument that to be charitable, or even to be just, Jews can just as easily be political conservatives as liberals. And in fact, the biblical writings on the subject weigh heavily on the side of the conservatives.

When one looks for the word *charity* in the general index of names and subjects in the Soncino Second Edition of the Pentateuch and Haftarahs, it is not listed. There are, however, some twenty-two listings for the word *justice*. This would seem to reinforce the seldom-mentioned fact that, in Judaism, the word "tsedekah," often used as a synonym for "charity," really does translate to mean "justice." Does this then mean that when Jews cite charity as their primary reason for remaining liberals, they would be more consistent with Judaism if they understood that what they really want is justice for all, and especially for the less fortunate? It therefore seems appropriate to explore the various meanings of justice in the Torah, to see if we can find some connection with that concept and modern liberalism.

The most prominent listing for justice is in Deuteronomy 16:20: "Justice, justice shalt thou follow, that thou mayest live, and inherit the land which the Lord thy God giveth thee." The notes for that section stress that the duplication of the word *justice* gives the greatest emphasis to carrying out justice for all in the most even-handed manner possible. "Do not use unjust means to secure the victory of justice," a Chasidic rabbi is quoted as saying in the notes. He continued, "In the eyes of the Prophets, justice was a Divine, irresistible force." The words "Justice, justice shalt thou follow" are defined as the heart of the humane (charitable?) legislation of the Torah, and following this law fulfills the demand for social righteousness by the Prophets and Sages.

The notes to Deuteronomy 16:20 continue to expand on the interpretation of justice and it is here that we find a link to charity. "Justice is a positive conception, and includes charity, philanthropy, and every endeavour to bring out what is highest and best in others. . . . To do justly and to love mercy is the Prophets' summing up of human duty towards our fellow-men." The notes add that justice even extends to asserting the claims of the poor upon the rich, and of the helpless upon those who have the means to help. Thus these Soncino notes suggest that although there is no pure Hebrew word for charity, charity can be considered an important subsection of the full definition of justice.

There are, however, other writings that must be considered. Exodus 23:3 says, "Neither shalt thou favour a poor man in his cause." The notes comment that the "Biblical view of justice is remarkable for its unbending insistence on the strictest impartiality." The judge is not to favor a poor man on the theory that the rich man would not miss any sum involved. "Sympathy and compassion are great virtues, but even these feelings must be silenced in the presence of Justice."

In Leviticus 19:15 it is written, "Ye shall do no unrighteousness in judgment; thou shalt not respect the person of the poor, nor favour the person of the mighty; but in righteousness shalt thou judge thy neighbor." The notes to this section quote the Talmud: "Judge every man in the scale of merit; refuse to condemn by appearances, but put the best construction on the deeds of your fellow men." The entire thrust of this section is that to be poor is no great honor, and that simply being poor carries with it no claim on a judge's sympathy or on any skewing of the equal application of justice.

So what are we to make of this scripture? What, if any, is the connection between justice and modern political philosophies? Is modern liberalism justified in suggesting that it is somehow in the Jewish tradition to use the force of government for charitable purposes? Nothing referred to above would tend to support this notion. The entire thrust of the Torah consists of Commandments to the *individual* to do what is right and to worship God as individuals, not as members of some organized force. It is only as individuals that we as Jews can dispense charity, and we should pay our political allegiance to that philosophy which emphasizes individual responsibility. The idea of individual responsibility is not a main component of today's liberalism.

It seems to me the best definition of charity is that we are each of us endowed with the emotions and passions and ability to do what is right or what is wrong. If we believe in the concept of justice and all that this entails, then out of the goodness of our hearts we will exert our energies as best as we can to dispense charity and help those less fortunate. Certainly we are fulfilling this goodness in this country to the tune of over 200 billion dollars of voluntary contributions a year. But nowhere do I find in our Jewish tradition any meaningful connection to the government-enforced "charity" that is at the heart of today's liberal dogma.

This use of force to accomplish what liberals want permeates all of their legislation and thinking, and thus downgrades and diminishes the importance of the individual citizen making up his own mind as to how to spend his hard-earned money. In view of the Torah itself, it is a false notion that only by being liberals can Jews satisfy their charitable instincts. Judaism stresses justice as one of its cornerstones, and charity is a subsection of that all-inclusive term. American Jews need to rethink their reasons for remaining liberals. The desire to be charitable should no longer be the justification for ignoring the conservative philosophy, which above all stresses individual freedom, responsibility, and true compassion for the less fortunate among us.

It is interesting that when Jews came to America, they founded societies to help immigrants get established. Those associations were not labeled charitable organizations. Rather they were known as "benevolent societies." Why "benevolent" instead of "charitable"? Perhaps because the true definition of "benevolent" is to do good to others, to express goodwill or kindly feelings, to act out of kindness with an altruistic, generous, liberal, benign, charitable, philanthropic feeling. "Benevolent" encompasses much more than simply being charitable. Also, nowhere in its definition is there any reference to the use of force, either privately or from some external power, such as government. Thus it would appear that Jews have always correctly used the word "benevolent" to express their deeply held feeling of doing good for others. It has only been since the 1930s in the United States that this feeling has been subverted into substituting the use of government force for the previous system of voluntary benevolence.

If we wish to use the power of government to achieve our Jewish goals, let that mighty power be used to secure justice for our citizens. Justice would include making sure that the playing field is equal for all of the players, that there is equal opportunity for all in pursuing their individual ambitions, that there are equal blessings and punishments for all based upon individual achievements or transgressions, and that each of us can enjoy the fruits of our own labors with as little interference as possible from any outside force.

Justice would also dictate that government must remain the impartial referee that sets the rules and enforces them without favor to any party, and that government limits its powers to only those necessary to keeping the peace among its citizens. If one accepts this position, then American Jews can no longer remain political liberals but must recognize that today's political conservatism more closely aligns with the principles and traditions of Judaism.

TO BE JUST LIKE
THE CHRISTIANS
✡

Throughout their history, Jews have resisted being absorbed by their conquerors. Whether those rulers were Greek or Roman or Christian, Jews have always fought to keep their own ways and traditions and religion separate from that of the ruling majority. For the 2,000 years of Christianity, one of the main reasons for the discrimination in its various forms against Jews during many of those years was that Jews stubbornly refused to accept Jesus Christ as their Messiah. In spite of their isolation into ghettos, Jews continued to resist being absorbed and retained their own identity as a separate people. Only in the past century has there been almost complete acceptance of Jews as a people separate and distinct from Christians, with the resultant decline of anti-Semitism. It is now official Catholic doctrine that Jews should not be held responsible for the death of Jesus Christ. This is definitely a change from when I was growing up in Chicago in the 1930s. Then the term "Christ killer" was not that uncommon to be heard from our non-Jewish neighbors.

Is it not thus somewhat ironic that instead of maintaining their own separate identity as they have throughout the ages, today's American Jews seem to want to emulate the liberal Christian majority in supporting the popular programs of government control and redistribution? Nowhere is there heard a call for Jews to stand apart, to resist these attempts to reduce individual freedom, to restate the Jewish tradition of the importance of the individual. In Jewish life it has always been the individual who was granted the greatest freedom and liberty. Yes, the community is important; yes, Judaism is a communal religion whereby we are to some extent our brother's keeper; but it is still the individual and the family around which the religion is based. Nowhere was it thought that some supreme government authority could force the individual to do its bidding. Jews recognized only the authority of God as revealed to them by their Bible and its interpreters. So from where does today's "me-tooism" stem? Why do Jews feel they must adhere to the ideas of the dominant Christian majority in this country?

Milton Friedman, the famed Jewish economist, had an interesting angle in an article he wrote for the *Freeman* in October 1988. Friedman was trying to determine why so many Jews seemed to exhibit an anti-capitalist mentality, while at the same time they gloried in the benefits derived from living under that same capitalism. He admitted it remained a mystery to him, but he did advance one theory.

Friedman wrote that because Jews in Europe in the seventeenth, eighteenth, and nineteenth centuries were channeled into business and money lending, two of the lesser regarded vocations in the eyes of the Christians, they were regarded as somewhat "lesser beings" by the dominant Christian majority. To show that they were really "nice folks," Jews tended to downplay their success in the business world so as not to stand out excessively from the crowd. Jews also wanted to portray themselves as the guardians of the poor and downtrodden. This would then somehow erase the image of Jews as being nothing but money-grubbing, profit hungry shylocks. Friedman thus concluded that this trait of always wanting to be in sympathy with the majority in the country wherein they resided has somehow persisted in the traditions of today's American Jews.

We see this somewhat in the positions advocated by some of our leading Jewish personalities. I cannot think of any prominent Jew in the Hollywood entertainment business that can be considered to be a political conservative. (Although he is not part of the Hollywood crowd, Jewish humorist/pundit Jackie Mason is a prominent entertainer and is definitely not a liberal.) Is it because they really believe in the liberal philosophy or is it the herd instinct at work, where no one wants to be the first to break out of the mold?

The need to be generous and magnanimous so as not to be called shylocks, plus the reinforcement from our religious leaders, has led Jews down the slippery slope to backing any feel good government programs designed to help the poor. If we could not accomplish all of our worthy goals from individual and community efforts, then it was a natural leap to support government programs, especially since the American majority advanced these programs, or so it seemed.

Whatever the polls showed approval for—whether it was affirmative action, expanded welfare, protecting the environment, pouring more money into public schools, denying school choice—the majority of American Jews wanted to be on the "winning" side. Seldom if ever would Jews support a minority position, even though that position may be more in harmony with Judaism. Certainly, we did not want to be portrayed as being selfish, money-grubbing shylocks! It seemed not to occur to most American Jews that they have become an elite group entitled to express their individual opinions on the issues of the day without bending knees to the current majority.

However, the big question is what if the majority opinion, as expressed in current polls, should turn in favor of conservative positions? What if the majority decided to back school choice in some form, an end to government-enforced affirmative action, or an end to the government-imposed welfare system? Will American Jews be consistent in their desire to be with the majority and change their political backing? Now we would hope so. One would think that if Jews and, most importantly, their leaders would be consistent and go with the new majority, a sea-change in Jewish voting would take place. Suddenly the mantra of "to be Jewish, means you must be a liberal" would fade away with all the other false theories that have bit the dust throughout history. The idea that we must go along to get along has never worked for us. We have always had to eventually fight the majority to gain and then maintain our individual freedom to be Jews.

Hans Kung, in his 1992 book, *Judaism*, quotes Abraham Joshua Heschel on this point. Heschel in his book, *God in Search of Man*, wrote,

"The spirit of Judaism is not the spirit of conformity to American secular society, but above all is the spirit of protest, embodied in the great prophets, against a confusion of the true God with the many earthly, false idols of this society. Also the protest must be made on matters of religion and law. To be a Jew is to renounce allegiance to false gods, to remain free of infatuation with worldly triumphs, and never to succumb to splendour."

In *The Jewish World*, edited by Elie Kedourie, it is written, "But it should never be forgotten that the fiercest conflicts between Jews and Gentiles in Antiquity erupted against kings who were considered enlightened, liberal and tolerant. Antiochus Epiphanes, Titus and Hadrian are typical examples. All three persecuted Jews with the declared objective of compelling them not to be different from other people. Thus, even these 'well-meaning' rulers had fallen victims to the disease of dislike of the unlike, the epitome of intolerance."

The notion that we Jews will somehow curry favor from a country's majority by blindly backing programs momentarily favored by that majority, conflicts with our tradition of independent thought. When the evidence is clear that these programs do more harm then good, why can we not use our own common sense and change our thinking. It is a fact that we gain the respect and admiration of others, mostly by standing up for our true principles no matter how unpopular they may be at the moment.

The problem here is that too often, we do not recognize what our true Jewish principles are, and our Jewish leaders are not very good in explaining them. So it is left to our religious leaders to show us the way, but alas, it appears there are few of them who seem to see the light. But we Jews have survived through the centuries by never losing our optimism that better days are ahead. We must continue to hope that Jews in America will soon see what their best interests are and vote accordingly.

The terrible calamities that have fallen upon the Jewish people in our own "enlightened" 20th century did not come about because Jews stood out from the crowd by backing unpopular programs or issues. It would not have made any difference to a Hitler or a Stalin whether or not Jews favored or opposed a higher minimum wage, or granted monopoly powers to a union, or were for or against abortion. No, we were singled out only because we were Jews, and we were considered to be a threat to those dictators, largely because of our tradition for independent thinking. If we are to prevent any repeats of this type of persecution, then we must be ever on the alert to resist any government from obtaining excessive power and control over the individual, no matter how attractive those programs of the moment may appear to be.

Today's liberal philosophy, when stripped of all its camouflage, is one that grants greater and greater powers to a central government. Many of the current liberal programs are ostensibly designed to correct some evil or solve some pressing social problem. From the "war on tobacco" to the "war on guns" to the coming "war on fat in our diet" to whatever the facile minds of the liberals can conjure, all of these schemes result in limitations on the freedom of the individual to live his or her own life. This has never been in the interests of Jews throughout their history and it is time that American Jews recognized that truism. If for no other reason than enlightened self-interest, American Jews should reject today's liberal doctrine.

It is somewhat ironic that liberals are now very concerned about the possible loss of individual freedoms under the Patriot Act enacted after 9/11/01. It is true that this act gives government new powers to intrude into the lives of our citizens, along with the ability of our intelligence agencies to share information. There was a general consensus that intelligence failures may have contributed to our inability to prevent the attack, and this is why the Patriot Act came into being. To date, there have been few, if any, instances of abuse of these powers. American Jews should be ever watchful for such abuses. Liberals, however, always seem to be able to choose which freedoms they support, so long as their own oxen are not being gored.

The fact is that throughout our 4,000-year history, Jews have been willing to endure the most terrible of consequences in order to speak their minds on what they believe. The history of persecution by the Christian Church from the time when Emperor Constantine declared Christianity as the official religion of the Roman Empire was due primarily to the unwillingness of the Jews to accept that religion as their own. If Jews had been willing, history would have recorded a far different fate for the Jewish people. This is why it is so difficult to analyze why today's American Jews present such a united front in their obedience to the liberal Democratic philosophy and programs.

We need more leaders like Norman Podhoretz, editor of *Commentary* for many years, who changed his political stance sometime during the course of his distinguished career, and is now an eloquent spokesman for the conservative cause. Because of his current beliefs, Podhoretz lost many of his closest friends, but has remained an effective champion of individual rights and freedoms. Irving Kristol, sometimes described as a "Neo-conservative," changed his beliefs as he evolved, along with his wife Gertude Himmelfarb. There are other outstanding Jewish conservatives—Rabbi Daniel Lapin, Michael Medved, Jeff Jacoby, Dennis Prager, Bruce Hershensohn, to name a few—so all is not hopeless. Unfortunately, there seem to be few Jewish conservatives who are prominent in the major media, and we could certainly benefit if we had more columnists like Don Feder, Mona Charen, and David Brook.

When one reviews the years leading up to the Nazi Holocaust and questions why German Jews in particular seemed so helpless during those years to try and change the political climate, the fact emerges that German Jews believed they were so much a part of the German fabric that nothing bad could happen to them. German Jews were very prominent in that society, garnering almost one half of the Pulitzer Prizes awarded to Germans. Ever since the liberation of Jews in Europe, stemming back to the French Revolution, Jews had been steadily improving their financial and social status in Western Europe. Now to be suddenly torn away from the German culture that so many Jews were a part of came as a tragic shock. One wonders what would have happened if German Jews had used some of their economic and political power to stand out from the crowd and oppose Hitler in the 1930s before he had attained absolute power.

I believe the lesson of that history is that American Jews must exercise their own independent judgment, apart from what may be the current majority, to oppose those laws, regulations, and programs which have as their ultimate purpose the limiting of individual freedom. It has been this freedom in America which has made possible the unbelievable successes of Jews here these past three centuries. Lipset and Raab write to this point, "Even constitutional restrictions are not necessarily forever. It is not paranoid and may even be healthy for a majority of Jews to harp on the possibility that anti-Semitism could conceivably become a serious problem in America's future."

The problem is that all the liberals have to do is to throw out the magic words of "social action" or "save the environment" or "help the minorities," and our Jewish leaders rise up to take the bait of supporting those government programs ostensibly designed to solve these sticky problems. And then, to compound their mistakes, these leaders ignore the failures of those programs and too readily buy the notion that the reason for failure is not enough money was spent or too few regulations were imposed.

Would they accept such an explanation from their associates in business if their business plans did not meet with the planned success? I don't think so. If our leading Jews would use the same God-given brains that they use to make their businesses and professions successful, the "war on poverty" would have lasted about as long as the first unsuccessful results began to become apparent. But then again, their motives were pure and how can you fault that? Liberals believe that as long as they try to solve problems this is all that counts, whereas most Jewish traditions look to results, not just intentions.

Liberals seem to seek out easy solutions to our difficult social problems. Pass a law and all else will fall into place. Don't bother to dig deep for the basic causes of problems. No, just wave a magic law over the mess and all will come out fine. And we Jews—noted for our intelligence, our ability to analyze and ferret out the truth of the most complex problems, as exemplified by our Einsteins, our Salks, and our Rubins—swallow this garbage.

Did the Jewish people solve any of their historic problems by the passage of laws? The only thing new laws did for Jews was to free them at times from the oppressive yoke of government so they could be free to solve their own problems through hard work and independent action. The 2.5 million Jews who fled Eastern Europe from 1881 to 1925 to seek a new life in the United States did not wait for any magic laws to be passed to permit them to seek that new life. They simply acted in their own self-interest. This is what American Jews should be doing, acting in their own self interests, which almost always is not following the path that the liberal Democratic Party advocates.

We Jews need to keep reminding ourselves that our exodus from Egypt, our Passover, was the central and most profound episode related in the Torah. The Soncino Pentateuch describes Israel's redemption from slavery as teaching mankind that "God is a God of Freedom." It goes on to state, "The Ten Commandments, spoken at Sinai, form the Magna Carta of religion and morality, linking them for the first time, and for all time, in indissoluble union." Jews need freedom as much as the air we breathe. If we want respect from our non-Jewish friends, associates, and neighbors, the best way is to be true to our Jewish religion and traditions, no matter how separate a path those beliefs may take us. Jews must use their intellect to think through the issues on their own and rely on Jewish principles to help them make informed decisions.

Judge Bork writes about Alexis De Tocqueville, the young Frenchman whose observations on America in the 1830s have proven to be extremely farsighted. De Tocqueville warned that a soft form of despotism consisting of a myriad of small complicated rules, would soften and guide the will of man to acceptance of a form of servitude, which would be disastrous to the liberties of the people. He thought that certain strong institutions, in defending their own rights, would help preserve the common liberties for all. Unfortunately in America today, we cannot depend on those powerful forces to fight this battle for us. Jews, as individuals, have an opportunity and a responsibility to stand up for their own rights and principles, because it appears no one else is going to do that for them. Hopefully our younger generation of Jews, encouraged by the multitude of opportunities available to them in this new Internet-driven age, will prove to be more independent of thought than were their forebears.

JEWS AND THE FREE MARKET (CAPITALISM)

Most observers of American politics would agree that between the two competing political doctrines of liberalism and conservatism, when it comes to promoting, encouraging, stimulating, praising, expanding, and identifying themselves with the free market, capitalistic system, it is conservatism that captures the prize. Of course, liberals welcome the fruits and benefits of the free market, but it is mostly to their liking because it creates sufficient wealth for their redistribution schemes and not because it is the most natural and productive system yet devised by man. Still liberals continue to want to tinker with it, to control it, and when necessary, to intervene with their own pet programs and ideas.

Again their thinking is that too much freedom in the marketplace is no good because too many people are just too dumb to spend their hard-earned funds on those goods and services and programs that liberals deem most important. When asked in 1999 whether the projected federal budget surplus should be returned to the taxpayers who provided the surplus, President Clinton replied that, "No, we could not do this because we could not trust our citizens to spend their refunds in the wisest way." This typifies the arrogance and feeling of superiority that today's liberals possess. Thus if we need to tax away the surplus funds that people have paid in order to "invest" in more education, or welfare, or animal rights, or whatever, then so be it. Isn't that what America is all about?

Conservatives on the other hand, seem to be generally more in favor of permitting people to spend their money as the individual sees fit. They are content to permit the free market to do its wondrous work, and with the "invisible hand" doing its thing, they sit back and enjoy the fruits of their endeavors. If Americans want to spend their hard earned dough to see Madonna, Barbara Streisand, or Michael Jackson in the flesh, at the ridiculous prices charged for those events, so be it. Conservatives may secretly wish that our citizens would agree to pay their teachers and policemen and firemen and garbage collectors more, and those celebrities less, but they realize this is the free market at work. If we want to enjoy the fruits of the market, one has to take the bitter with the better, and then we must make it work as best as we can. To paraphrase Winston Churchill, capitalism may be a sometimes cruel and ineffective system, but it is still the best economic system yet devised by man.

So what does this have to do with American Jews being liberal? If we agree that it is the conservatives who do the best job of growing the free market; and if we agree that the free market is the best system yet devised by man to spread the wealth created among all the participants; and if one of the cherished goals of Judaism is to help solve the problem of poverty, then doesn't it follow that American Jews should be the foremost champions of growing the free market, and to do this they should be conservatives?

In spite of this apparently irrefutable logic, the overwhelming majority of prominent, wealthy, American Jewish capitalists—and we could name dozens—remain strong supporters of the liberal Democratic Party. What if we could demonstrate that Jewish law and tradition are much closer to today's conservative philosophy than to the liberal position? Would this be enough to turn them politically? Let us give it a try.

In his book, *With All Your Possessions: Jewish Ethics And Economic Life*, published in 1991, Dr. Meir Tamari, formerly chief economist of the Bank of Israel and a Biblical scholar, interprets the Bible and the Talmud as they relate to the business world. Dr. Tamari wrote that society is free to determine the degree of competition it desires, provided that the demands of justice and mercy are met. However, Jewish law tended to prefer a free market, which would provide for the benefit of the majority of the people.

Tamari explains further that economic wealth and prosperity were desirable; they were a gift of God. There is a joint ownership of wealth between God, the individual owner, and his fellow man, Dr. Tamari writes, but Judaism recognizes the legitimacy of private property, profit motive, and the market mechanism. The merchant or entrepreneur is legitimate and is morally entitled to a profit for fulfilling a function. Price controls always distort the market, although they were allowed for some basic commodities, while the pricing mechanism was always to be based on free markets. Halakhah sources encouraged a competitive market even in the ghetto where political freedom was absent. There was no trace of the Marxist labor theory of value, and wages were to be determined by the market. Also, unions could not use force to prevent the free entry into the market of non-organized workers. (The Talmud as interpreted by Dr. Tamari, sounds as if Milton Friedman had written it.)

Each individual has the right to perform with his property whatever economic activity he sees as most profitable to him. Morality and kindness are part of the market mechanism, even when they cannot be legally enforced. The bottom line according to Dr. Tamari was that the free market is really the only economic system sanctioned by Jewish law and tradition. The community could interfere with the workings of the market only if the weak and ignorant were not benefiting, but such interference was to be of a short and limited duration. Does it not follow that Jews should be doing everything possible to strengthen and enhance the free market system in the United States and that being a liberal is not consistent with that goal?

When it comes to welfare, Dr. Tamari wrote that welfare's aim is to provide a means of breaking the poverty cycle or to prevent a descent into poverty. One should accept the most menial of jobs before accepting welfare. Although acts of welfare are considered to be characteristic of the Jewish people, poverty carries with it no spiritual connotation. There is a line in *Fiddler On The Roof* that sings, "It is no great honor to be poor." In Jewish tradition there is a strong bias against being dependent on others or on the communal purse. Dr. Tamari did write that assistance to the weaker members of society is an obligation placed on the individual and on the community, so that its financing falls both on the public purse, through taxation and on voluntary donations. Again though, this help was to be only temporary. There was no automatic support for the forced re-distribution of wealth as this would not be consistent with the principle of controlling one's own private property.

The Jewish system of welfare differed radically from the modern system because of basic Jewish concepts of the role of wealth, economic justice, the dignity of the individual, and the moral responsibility of the individual. Welfare was considered to be an act of *imitatic dei*—imitation of God's ways. It appears that throughout Jewish tradition there is the respect for the individual and the need to help him get back on his economic feet as quickly as possible.

If we accept Dr. Tamari's analysis, and there seems to be no reason not to do so, where does that leave today's liberal with his championing of our coercive welfare system, which after sixty years and five trillion dollars, still leaves almost as many people below the poverty level as there were at the beginning. If we were following Jewish tradition, the welfare given would have been only of a temporary nature, the emphasis would have been to teach those on welfare a trade or a skill to enable them to earn their own living, and there would have been direct, personal help given voluntarily to those in need. Instead, the liberals created a monstrous bureaucracy that only recently is being whittled down to a more localized creature with the goal of actually removing people from the welfare rolls instead of finding ways and means of keeping them and their descendants wards of the system. I don't hear any big apologies from the liberals for having foisted this miserable, demeaning system on the American public for so many years. Nor do I hear most of our prominent Jews rendering any type of apology.

The link between Judaism and capitalism is well described by Ellis Rivkin in his book, *The Shaping of Jewish History*. Rivkin wrote that it was the onset of capitalism beginning in the late seventeenth century that began to bring freedom to European Jews. Where Jews had been forbidden to live for centuries, as in Holland, England, and France, they were permitted to resettle. In Germany it took until the end of the nineteenth century for capitalism to free the Jews. Where Jews participated in the creation of a capitalistic society as in America, they enjoyed a high degree of equality from the outset. Where capitalism failed to gain a secure foothold, as in Spain, Portugal, and Eastern Europe, Jews were either expelled or persecuted.

Capitalism and capitalism alone emancipated the Jews, Rivkin writes. The reason for this is that developing capitalism generates individual freedom, which is necessary for the entrepreneur to be free to seek a profit. Paul Johnson writes, "Jews made contribution to the creation of modern capitalism disproportionate to their numbers." Their motto was if there is a better way to do it, then let us find it.

The history of Jews in the modern world makes explicit the connection between individual freedom and developing capitalism. And yet, there seems to persist the notion that somehow capitalism breeds too much greed and selfishness, and we Jews must be the guardians against such evil spirits. It is okay for us Jews to become wealthy and to accrue power and influence through the workings of our marvelous free market, but we've got to protect society and the poor and the children from the evil inclinations that must reside in those "other rich and powerful" folk. Apparently only wealthy Jews (and liberal Democrats) possess that kindness of spirit that entitles them to possess the wealth they accumulate. So we Jews must continue to support the liberal cause because that is the only doctrine that seems to be consistent with our Jewish calling of *Tsedekah*, and which can control the evil impulses of those other rich guys.

We Jews are supposed to have high intellects, the result of the survival of the fittest throughout our 4,000-year history. We excel in business and the arts and all of the other modern skills, and still we cannot seem to get it through our heads that it is the free market, capitalism, and political freedom that constitute the foundation for our great, good fortune in these United States. When will we wake up to the fact that today's liberalism, if left unchecked, works to diminish that political freedom, to chip away at the workings of the free market, and will eventually bind us up with thousands of rules and regulations which inhibit our freedom to live our lives as we choose?

One rabbi wrote me that the free market had to be regulated and controlled because the Talmud set specific guidelines for prices. A seller could not sell for more than one-sixth or less than one-sixth of the fair market value of a commodity. In a way this is a non-statement. By modern definition, fair market price means the value of any good or service that a willing seller will sell for and a willing buyer will pay. So if the fair market price is used to consummate a transaction, then by definition, the one-sixth rule would not apply.

But to carry on the argument of the one-sixth or 16%, this could mean that a company could not make a net profit of more than 16%, after taxes of course. In reviewing the profit margins of the 1,000 top companies in America, there were just twenty companies that exceeded that margin. The only regulation the market requires is that of preventing fraud and deception wherever possible, and policing the rules that ensure open entry into any industry or occupation. In the final analysis, the best protection is the market itself. If companies persist in cheating their customers, they simply do not last. As long as competition is fostered and there are no artificial barriers from government or elsewhere to prevent new entrants into an industry, then we must rely on the market to police itself.

Competition, 1992 Nobel Prize winner for economics Gary Becker writes, is the "tonic for meeting human needs." Becker writes that competition fosters the variety that meets the needs of a free society. "Competition is the foundation of the good life and the most precious parts of human existence; educational, civil, religious and cultural as well as economic." Thus was Becker quoted in the Heritage Foundation autumn 1999 quarterly report.

Werner Sombart, author of *The Jews and Modern Capitalism*, written in 1913, theorized that the Jews were really the first capitalists. This is disputed by Rivkin who claims that it was the traders of Venice in the 1500s, non-Jews, who were the first. Regardless of who was first, Sombart made some interesting points. He wrote that Jews championed the cause of individual liberty in economic activities against the then dominant views of the majority who seemed to avoid competition. It seems that Christian traders maintained prices, while the Jews broke into their markets by under-selling them. Does this sound familiar? (Another example of Jews separating themselves from the dominant majority, and to the benefit of all.) Although Jews in Europe were at best, "semi-citizens," they made their mark in business particularly in the money-lending business (forbidden to Christians) that Sombart claims is the root idea of capitalism. Without credit and lending, nothing would get accomplished.

Sombart wrote that the Jewish religion was a contract between God and His chosen people and that the getting of money was a means to do God's work. A non-Jew, Sombart praised the Jewish traits of self-control, love of order and work, moderation, chastity, and sobriety. He claimed that the restriction of sexual activity released energies to economic activities. (Perhaps "prudish" conservatives are not so backward.) Jews believed in free trade without restrictions and welcomed anyone who wanted to compete. One would think that Sombart's book, although somewhat overly favorable to Jews in certain phases, would still be one that should be studied by today's young Jews to give them a better perspective on their economic history.

When we weave together the historical bias of Judaism for the free market, the fact that capitalism is closely linked to Judaism and has liberated Jews from the ghetto in Europe, that Jews were instrumental in at least the expansion of capitalism, and when we know through our history here in America, that to truly benefit those less fortunate, it is only the growth of the free market here that has accomplished this, there would appear to be an air-tight case for Jews to be the most active champions of that same free market. And to accomplish this, the political philosophy that makes the best case for its support of the free market, and for the limiting of the power of a central government, has to be conservatism.

When one strikes to the core of modern liberalism, one will usually find a secret distaste for the apparent chaos of the free market, and a not-so-secret desire to legally control it by enforcing the wondrous intellectual powers of those same liberals. Liberals are great for championing the rights of the individual when it comes to abortion or the right not to pray in public schools, but when it comes to the right of individuals to retain their hard-earned monies to spend as they choose, suddenly the liberal turns deaf. Is that what Judaism really says? Rabbi Lapin writes that of the 613 commandments in the Torah, a great number relate to property and money. "No area of law is given as much attention in the Torah as the area dealing with free market transactions between free and independent citizens." These laws presuppose private property, and the right of the property owner to dispose of that property as he chooses. This puts the lie to the liberal position that only certain individual rights are sacrosanct.

How often does one read statements by Jewish leaders that praise the efforts of Bill Gates or Intel's Andrew Grove (a Jewish Hungarian refugee) for their success in helping to create the wonder of the twentieth century, the computer industry? These two men have done more to grow the American economy and provide jobs for thousands, than have all of the war on poverty programs of the past forty years. Yet the people who receive the Jewish merit badges are usually the politicians—Democrats mostly—who talk and talk and talk, and pass more and more useless laws that provide employment mainly for the attorneys of the world. How can we return to the political climate that existed with Jews prior to the FDR phenomena? It will never happen if Jews remain political liberals!

Where Jews should be making their contribution to our market economy is by exhibiting the highest morality in their dealings with others in the business world. Our capitalistic system depends on honesty, integrity, and the carrying out of one's promises. It is when fraud and deceit enter the picture that the worst excesses occur, and when people begin to doubt the value of our system. If Jews who are already so prominent in the business world would stress the positive aspects of the free market and set great examples of honesty in their business dealings, they could do more to help the economy grow and provide jobs than any government program existing. In the process, they would also demonstrate some of the basic morality of our Jewish religion.

The notes to Exodus of the Soncino Pentateuch state that Judaism "continues to proclaim that there is an everlasting distinction between right and wrong...and that weak and erring man needs an authoritative code in matters of right and wrong." The portion of the Decalogue and its commandment that thou shall not steal, constitutes one of the sturdiest pillars that supports today's successful American free market economy.

It is not enough merely to do what is legally correct, we Jews should go beyond that and do what is morally right in our dealings with our fellows, so said a Hasidic rabbi recently. Shubert Spero writes that basic to the legal system is the concept of justice, which is a moral principle. Justice, fairness, and equity are universal moral principles. As Spero states, "In Jewish view from the very beginning men were considered moral agents and responsible for their behavior."

When we read about a Jew who has cheated in business, and there have been several recent examples, it hurts. There is something that is inborn in most of us that wants to do what is right, and we are particularly sensitive about the actions of our fellow Jews, especially the prominent ones whose actions catch the headlines. On the other hand, the positive stories seldom receive sufficient attention. Most heartwarming was the story of the Jewish manufacturer, Aaron Feuerstein, an Orthodox Jew. In 1995, Mr. Feuerstein's company, Malden Mills in Lawrence, Massachusetts, suffered a devastating fire in its main factory. Mr.

Feuerstein not only maintained his entire staff of workers on salary for several months until he could resume production, he also gave out his traditional Christmas bonuses to his employees. His workers could hardly believe he would do this, but he believed that it was the people working for him that had made his family business a success and that he was only doing what he thought was right.

In early 2003, Malden Mills was forced to declare bankruptcy due to declining sales and increased foreign competition. Mr. Feuerstein, however, has plans to personally revive the company soon with his own funds. When asked whether he regretted paying out all of that money several years ago when his factory burned down, thereby depleting his company's reserves, he said no—he had acted not for the moment but rather for a larger goal.

Today, I like to think that deep down in their innermost gut, many American Jews really do believe that big government is not the answer to our social and economic problems. In fact they may now suspect that big (liberal) government may be a large contributing source of our problems. Many American Jews recognize that the noble sounding programs of the 1960s—the war on poverty, the war on illiteracy, the war on unemployment of the less fortunate, etc.—have not accomplished their avowed purposes. Jews frequently find themselves opposing these programs in cases of quotas and affirmative action. One could almost conclude that many Jews are "closet conservatives." Perhaps what is needed to bring them out of this "closet" is a fable that may illustrate the basic point about the capitalistic, free market system, and the wondrous benefits that flow from it. And this brings us to what I will call "The Mahi--Mox Story."

Once upon a time there was a young Jewish lad growing up in Chicago. It was a tradition for this lad and his family to shop at their local deli on Saturday nights to buy the fixings for Sunday breakfast. Naturally these fixings consisted of lox, cream cheese, and bagels. All through his youth, our "hero-to-be" feasted on these delicacies, never giving a thought to their cost.

When he became of age, seeking his fortune he moved to Los Angeles, studied hard, and became a CPA. While raising his own family, he naturally carried on the Saturday night tradition of buying lox, cream cheese, and bagels for Sunday's breakfast, which in California language became "brunch."

Of course, the prices of these precious ingredients rose with the increase in the general price level, but it seemed that the price of lox had its own special multiplier. Our "hero-to-be" became accustomed to paying at first $6.00 per pound, then $9.00, then $12.00, but when the price hit $16.00 per pound, this really caught his attention. Since he was still just a low level CPA, he seriously considered eliminating lox from their Sunday brunch. When he asked the local deli owner, Mr. Kaplan, for an explanation for the continuing price increases, the only thing Mr. Kaplan could answer was that it was simply "supply and demand."

Before giving in to his miserly and conservative instincts and eliminating Lox, the creative juices of our "hero-to-be" began to percolate. After all, CPAs are not just bean counters. What if someone could invent a cheaper, more plentiful substitute for lox?

Not only would this creation be welcomed by the millions of lox lovers around the world, but the inventor could possibly make a great deal of "gelt," otherwise known as real money.

So our young CPA began to experiment with various recipes in the privacy of his kitchen between preparing tax returns for his clients. After months of trial and error, he discovered that the plentiful mahi-mahi had many of the same characteristics as the salmon, of which lox is the smoked variety. Further, through intensive reading of the Dead Sea Scrolls, he discovered an ancient smoking and seasoning process that magically transformed the taste and looks of the mahi-mahi into an almost perfect replica of the precious lox. (Perhaps, he reasoned, this is how the early Jews could afford their Sunday brunches.) Best of all, he could produce this wondrous substitute at a fraction of the cost of lox. He decided to call his new product "Mahi-Mox."

At this point in our story let us pause for a moment. After all of his work, our "hero-to-be" still had not created any new jobs, nor had he created any new wealth, nor had he provided any help to the less fortunate. There remained many problems to be solved. What he had accomplished was to imagine that there might be a market for a low-cost substitute for Lox that he could produce profitably, and that he alone, through hard work and research, had developed this product. Unable to afford any focus groups to test his idea, he had to rely on his own God-given instincts to pursue his dream. And perhaps most important to remember, our "hero-to-be" lived in a society under a system which granted him the freedom to pursue his imagination and his dream, in spite of various restrictive government rules and regulations.

The rest of the story is somewhat predictable. He takes out a second mortgage on his home, rents a small seasoning factory, contracts to buy mahi-mahi from San Pedro fisherman who have a plentiful supply, hires at first his unwilling kids and wife to do the dirty work while he continues on his CPA job, prepares some samples and takes them to some local delis, sells them their first orders on a money-back guarantee, shows them they can sell "Mahi-Mox" at one-half the price of lox and still make twice as much profit, does some local advertising, and before one can say "Mahi-Mox" ten times, his product's sales take off.

One year later he quits his CPA job, expands into a modern 50,000 square foot plant with 150 employees, including all of his local relatives and friends, plus some recent importees from across the border to do the hard work, because our new welfare programs had not yet fully kicked in. As he banks his first million, our "hero" reflects that in just one year he had provided the market with a new product that sold by the ton, and amazingly the makers of lox did not seem to have been hurt at all. With a lower cost alternative to lox, the total market expanded so dramatically that those who could afford it continued to buy the original lox, the status product, while many new buyers loved the pure taste of the "Mahi-Mox" at its bargain price.

Most importantly, he had created hundreds of new jobs without any help from government. Just like Ford, Edison, and Gates, he had created new wealth by pursuing his own selfish self-interest. It was enlightened self-interest though, because he furnished all of his employees with an unlimited supply of "Mahi-Mox" plus all the soap and deodorants they needed. And all lived happily ever after.

Stories like this are repeated over and over in this country. Individuals pursuing their own selfish, frequently enlightened, self-interest create jobs. Jobs are not created by government taking money from some to give to others, and in the process wasting half of it. If that were the answer, the Roman Empire would still be with us, all of us would still be running around in bed sheets, and living off of the State.

Jobs are created by producing goods and services that fill a need in the marketplace. To create more jobs we need to strip away the regulations and restrictive rules that make it so difficult to start or to expand a business, permit people to retain more of the fruits of their own labor, and confine government to its proper role of enforcing fair laws without favoring one side over another. If we can stir these simple ingredients together, ease in starting and expanding businesses, increased incentives for keeping and reinvesting the money we earn, and a sharply reduced role for government, then this wonderful American free market system can retain its place as the world's freest and most productive economy.

If there is any one group of immigrants who has flourished the most under our system, it has certainly been the Jews. Wandering from nation to nation throughout our 4,000-year history, only in America has it been possible to achieve what we have within the space of a few generations. For us not to recognize the value of the system that has permitted this progress is simply pure ignorance. Let us now make sure that others have the same opportunities that our ancestors and we have had. We can do this only by strengthening our free market system and not by strangling it with the deadening hand of government regulations.

Who knows how many more "heroes-to-be" are out there waiting for their "Mahi-Mox" to be discovered? And now with even McDonalds serving them, if only someone could invent a cheaper bagel!

JEWISH VOTING PATTERNS

Since the days of Abraham, Isaac, and Jacob, right up to the present conflicts between Orthodox vs. non-Orthodox, Jews have always been a fractious people. Never being able to present a truly united front on many of the major issues confronting our people throughout the ages, we still have managed to survive numerous persecutions and dislocations. Israel currently is a politically divided nation. Why is it then that in these United States, Jews continue to show such uniformity in their voting habits? Why is it that for the past seventy years, from 60-90% of American Jews routinely vote the Democrat ticket, no matter who the presidential nominee is? This was not always the case here. In the presidential election of 2004, it is estimated that the Jewish vote for the Republican incumbent, George W. Bush, "soared" to 25%, still an improvement over the 19% recorded in 2000. A most interesting footnote to Jewish voting in 2004 was just released. It seems that Jews who attend religious services on a regular basis split their votes 50/50 between Bush and Kerry. Is this another argument for Jews to abandon their secular liberal philosophy?

In the eighteenth and nineteenth centuries, the first great waves of Jewish immigrants from Germany and Western Europe established themselves eventually as merchants, financiers, and generally became part of the capitalistic fabric of America. They tended to vote their pocketbooks and were politically conservative. The memories of their European origin were not excessively burdened with pogroms and brutal persecution. Nathaniel Weyl writes in *The Jew In American Politics*, "(T)o the extent that they were politically committed, the majority of American Jewry remained faithful to the party of Lincoln between the

Civil War and the Rooseveltian New Deal." The main reason for this was that American Jews, mostly of German heritage at the turn of the twentieth century, had succeeded in their new homeland and were now firmly established in the middle and upper classes of American business and social life.

They backed the Republican Party, Weyl writes, because that party was the one of business and espoused the virtues of individualism. The Republican Party, he writes, "was more Protestant than Catholic, more mid-Western than Eastern, more North European than representative of the newer immigrant stocks, more middle class than proletarian." When they were followers of the Democratic Party, such as Morgenthau and the Strauss brothers, they were moderates, and probably in today's political definitions would be classified as moderate Republicans.

In Stephen Birmingham's book, *Our Crowd*, a history of the one hundred German Jewish families who attained great wealth after coming to this country in the 1800s, he relates that almost without exception, these Jews became Republicans. Joseph Seligman, Jacob Schiff, and Otto Kahn, among others, were the outstanding figures who went from peddlers to becoming giants of finance. When one of their descendants or associates became a Democrat, this was regarded with horror. Sadly, future generations of these great achievers did not retain much of the political conservatism of their ancestors.

In 1881, the mass immigration of Russian and East European Jews to America began. These Jews, escaping from the persecution and the pogroms, were poorer than the German Jews who had preceded them, and had little in common with the established 250,000 mainly German and Sephardic Jews already in the United States. They were escaping from the tyranny of the czar and tended to support those attempting to overthrow the czar, including the communists. Many Eastern European Jews had become socialists to defend themselves from the tyranny of the czar. Paul Johnson writes that some Jews became Bolsheviks and revolutionaries to escape their Jewishness. Jews, who were in reality "non-Jews" when it came to observing their religion, were prominent in revolutionary parties in many countries in Europe. One example was Leon Trotsky, a Jew, who helped bring Lenin into power in 1917.

Once arriving in this country, many gravitated into the needle trades and light industries with which they were familiar. Jews became leaders of some of the more prominent labor unions: Samuel Gompers, first with the cigar makers, and then as president of the AFL, and Sidney Hillman with the garment workers. Weyl writes that the first generation of Russian Jews concentrated on giving their children an education and moving themselves out of the sweatshop labor into that of skilled labor, contractors, and independent businessmen. The number of firms in the garment industry in New York increased from 234 in 1882, to 16,552 in 1918, employing over 300,000 people. The second generation moved into other small businesses and those professions that did not require more education than they could afford, such as lawyers, accountants, and pharmacists. Not until the third generation did they begin to reach the medical professions that required extensive education and training.

Although these Russian and East European Jews settled in major American cities, which were mainly controlled by the Democratic Party, as they gradually moved up the economic and social scale, by no means did they uniformly move into the Democratic Party. Apparently enough of them remembered the tyranny of the czar and were determined to deny the American government those supreme powers that had forced them to leave their mother countries. To many Russian Jews, the concept of liberalism meant that this would liberate them from the control of government or the czar. When they found that American liberalism tended to increase the powers of government over their individual activities, a goodly number of them rejected the Democratic Party.

Thus from Lincoln to the beginning of World War I, the majority of American Jews were Republicans. A succession of American presidents had been friendly toward Jews and had vigorously protested anti-Semitic pogroms in Eastern Europe. Also, the Irish controlled most Democratic political machines in the North, and there existed hostility between the Irish and the Jews at that time. Theodore Roosevelt, in particular, was a strong favorite of Jewish voters. Roosevelt even predicted that a Jew would someday be president of the United States, and appointed the first Jew to a Cabinet post: Secretary of Commerce and Labor, Oscar Straus. The leading Jews in America, Jacob Schiff, et al, supported Theodore Roosevelt. Even though the bulk of American Jews, now numbering almost three million, were of Slavic origin, and were more of the working class than the original German immigrants, they tended to continue to accept the leadership of the German Jews, who were still heavily Republican. Also the German Jews in America, even though they disagreed with the politics of many of the Eastern European Jewish immigrants, still contributed heavily to help the new immigrants become established here.

In 1920, eleven Jews were elected to Congress: ten Republicans and one Socialist. Then things began to change. One of the factors bringing about the change was, strangely enough, the rise of the Ku Klux Klan. The rebirth of this organization in 1915 stressed the supremacy of the Caucasian race, and was against Negroes, Catholics, and Jews. By 1924, the Klan claimed a membership of six million and was strong in Southwestern cities. At that time the South was solidly Democrat. Thus the Klan became an important element of the Democratic Party, and in the 1924 Democratic Convention was the cause of a debate that almost split the party into two pieces. Alfred Smith, a Catholic, former governor of New York, demanded that the Party repudiate the Klan. His motion lost by one vote, but Smith went on to win the Democratic nomination for president in 1928, when the Republican Herbert Hoover defeated him.

The effect of all this, strange as it may seem today, was that America's Jewish voters, one half of whom were concentrated in New York, became impressed with Smith's denunciation of the Klan, and began to switch to voting Democrat. This was ironic because the issue of the Klan was never a divisive issue in the Republican Party. Perhaps the

Republican Leadership did not speak out loudly enough against the Klan. For whatever reason, history records that the Democratic Party took the credit for defeating the Klan, and thereby earned the gratitude of many Jewish voters. This was almost akin to setting up a straw man, knocking him down, and claiming credit for a real knockout. In heavily Jewish precincts in New York and Chicago, Smith won 66% to 75% of the vote. Two years later, in 1930, six of the eight Jews elected to Congress were Democrats. (In 2001, 25 of the 27 Jews in the House of Representatives and 10 of the 11 Jews in the Senate are Democrats. The trend has continued.)

Then came the election of 1932, Franklin D. Roosevelt against the Republican incumbent, Herbert Hoover. This was the third year of the Great Depression. Hoover was trying unsuccessfully to cope with the Depression. Jews as a group had been hit by the Depression, but no more and perhaps less than other groups. There were no particular Jewish differences between the two candidates. Nazism had not yet become an issue; domestic anti-Semitism was not a big problem; Hoover was considered to be an honest, capable president. Yet Jewish support for Roosevelt in 1932 was overwhelming. Illinois recorded Jewish votes of 85% to 95%. New York was up in the 90 percentile. Roosevelt won forty-six of the forty-eight states.

Why this massive swing in the Jewish vote? FDR was a charismatic leader. Endowed with a deep, resonant voice—remember there was no television—FDR talked about helping your fellow citizen, about charity for all, about helping the average man to achieve his goals. In other words, he preached charity, brotherly love, repair the world, all themes dear to Jewish hearts.

Weyl writes, "Jews, even those of a secular bent, saw in Roosevelt's programs the embodiment of ideals of brotherhood and charity which were deeply embedded in the ethical teachings of Judaism. The intensity of Jewish religious and ethical education made these concepts a vital part of the everyday lives and aspirations of ordinary Jews." Paul Johnson wrote that Jews voted Democrat because of sympathy for the poor and the underdog, a position that many had escaped from in Europe. FDR sold himself and his party to America's Jews as the group that was best equipped to achieve the goals that Jews sought here.

So there we may have it. Having become fairly well established in their new American environment, Jews still longed to implement their inborn desire to do good and be charitable. In their infinite wisdom, American Jews saw FDR as a modern Messiah. FDR with his undeniable charisma, magnificent speaking ability, and brave disregard for his own physical handicaps, seemed bigger than life. Elected to an historic four terms, climaxed by his leadership in helping to defeat Hitler, FDR became a giant figure in Jewish eyes, and remains so to this day. This appears to continue to be one of the primary reasons that the great majority of American Jews have remained Democrats to this very day.

As Thomas Sowell writes in *Visions Of The Anointed*, liberals create or seize upon a crisis, develop a solution for it that involves government programs, and then walk away from it to await their next crisis opportunity. The fact that their programs fail, and frequently bring about the opposite result from that intended, has no meaning to the liberals. And so it is with the FDR myth and his programs. Jews thought they would bring about universal brotherhood and prosperity for all. At this they failed miserably. After seven years of the New Deal and all the make work programs inherent in that doctrine, as late as 1939, there still existed a national unemployment rate of 20%! As for universal brotherhood, it was during the late 1930s that anti-Semitism in this country reached its heights.

It has only been the marvelous workings of our free market system that has brought unparalleled prosperity to America. All of the government welfare programs, with the possible exception of the GI Bill to educate returning veterans from World War II, have had on balance probably a net negative effect on the growth of our economy. Yet American Jews still cling to the outmoded and obsolete reasons that first influenced their swing to liberalism.

Studies have shown that the way one's parents vote has a great influence on the political leanings of their children. I did not realize it at the time, but my parents were Republicans, at a time in Chicago when almost all Jews were Democrats. We read the *Chicago Tribune*, which then was a staunchly Republican newspaper. When FDR died in April 1945, I remarked to Ellie, then my girlfriend and later my wife, that this was possibly a good day for America. She was somewhat horrified at my statement, and frankly, I don't remember from where it came. It was probably from some deep feeling that came from overhearing conversations of my parents. Fortunately it did not spoil a beautiful romance and today we think alike on all things political.

Perhaps now with a third generation coming of age since the 1930s, Jewish votes will begin to shift. There are hopeful signs that the young American Jews of today are questioning more and more the political leanings of their elders. In the new age of computers, the Internet, and the wide dispersal and availability of information, it appears that many of the old myths are slowly disintegrating as more light is cast on the lack of results of the liberal programs. Also it appears that many young Jews do not have the emotional attachment to the old liberal dogma that prevents many of their elders from rationally thinking through just what it is that is so great about liberalism.

One recent example of changes that are taking place was reported in 1999 in the *Orange County Register*. Several young Orange County readers were interviewed about their reasons for their recent conversions to different religions. A recent convert to Judaism was quoted as follows: "I'm a libertarian, so liberty, self-responsibility and acting on your own volition are important to me...the heart of Judaism's history is its struggle for freedom amid mass persecution. It is a story of the tragic price paid when people cannot exercise free thinking." As more young Jews enter the business world and come face to face with the multitude of government rules, regulations, and taxes, the Jewish tradition of the importance of freedom of the individual to act in accordance with his own enlightened self-interest may well contribute to a meaningful change in their inherited voting patterns.

One never knows how attitudes are influenced. Change is coming, although it is sometimes difficult to see. Old habits are hard to break, but break them we must if American Jews are to finally become convinced that liberalism is a philosophy that is truly not in harmony with Jewish law and tradition.

LIBERALS' BELIEF IN THE MAGIC POWERS OF GOVERNMENT

Of all of the ties between Jews and liberalism, the one that is perhaps the strongest and the strangest is the devotion and dedication that Jews in America have had to the "wondrous" powers of a strong, centralized federal government. Ever since 1933, when FDR converted the federal government from a fairly insignificant entity into the powerhouse it has become, American Jews have hailed and championed the federal government as the answer to all of our social ills. If only more of them had read and believed what the great French economist Frederick Bastiat wrote in the 1800s—"Government is the great fiction, through which everybody endeavors to live at the expense of everybody else"—we would not have created the monstrous governmental structure we have today.

Somehow in the minds of the Jewish leaders and the organizations they head, the best and in most cases the only solution to our social, economic, environmental, and assorted difficulties, was to grant the federal government those powers that they believed could bring about the desired ends. As to the results that accrued from granting those powers, that was left to the historians. So long as the "sound good" and "feel good" laws were passed, with their invariably rosy predictions, then we Jews believed we had done the right thing. As Dennis Prager has said, liberals believe that it is not results that count; it is only good intentions.

The fact that in 1939, after seven years of the New Deal, the unemployment rate in the United States was still close to 20% is unknown by most Jewish voters. It was only the onset of World War II, with the massive war effort financed only partly by taxation and mostly by the issuance of government bonds, that eventually created a wartime boom period. Our national debt skyrocketed during that period with the issuance of massive amounts of government bonds, along with deficit spending. In hindsight, most economists agree that most of the New Deal programs passed in the 1930s served mainly to prolong the length of the Depression, rather than bringing it to an end. In a free economy, if left reasonably alone, the natural forces of the market will tend toward balance, not imbalance.

One effort to try and pull us out of the Depression was the establishment of Social Security, inaugurated in 1935. This program was supposed to establish a minimum form of retirement income and most Jews hailed its passage. No matter that at the time the average mortality age for men was sixty-three and benefits began at age sixty-five. No matter that the tax was only 1% on the first $3,000 of wages, or $30 per year. This would still somehow provide some minimum income at age sixty-five to keep the wolf away from the door. Perhaps it could not have been predicted by anyone at the time that after opening the door to such a system, the politicians of both parties would succeed in expanding that program until in 1999, many Americans pay more in Social Security taxes than they pay in income taxes, and that today the program is seriously in need of oxygen.

What should have alerted Jews to the potential dangers of such a system was their historic experience with granting a centralized government the power to tax and re-distribute income. Jews in Europe were skilled in bargaining with the governments of those countries in which they were permitted to live in order to continue to preserve their very existence. Jews willingly paid taxes to their local governments, as compensation or bribes, to secure their permission to exist in that area. Whatever types of retirement programs they wanted were always set up through their own organizations and were private and voluntary.

Somehow all of that was forgotten when they arrived in the "Goldena Medina," America. We were so enjoying our unprecedented freedom here, to live and work as we chose, that we were willing to give the benefit of the doubt to the New Dealers and the Fair Dealers. But does that excuse the current attitude of most Jews in America towards these government programs that are slowly but surely sliding into black holes? One would think that after two generations of enacting and expanding government programs and observing their results, Jews would begin to question their support of them. This certainly does not show up in their voting. Jews continue to vote Democrat, or liberal, in overwhelming numbers, in the face of almost disastrous results.

The war on poverty, which accelerated in earnest under Lyndon Johnson in 1964-5, has led to the expenditure of over $5 trillion to this date, and still the number of citizens below the poverty level is approximately the same number as when these programs began. The collateral effects of this war have been equally dismal. We have spawned an entire generation of fatherless youth, due to our subsidizing unmarried women when they had children, and continuing that support indefinitely. Now we are reaping the results. Crime, illegitimacy, illegal drug use, and many of our current social ills can be traced to the enormous rise in the birth of babies out of wedlock. All of these unintended results came about from well-meaning politicians, but Jews could have predicted what would happen based on their own prior experiences with governments.

An Irishman, and a future Senator, Daniel Patrick Moynihan of New York, was amazingly perceptive when he wrote in 1965 in *Family and Nation*, "There is one unmistakable lesson in American history; a community that allows a large number of young men to grow up in broken families, dominated by women, never acquiring any stable relationship to male authority, never acquiring any set of rational expectations about the future—that community asks for and gets chaos. Crime, violence, unrest, disorder—most particularly the furious, unrestrained lashing out at the whole social structure—that is not only to be expected; it is very near to inevitable. And it is richly deserved." If only this nation had listened to Moynihan then, we would probably not be reading about all of the crime and murders perpetrated by young people today.

As for the granting of great powers to government, we Jews could have hearkened back to Deuteronomy 17:14, which defined the powers that were to be granted to any king. Although God promised His people a king when they entered the Promised Land, that king was to have very limited powers. He was to be one of the people, could not multiply horses to himself, nor order the people back to Egypt. He could not have multiple wives, nor gather to himself inordinate amounts of gold and silver. His main duty was to keep a copy of the law with him, read it all the days of his life, keep the words of the law and the statutes, and do them, so as to prolong his days and the days of the people in the land of Israel. It seems that these words of Deuteronomy 17:15-20 were meant to establish a king from among the people through a prophet's choice, and then have that king serve his people mainly by helping them to live by the words of God. Most importantly, such kings were always to be subordinate to the one God, the invisible God, Yahweh.

One could almost see those thoughts replicated in the part of our own Declaration of Independence which reads: "(A)ll men are created equal; that they are endowed by their Creator with certain unalienable rights; that among these are life, liberty, and the pursuit of happiness; that to secure these rights, governments are instituted among men, deriving their just powers from the consent of the governed." Thomas Cahill in his recent book, *The Gifts of the Jews*, writes, "There is a direct link between the ancient Jews and the American Declaration of Independence."

Thomas Jefferson, author of the Declaration, also wrote that "A wise and frugal government which shall restrain men from injuring one another, which shall leave them otherwise free to regulate their own pursuits of industry and improvement, and shall not take from their mouth of labor the bread it has earned; this is the sum of good government." Thus both the ancient Jews and the eighteenth century Americans appeared to have had a similar fear of what can happen when a king, or a congress, or a president is granted unlimited powers.

As if to prove the truth of what Deuteronomy and the Declaration declare, the history of Jews and powerful, centralized governments is a sorry one. From the time of the Egyptian pharaohs, to the Roman emperors, to the European kings, to the mad dictators of the twentieth century, Jews have been the convenient "sacrificial lamb," on which the problems of the day could be blamed, for all of those tyrannical leaders. It was always the power of a centralized government, by leading the persecution, sanctioning it, or participating in it with other willing allies, that kept the Jews on the run. Now in America, where there has been no government supported discrimination or persecution (other than some early state laws which were soon abandoned), Jews have enjoyed unprecedented political freedom. As a result, it appears that Jews have relaxed their guards and somehow have come to regard government with a kindly, almost benevolent, gaze.

Maybe it was that the people elected to public office seemed to be so brilliant. The prevailing thought seemed to be that they must know what is right and best for our country since they came from all those prestigious schools in the East. During the period when it was difficult for Jews to enter those schools, and when the local city colleges were the most open avenue to obtaining a higher education, it may have been only natural for American Jews to swallow the propaganda coming out of the East that the federal government had all the answers to our social ills. After all, socialism by another name wasn't too bad. Were not many of our people prominent in the American socialist and communist movements? And were not the government programs being advanced simply a milder form of that socialism?

An observer can perhaps rationalize those views as occurring back in the 1930s and 1940s. But to still believe that government contains such magical powers today at the beginning of the twenty-first century when we have two generations of dismal results from those federal programs to examine, stretches the bounds of reason. For Jews to still so over-whelmingly continue to be strong supporters of federal programs to cure all of our social and economic ills is truly astounding. For our captains of industry, the arts, the media, the professions, who by their own talents and skills have created vast empires of business, who have created thousands of jobs without any federal aid, to still tread the path of disguised socialism, and march in lockstep with the liberal Democratic Party, defies rational explanation. To do anything that does not strengthen this wonderful free market system of capitalism is to defy Jewish roots, Jewish traditions, and their own experience.

In the book, *The Jewish World*, edited by Elie Kedourie in 1979, the author writes that all through the Bible is the Jews' mistrust of merely political authority. They were skeptical about the ability of rulers to act justly. The body politic being only human and subject to decay and failure, is not one that gives meaning and coherence to human life. Only God's judgment as revealed through the prophets and Moses should be our guiding lights. As God's "chosen people," the Jews believed they had the right to political freedom and to worship the one God, thus renouncing all other gods.

Even when it came to the kings of Israel, as the notes to Deuteronomy in Soncino Pentateuch relate, it is God who is the real king and the sole supreme authority. The king is only the agent of the Divine King, and serves as the leader of the people under the law to "respect the life, honor and possessions of his people." It was not the king who had sovereign rights; those belonged to the people and they were free to impose new restrictions on each new king. The essence of our Biblical history is that our ancestors had a wonderful capacity for self-government. The late Justice Mayor Sulzberger is quoted in those pages as writing, "the Jewish people at large had as keen an outlook and as wide a vision in political as in religious affairs ... and that the modern conception of a rational, democratic, representative government owes its origin to the same (Jewish) ancestry." The Old Testament provided inspiration and guidance to the founders of this country, and it is sad that our modern Jews have strayed so far from their roots.

In spite of this glorious history, there remains still imbedded a myth that is difficult to eradicate from the American Jewish psyche. That is the notion that the people we elect to send to Washington, DC are somehow endowed with a magic power that gives them a far-seeing wisdom with which to solve our national problems. No matter that in their previous lives in California, or New York, or wherever, these bright folks may have had trouble making an honest living, or raising a decent family, or doing a commendable job in the local government position many held prior to going to Washington. Now these same folk would be magically transformed into all-knowing, all-seeing wizards. Perhaps one out of fifty, or at best one out of twenty, could fit the description of being a truly enlightened person with honor and integrity, who had studied the issues and had developed a formidable, reliable, personal philosophy of government and what the true role of government should be. I don't know how others feel, but I want people that I vote for to have that type of honor, integrity, and knowledge.

In my personal dealings with our elected representatives, and in listening to them over the past half-century, I can count on perhaps both hands and feet, the number of men and women whom I would acknowledge fit that description when it came to analyzing and dealing with the complex issues they face. The biggest problem, of course, is that government, particularly at the federal level, gets involved in so many facets of our lives, they cannot do a decent job in any of them. That, I believe, is at the root of the problem. If we would insist that our Congress limit its efforts to maintaining a sound currency, reducing to minimum the intrusion of government into our private lives, providing for a strong national defense, ensuring the integrity of our judicial system, and eliminating as much as possible the rules and regulations that restrict our individual freedoms, perhaps then these folk could do a decent job and really earn their salaries and perks.

In fairness to our elected representatives, both state and federal, one can see how easily they become seduced into believing that only they can make decisions that will solve our most pressing social and economic problems. When you visit Washington, DC and wander into the magnificent museums, memorials, and capital buildings, it is natural to begin to assume that you too, the newly elected representative, can also exhibit the wisdom and courage that those men and women of past years did in the service of this country.

The problem is that the best decisions of those revered figures were almost always the ones that enhanced the freedoms of the citizens of this country to maximize their own individual lives, and not the ones that expanded the powers of government. The swing to thinking that government laws and the concentration of power in Washington and in state capitals is somehow in harmony with the principles of our founding fathers is one of the great myths of our time. Again to quote Thomas Jefferson, "If we can prevent the government from wasting the labors of the people, under the pretense of taking care of them, they must become happy." One would think that based on our historically bad experiences with the powers of centralized governments, Jews would know better!

Yet our prominent Jews, both in the business and religious worlds, continue to call for ever-increasing federal regulation on how we live. Whatever popular cause of the moment grabs the fancy of the media and the TV-watching public, I don't hear many Jewish leaders speak up for the defendants of the day. When the tobacco hysteria came along, with the mostly successful financial pillage of the tobacco companies, where were our Jewish leaders to protest this invasion of privately owned companies? The only voice I heard was that of Dennis Prager.

In a special issue of *Prager Perspective* written in May 1998, Prager made a convincing case that the anti-tobacco campaign was due to several factors, none of which are directly tied to Judaism, but were still relevant to our subject. One factor Prager stated was that activists are often totalitarians. This should be an alarm call to Jews.

The way he explained it is that those who seek to control the behavior of others, by definition, are often totalitarians. Also the argument that only the anti-smoking crusaders in school can be the moderating influence over children takes away and reduces the parental influence over their children. Prager writes, "If anti-smoking activists are sure of anything it is their moral superiority. And the combination of moral superiority, an ability to coerce, the means and will to indoctrinate the young, and almost unlimited resources for media propaganda comprises what is known as totalitarianism."

In my opinion, Prager's analysis of the tobacco matter is equally applicable to most of the other liberal sponsored laws that attempt to regulate peoples' behavior. If there is a problem in our society—from smoking, to drinking, to using too much water when we flush our toilets, to being too fat or too lean—then let us pass a law to punish, control, regulate, and change that behavior. We tried to eliminate the "sin" of drinking alcohol with prohibition in the 1920s, and although that failed miserably, the liberals continue to try and try and try. Give them credit for their persistence, but it is at our expense.

We Jews, especially the Anti-Defamation League, respond quickly whenever there is the faintest smell of Jews being discriminated against or when some effort is made to introduce prayer in schools. When however, any movement seeks to control our individual behavior for the sake of some preconceived benefit, ADL and the other Jewish organizations fail to make the connection between loss of individual rights and our traditions of Judaism. What comes to mind here is probably the counterargument about conservatives and abortion, which requires a section all of its own. Suffice for now, the point is that American Jewish leaders apparently do not have a clue that when they sit by and watch individual freedoms erode, that somehow this is not in the Jewish tradition of protecting individual freedom. They seem to disregard what George Washington wrote: "(G)overnment is not reason, it is not eloquence—it is force! Like fire it is a dangerous servant and a fearsome master."

This reminds me of the story my former boss told me many years ago when he worked as a gas station attendant. In those days, he preferred to wait in the station's office until he saw a car drive up for service. The result was he frequently did not respond to a customer as swiftly as the manager desired. His boss told him that whenever he heard the bell sound when a car drove over the cord that sounded the bell, that was the instant he should leap out of the office to start his duties. My boss replied that he frequently did not hear that bell. After a warning that he better tune his ears to hear that bell at all times or else he could find another job (this was during the Depression), he somehow became very alert to the slightest bell sound.

That is the instinct I would like to see our Jewish leaders develop. Whenever and wherever our individual liberties are attacked here in these United States of America, whether or not it is a cause that they are in favor of, that they respond to this bell and speak up on behalf of American Jewry because as Jews, we must be ever vigilant to protect our individual freedoms. In *The World of the Talmud* by Morris Adler, the author cites the Talmud's preference for democratic politics and limits on the power of kings. The rabbis were concerned that all too easily could a government impose on its subjects a heavy yoke of its unrestrained passion for power. The State could be subverted to the service of the few at the expense of the many. (How prescient they were.) Although we needed some government, loyalty to government always was to be subservient to loyalty to God. Absolute power was never to be wielded by any government, and the law of Torah for Jews was to be the paramount guide of right policy and action. When we are in doubt as to the position to take on a particular issue, it is these Talmudic principles that should guide our thinking and our actions.

Why are most Jews afraid to stand out from the crowd of other Jews who have voted the liberal line these past two generations? There is within all of us that certain quality that makes marketing people happy. That is the "monkey see, monkey do" syndrome. The big thing in selling your merchandise or ideas is to attract a sufficient number of buyers and then the masses seem to follow along. This is known as achieving your critical mass. So once an idea takes over, or a product becomes a household name, the purveyors of those ideas or merchandise can count on a prolonged life of prosperity and acceptance, at least until a better idea or product emerges or until the successful company commits grievous mistakes and ignores the desires of its customers.

It seems to me that this is part of the explanation of why Jews, who normally argue about most ideas and people (two Jews, three opinions), have come to accept liberalism as we know it today, as "the political cloak" they all must wear. To be a Jew who speaks up and disavows liberalism, even in the most conservative communities in America, is to risk wrath, insults, and isolation from their brethren. I know whereof I speak because I have lived that life for many years. It has been almost a lifelong search for a rabbi and a congregation where at least there was a reasonable division between the various political philosophies. Unfortunately, I have not been able to absorb and practice the Orthodox beliefs where I would have found more sympathetic political allies. Thus I have labored within the Jewish Reform and Conservative worlds for these many years, and I know how difficult it is to stand out.

I heard Dennis Prager, the brilliant Jewish commentator in Los Angeles, say that coming from the Orthodox home where he was raised and where being a Jew meant being a Democrat, that it was more difficult for him to vote Republican than it was to eat ham! And yet he did finally change his political affiliation to Republican because he concluded that the Democratic Party no longer represented his core beliefs. I think that statement illustrates the point. Once the liberal philosophy took hold among the Jewish intelligentsia in this country, and once the Hebrew colleges began turning out social action-minded rabbis with apparently little attention paid to being at least politically neutral, the trend was established which continues to this day. Here and there pop up a few rebels, but they are so few and so muted that their influence is barely felt.

One of my darkest memories was in the 1960s in California, when the rabbi at our local congregation told us on Yom Kippur that is was a sin for us Jews to vote in favor of a statewide proposition that would have protected the right of property owners to exercise their right to choose their own tenants. The aim was to open up more housing selection for minorities, a laudable goal. But no regard was paid to the rights of the property owners to use their buildings as they wanted to. Where the rabbi found his position in Jewish tradition, he never said. The message was simply that since this was a noteworthy goal, that it was fine to use the coercive powers of government to achieve that goal, regardless of the rights of the landlords. At that time the measure passed, but now with all of our fair housing laws, we have gone far beyond that modest provision. Incidentally, that rabbi in his later years seemed to be turning around in his reliance on the powers of government to achieve his goals and became more of an advocate for voluntary action to right the wrongs of the world.

In his book, *Who Needs God*, Rabbi Harold Kushner writes that just as the civilized world had difficulty in accepting the findings of Copernicus and Galileo in the 1600s about the way the solar system works, the Christian Church could not bring itself to acknowledging that its treatment of the Jews was wrong. To admit that, Kushner wrote, would have been to destroy the entire framework of much of what they had believed and practiced for 1,500 years.

It seems that this is similar to the situation that perhaps many Jewish liberals find themselves in today. They have swallowed the liberal line that forms the foundation of their political philosophy for so many years, that at this point in time to change would create a massive upheaval in their thought process. And the question they would have to ask themselves is why? Why should they change their comfortable existence as a mainstream, politically correct thinking Jew, to become a person apart from the group? So what if they have been wrong all these years? Who is going to notice, until many more of their co-religionists begin also to turn?

This is the problem today of bringing about such a change. But change we must accomplish, both to preserve our Jewish traditions and to preserve the freedom and independence of these United States of America. For the American Jews, although small in number, exercise an influence on the body politic far beyond their numbers. A dramatic swing in the sentiments of prominent Jews in the business, entertainment, political, and religious worlds would bring about a profound change in the political make-up and philosophy of this nation, and all for the better.

Can you imagine if Barbara Streisand, Steven Spielberg, Jerry Seinfeld, Robert Rubin, Michael Eisner, or even Ed Asner should somehow wake up one morning and proclaim themselves reconstituted political conservatives? The heavens would truly shake and the media would probably post this news on the back pages of the classified ad section. As much as I believe that celebrities in general have not devoted sufficient time to truly informing themselves on the great issues of the day, still it would be sweet if some of them should turn around their political faces. On the religious side who knows what the effect would be if some of our leaders in that field should suddenly announce their "conversion" to the politically conservative cause. What would it take to accomplish this?

I had a recent experience in my own home area of Orange County, California. I challenged the twenty Orange County rabbis to comment on my argument that Jews everywhere, in particular our Jewish leaders, should be champions of the cause of school choice for parents. The reasons are fairly obvious. Without the necessity of supporting public schools with their tax dollars in addition to paying tuition to Jewish day schools, many Jewish parents would be able to afford to send their kids to the Jewish schools, both for a better education, and to make them better Jews.

I wrote that I attended UCLA under the GI Bill and I could have chosen religious studies as my major, eventually perhaps becoming a rabbi myself. If that had happened, Orange County would have had at least one politically conservative rabbi, I said somewhat tongue in cheek.

The editor of the local Jewish paper wrote back that there was one politically conservative rabbi in Orange County. He was even a prominent one, so the editor wrote, but he could not be revealed as such because "he is the spiritual leader of all his members." Apparently what is "sauce for the goose is not sauce for the gander." All the years that I was paying my dues to temples led by liberal rabbis, were they representing my side? I don't think so. Incidentally, I am still waiting to read some responses to my challenge.

One of my major hopes in writing this book is to incite some meaningful responses from rabbis and Jewish leaders and to invite them to argue their Jewish case for remaining political liberals. I am waiting to read or hear a Jewish liberal cite any Jewish law or tradition that supports his liberal positions on any subject. Any relevant Jewish law or tradition does not support much of what liberal Jews proclaim as Jewish positions. I recently heard one of the prominent liberal rabbis from New York insist on a cable news program that unlimited abortion was absolutely a traditional Jewish theme and was well documented in the Torah. When the interviewer expressed his astonishment at that statement and recounted that he had discussed this with Orthodox rabbis who made no such claim, the liberal ended the conversation by saying simply that "he knew" and that was that. This again appears to be an example of liberal Jews attempting to dominate the issues because they believe they represent the majority of American Jewish thinking. Perhaps they are correct in that assumption today, but that does not mean they should continue to go unchallenged. There is no question we need new leadership in the Jewish community, and the question is from where will this new leadership come?

JEWISH LEADERSHIP

In an effort to learn what factors have influenced the political thinking of prominent Jews, I recently mailed another brief letter to the twenty rabbis in Orange County, California, asking questions about where and how they have come to believe as they now do. Why are they liberals? How did they become liberals? What is the linkage between their politically liberal views, and Jewish laws and traditions? The responses numbered three.

One said he was a "pragmatist" meaning to me he had no particular philosophy or set of political principles. This sounded as if he would judge each episode or problem on its own merits without having an anchor of principles to direct that judgment. This would appear to be contrary to the basic tenets of Judaism, founded on the Ten Commandments, which are not open to varying interpretations. Still he is a nice man who just hasn't been politically enlightened to see the link between Judaism and political conservatism.

One rabbi said he was a liberal because that was the only group that truly cared about helping the poor and downtrodden. This is probably the same answer I would have received from most of the seventeen that did not answer. Somehow these religious leaders forget their religious training that teaches them that most human beings, liberals and conservatives alike, are similar in their basic desire to help those who are less fortunate than they are. Only the methods differ, but this is a huge difference. Apparently after years of indoctrination, however, this rabbi concluded that only his political group, the liberals, had the heart, desire, and ability to bring about the results he desired.

The third rabbi who answered said to me verbally, "Hey, I'm no liberal; I believe in school vouchers, and eliminating welfare, and all the rest of the conservative agenda." When I recovered from my shock at hearing these answers, I asked, so what makes you so different from the other nineteen Orange County rabbis? His comments were enlightening. He said he had been educated in England, not in the United States. Although his father was now a rabbi in this country, he himself had not been exposed, as he put it, to the teachings of the Hebrew Union College in Cincinnati. Instead he received a traditional Jewish education in England, where he studied for the rabbinate and was thus free to form his own opinions on the American political scene, as it relates to his religion. He had then come under the influence of some learned conservative thinkers in California and had become, if not a "true" conservative, at least a non-liberal thinker with a fairly open mind.

Does this admittedly limited survey reflect part of the reason why American Jewish leadership has been so predominately politically liberal these past two generations? Is it the teachings of our rabbinical schools that are responsible for turning out these robotic, liberal theory espousing, Reform and Conservative rabbis? This would appear to be the case. If there are Reform or Conservative rabbis who believe otherwise, they must be few and far between and they are certainly not given much publicity. I have written several letters to the Jewish Studies Institute, the school for Conservative rabbi students, and the Hebrew Union College, the school for Reform rabbi students, asking if perhaps they would consider adding this book to their study programs. Surprise, surprise, I have received no answers to date.

Elliot Abrams in *Faith or Fear* states that the strategy of American Jewish leadership has been to downplay Jewish tradition in public life. He writes that Jewish leadership assumes that any expression of religious faith or association is dangerous to American Jewry, and as such it must be resisted. These leaders have taught that there is safety through secularism; integration rather than separatism; and life under the Constitution rather than the Torah. These views are exactly opposite to those of the Jewish Orthodox rabbis, who seem to glory in and emphasize their Jewish differences from modern society. Abrams explains that the thinking by Jewish liberals that a more religious society threatens Jews is founded in fear and Jewish history of persecution, and should be rejected and condemned by Jewish leaders.

It appears to me that today, more respect is given to almost all Jews who openly proclaim their Jewishness. This is most noticeable in the political and sports fields. In Los Angeles there is still respect for the baseball pitcher, Sandy Koufax, who refused to pitch for the Los Angeles Dodgers in a World Series game when it fell on Yom Kippur. This happened back in the 1950s and is still well remembered. Most recently those same Dodgers acquired a young Jewish outfielder, Shawn Green. When Green was choosing among the teams he wished to play for, he is reported to have said that he wanted to play in a city where there was a large Jewish population. He also declined to play in an important Dodgers game that fell on Yom Kippur, September 2001. We hope that Green maintains this discipline with his new Arizona team.

It is with some irony that several top executives in the Clinton administration were either Jews or were of Jewish heritage. Robert Rubin, William Cohen, Sandy Becker, and Madeleine Albright all served with Clinton during his two terms. Unfortunately for the premise of this book, none of them qualify as political conservatives, although Cohen is an identified Republican. He also however, does not practice as a Jew, nor does Ms. Albright, who apparently was not aware of her Jewish heritage until very recently.

In August 2000, Democratic candidate for president, Al Gore, shocked the political world by selecting as his vice presidential running mate, none other than the previously referred to Orthodox Jewish senator from Connecticut, Joseph Lieberman. Although Gore and Lieberman were friends of long standing, the general consensus was that Lieberman was selected mainly because of his outstanding reputation as an "ethically pure" politician, which the Democrats were hopeful would help sanitize their ticket from the moral disrepute of being associated with President Clinton. Also, the fact that Lieberman was an Orthodox Jew apparently was not a negative for Gore. In fact, the hope was that this could prove to be a positive in swaying undecided Jewish voters to their ticket. Almost immediately upon being selected, the good senator began to back away from some of his more conservative, previously held positions on school vouchers, privatizing Social Security, affirmative action, and other issues. Perhaps this was part of the price to be paid by Lieberman to qualify as a national ticket candidate.

The point is that the previously held strategy of Jewish leaders to downplay and minimize their Jewish religion is no longer a viable strategy. In fact it is almost a badge of honor as a public figure to now be identified as Jewish. In the 2004 Democratic presidential nominating process, several candidates "suddenly" discovered they had Jewish roots via a parent or grandparent. The leading candidate for a time, Vermont governor Howard Dean, is actually married to a Jewish woman who made no secret about her religion. The ultimate Democratic candidate for president, Sen. John Kerry, also disclosed that one of his grandparents had been Jewish. For a time, Senator Lieberman, an Orthodox Jew, also led in the national polls, but his views were not radical enough to please the Democratic voters, and he soon gave up the struggle. The greater danger to the survival of the Jewish community in America today is assimilation. The more religious a country becomes, it would seem the more respected and honored are the various religions. As long as there is no government mandated control by one religion over the others, as long as one is not forced by government to financially support a particular religion, as Jefferson feared, and as long as there are no political restrictions on practicing one's religion as one chooses, then it would seem there is little for American Jews to be concerned about.

Still when one searches for a single Jewish leader who reflects the political sentiments of American Jews, there appears to be no one. Nor is there any small group of prominent Jewish leaders that can be identified as representing the majority of American Jews. Instead, it seems to this observer that the liberal dogma is carried on through a number of channels. Certainly there is the group of American rabbis, Reform and Conservative, who spout the liberal line. There are the heads of the prominent Jewish organizations. Then there are the influential Jewish media personalities. But again there do not seem to be any outstanding Jewish commentators who are influential liberals. And of course we must not forget our prominent Jewish entertainers who constitute an almost monolithic bloc supporting the liberal line. (The amazingly astute Jackie Mason as perhaps the lone exception.) Does the preaching of these folk really have an influence on the average Jewish voter? It is possible that in this age of TV and visual impressions, that the opinions of prominent personalities do have some effect on the leanings of many Jewish voters.

Perhaps our Jewish liberal leaders belong to that special group of Americans that Thomas Sowell describes so well in his brilliant 1995 book, *The Vision of the Anointed.* These are the folks who consider themselves to be the intellectual and political elite of our time, who have the vision that must prevail over that of all lesser beings, the "benighted" as Sowell defines all of us lesser mortals, who do not possess that same vision. Those who may disagree with this privileged group are not just inferior thinkers, but in most cases, are mean-spirited if they do not agree with the prevailing visions of the anointed. Sowell writes, "People are never more sincere than when they assume their own moral superiority."

For those of us who challenge this prevailing attitude of our Jewish leaders, we can identify with those words. How many times have we been accused of being "John Birchers" or worse, if we disagree with the liberal political positions of our leaders? It is not just that we are wrong, they say. Oh no, we are evil, cynical, hard-hearted, and mean people to differ with their pronouncements from "on high." Sowell quotes Joseph Epstein who wrote in a 1985 article, "Disagree with someone on the right and he is likely to think you obtuse, wrong, foolish, a dope. Disagree with someone on the left and he is more likely to think you selfish, a sell-out, insensitive, possibly evil."

I remember an episode back in 1966 when I was speaking to a Jewish group on behalf of Ronald Reagan in his successful campaign to become governor of California. I gave what I thought was a fairly good talk on why I was a Republican, why my belief in God as the rightful giver of our freedoms was in harmony with the Republican view on limiting the powers of the State, and why Reagan was the man for our time. A lady came up to me after my talk, ostensibly I assumed to congratulate me on my eloquence. Instead, she proceeded to castigate me for my views. How could I, a nice, young (at that time) Jewish boy, support such a reputed anti-Jew as "Dutch" Reagan?

When I sought to repeat my argument that Reagan was for reducing the powers of government, that he was a strong supporter of enhanced freedom for all, and that is what I thought Judaism stood for, she walked away muttering under her breath. As it turned out, "Dutch" Reagan did not have an anti-Semitic bone in his body, and was a great supporter of Israel while president. I should have known then that I was fighting an uphill battle in my desire to "convert" my co-religionists away from their liberal views. Still, the battle needs to be waged and eventually won! After all this is certainly not the first time that the Jewish people have followed the wrong course and the wrong leaders, and have eventually seen the light as to where their true interests lie.

I like to think that it would not take a large number of Jewish leaders to spark a turn-around in the thinking of American Jews. Rabbi Adin Steinsaltz writes in *The Essential Talmud*, that in most periods, learned men, leaders of each community chosen from its best scholars, ruled Jewish society. That was aristocracy in its truest sense. Those Talmudic scholars who became the leaders of their communities were endowed with spiritual and humanitarian qualities, and practiced what they preached. He also wrote, and this should be applicable today, that the Talmud specified that a man, however erudite, whose conduct was contemptible, should be condemned and despised. The Talmud often related that learned people of dubious character were punished, chastised, or excommunicated.

If we have such spiritual leaders today, and they may come from the ranks of rabbis, writers, media people, teachers, plain citizens, or even politicians, who would meet these standards, let them rise up and devote some of their precious time and scholarship to changing the political thinking of our people as we enter the twenty-first century. I suggest that next to keeping our American Jewry alive and well, there is not a more important cause that is as worthy of their time.

One would hope that in the twenty-first century with the growth of the Internet and the vast amount of information available, more and more Jews will assume leadership roles and transmit the sustaining values, responsibilities, and texts of our Jewish tradition. As Rabbi Daniel Lapin writes in *America's Real War*, what must be reversed is the secular humanism of modern liberalism that preaches that their "faith" is identical to Judaism. Rabbi Lapin believes that the reason many non-observant Jews pursue liberalism is frequently to escape from the eternal laws of God. But that yearning for God exists at the core of every Jew, and no matter how much we observe or do not observe the traditional rituals of Judaism, we must never abandon the essential core of our religion, the worship of and belief in the One and Holy and Eternal God.

Although there does not appear to be one large national organization today of Jewish political conservatives, there are some smaller ones, such as the Republican Jewish Coalition, who are fighting the good fight. I tend to believe there are more Jewish conservatives hiding in the underbrush than we know about, and who perhaps are just waiting for a call to arms. I am hopeful that out of these groups will emerge a new, strong cadre of politically conservative Jews to serve as a needed counterbalance to the current Jewish liberal leaders.

I am encouraged in reading about the worldwide activities of Chabad-Lubavitch, the Hasidic movement, as reported in the August 2000, edition of *Moment* magazine. Chabad now has emissaries in 109 countries around the world, where their young emissary couples are working to create active Hasidic branches. The key to the movement's success in its expansion is due to the thousands of smart, idealistic men and women who leave their comfortable homes and travel to a foreign county to build and establish Chabad Centers and to stay in those countries for the rest of their lives.

The Chabad emissaries, or *shlichim* as they are known, are encouraged to be quite lenient with other Jews' observance levels, while at the same time, maintaining their own strict observance of Jewish law. Although politics is not really a part of Chabad, it is a fact that Orthodox Jews are much closer to political conservatism and tend to vote that way quite consistently. As this movement grows worldwide and here in the United States, I hope it will spill over into other branches of Judaism.

Just as liberals never seem to abandon their favorite causes, so it is that we conservative Jews must not waiver in our struggle to recruit more of our co-religionists to our banner. Our cause is just, our goals are pure, and eventually I pray, our efforts will be rewarded. There is a new generation of young Jews coming on the scene. It may well be that only when they assume the mantles of leadership, and hopefully this book will serve as an aid to them, will we see a true change in the political complexion of American Jewish leadership.

I am particularly anxious to have my message conveyed to young Jews. I have written several letters to the Hillel Foundation headquarters asking for their assistance. Hillel is making a strong drive to help young Jews combat anti-Jewish sentiments on their college campuses. I had hoped that the Hillel leadership would at a minimum be interested in reading my book and using it in their classes. Alas, the only letters I have received to date are requests for additional donations.

WHO ARE THE TRUE FRIENDS OF THE JEWS?

During my lifetime, any discrimination I experienced whether in trying to obtain a job, or in some business or personal situation, could not be connected by me to any hate group or organized anti-Semitic group. Rather it came from individuals who had their own opinions and prejudices against Jews. One incident that I do remember is when I was being interviewed for a job as an agent with the Internal Revenue Service shortly after graduating from UCLA in 1949. I wanted that job badly for two reasons. One was to get the tax experience to further my accounting career, and second was that it paid $277 a month, which was higher than most auditing jobs at the time. The two men who interviewed me somehow left me with the impression that perhaps my Jewish sounding name was not exactly the optimum one they had in mind. I did not get that job, which may have been a blessing in disguise, because I could have become a career income tax sleuth and have been hated by all instead of just by the liberals.

However, these occasional incidents were never career threatening or that personally distasteful. Even when as a teenager I spent a month working on a farm in De Kalb, Illinois, where the town boys unknowingly described all Jews as "kikes" was there any real animosity. Perhaps I have lived a charmed life in this regard, but I don't think my experience is that much different from most Jews of my generation.

On the contrary, as the years passed by it turned out that my closest friends and business associates were non-Jews. Some were strong Christians; some were lukewarm Christians. Some were simply deists. They all had one thing in common. They looked to me in business for the contributions I could make to helping grow their business or further their individual careers. There may have been occasional attempts to enlighten me on the joys of Christianity, but these were never intense or threatening. In personal relations, it was rather the community of interests that governed our relationship, not our different religions. And so it appears is the case on the national or political scene.

It has not always been our American Jews that have been the strongest supporters of Israel these past fifty years. It was President Harry Truman who was quick to recognize the new State of Israel when it declared its independence in 1948. It was another non-Jew, President Richard Nixon, who saved Israel during the 1973 war by insisting that the United States send all the war materiel it could supply to Israel during those dark hours soon after the Arabs' sneak attack. This insistence, so I have read, was over the objections of our fellow Jew, Secretary of State Henry Kissinger, who is reported to have counseled to let the Jews bleed a little more so they will be more malleable at the next negotiation session. Yet Nixon is regarded by many non-knowing Jews as one who was at worst anti-Semitic, and at best, a less than enthusiastic supporter of Israel.

One of Nixon's shrewdest political managers, Murray Chotiner, was Jewish. My wife and I knew Murray, who met an untimely death in an auto accident just before the Watergate incident became public. We have always thought that if Murray had still been alive, he would have guided Nixon to confess his sins before the American public, who would probably have quickly forgiven him and permitted Nixon to serve out his full second term.

As the new millennium approaches, the strongest supporters of Israel are not the Jewish organizations, but rather the leaders of the Religious Right. It is the Evangelical Christians who will defend Israel's right to exist, while many American Jews are perfectly content to live with a Palestinian State, which may eventually lead to a complete takeover of Israel by the Arabs. (Although God will not permit this, I pray.)

I remember a personal incident in October 1981, when my wife and

I were in Israel for the first time. We wandered into a large convention hall in Jerusalem where the Feast of the Tabernacles pageant was taking place. Delegations of Christians from all over the world were present, marching into the auditorium with their banners and their joyful singing. It was an awe-inspiring sight. The featured speaker was the then Prime Minister of Israel, Menachem Begin. When the diminutive Begin rose to speak, the thousands of Christians in that auditorium leaped to their feet and roared ovation after ovation in tribute to both Begin and the State of Israel. I'll never forget what Begin's opening words were. "And they say we have no friends," he began, at which point the crowd again expressed their love and devotion for Israel and the Jewish people with thunderous applause.

The point to all this is that too often American Jews do not know, or refuse to recognize, who their true friends are, not only from the standpoint of protecting and preserving our individual freedoms which are inimical to Judaism, but from the point of supporting the cause of Israel, which is still of vital importance to most American Jews. Since 1948, it has been the emergence of Israel that has helped give us that additional pride in our heritage and which has, at least until recently, been the one cause that could unite most Jews in America. Keeping Israel strong was the dominant theme. As of this writing, there is a division of opinion. Can Arabs be trusted to live up to any peace agreement by giving up increasing slices of that small country's territory, or is it simply part of a plan to eventually take Israel over and eliminate the Jewish State from the face of the globe? Only time will tell, but many of us counsel against taking that chance.

Our true friends are those who are saying we should slow down and make the other side live up to their commitments before moving ahead. The liberals, on the other hand, and our fellow Jews, who were in power in the State and Defense Departments, kept pushing Israel hard to grant more and more land and authority to the Palestinians. Israel apparently cannot get an even break from our American Jewish leadership when it comes to support for any policies other than the current Oslo "peace" process. And where are the Jewish liberals here? Few and far between, when it comes to supporting a hard-line position for Israel.

This appears to be another example of the belief of liberals that all people are really good at heart, and you only have to treat them decently to obtain the desired results. This disregards the fact that others may have a different agenda from yours. The other side may not consist of honorable and trustworthy individuals. Perhaps the Arab leaders really cannot stand the thought of permitting Israel and the Jewish people to continue to exist in the middle of the Arabs' "Golden Crescent." Certainly this is what Arafat was saying to his followers when he spoke to them in their own language, as contrasted to his more moderate words of peace when he spoke in English. Arafat's death in late 2004 may open a window to friendlier relations between Israel and the Palestine Liberation Organization (PLO), but nothing will change until the Arabs cease their murderous activities and accept Israel without conditions.

One of the few Jewish organizations in this country to have figured out the real agenda of Arafat is AFSI, Americans For A Safe Israel, headed by Herbert Zweibon. In their monthly publication, *Outpost*, Zweibon and his associates appear to be a lonely voice in warning Jews everywhere of what the Arabs are really planning, and that the Labor-dominated Israeli government was endangering the future security of that nation with its position of blindly implementing the Oslo agreements. Another organization doing exemplary work on behalf of Israel is FLAME, Facts and Logic About the Middle East. All one has to do to become knowledgeable about Israel and the PLO is to read the beautifully written ads placed by FLAME monthly in various national publications. FLAME represents a labor of love for its president, Gerardo Joffe, the direct-mail wizard, who donates all of his time without compensation. We do not hear these same warnings from the major Jewish organizations, and this may be another example of how wrong the majority can be on a critical issue.

Dennis Prager again points out that one of the main differences between liberals and conservatives is the liberals' belief that all people are basically good, and that if they do bad things it is only because of some outside force. Conservatives, on the other hand, are more in tune with Jewish traditional belief that people are a mixture of good and evil. We possess an inclination to evil and to good, and each individual is responsible for his own actions. This basic difference is at the root of many of the disagreements between liberals and conservatives over how to solve our social problems. Until Jewish leaders in this country recognize the errors of their ways on this important point, we shall continue to see American Jews on the wrong side of most social and economic issues.

Nowhere is this expressed more clearly as in Deuteronomy 30:19-20, which reads in part, "I have set before thee life and death, the blessing and the curse; therefore choose life, that thou mayest live, thou and thy seed; to love the Lord thy God, to hearken to His voice and to cleave unto Him..." In the Soncino notes, Maimonides is quoted that "Free will is granted to every man. If he desires to incline towards the good way, and be righteous, he has the power to do so; and if he desires to incline towards the unrighteous way, and be a wicked man, he has also the power to do so. Since this power of doing good or evil is in our own hands, and since all the wicked deeds which we have committed have been committed with our full consciousness, it befits us to turn in penitence and forsake our evil deeds; the power of doing so being still in our hands. Now this matter is a very important principle; nay, it is the pillar of the Law and of the commandments."

So we are a mixture of good and evil, and we are responsible for our own actions, and it is not society that is responsible for our misfortunes. It is only by improving our own natures and choosing to do the right things in life that we progress to ultimately fulfilling our individual destinies.

If we Jews believe what is written in our Holy Book, how can our leaders then tell us that all that is necessary is for us to have good intentions in what we advocate, regardless of the results that flow from those good intentions. Until we understand that we cannot do for others what they do not want to do for themselves, all of our "feel good' and "do good" programs are doomed to failure. Conservatism seeks to assign accountability to each of us for our own actions, and if we need help at various times in our lives, we must look to our families, our religion, our faith, and our God for that help; not to Washington, DC or Sacramento, California or any other political entity.

Throughout our 4,000-year history, Jews have traditionally been known as a "stiff-necked" people, which the dictionary defines as being "haughty and obstinate." I would add to that definition that Jews in general have been less than anxious to rush to make friends with their non-Jewish neighbors. We have had to develop a healthy skepticism towards others in our communities because we were never quite sure when the other shoe might fall, and we would no longer be welcome neighbors because we were Jews. For hundreds of years we congregated in ghettos and had little contact with the outside world.

In America, we did not seem to have had this problem. We were accepted almost from the beginning as equals in the development of this nation. Still, we faced prejudice in many fields, although it was never inspired by the federal government. So it is perhaps natural that we tend to find it difficult to accept help from Christians, especially those Evangelicals that we cringe from in fear of their persuasive conversion tactics. From my personal experience, these Evangelicals are the very friends that are today most steadfast in helping us maintain the independence of Israel, without ever seeking to convert us to their own religions. They truly believe Genesis 12:3: "And I will bless them that bless thee, and him that curseth thee will I curse; and in thee shall all the families of the earth be blessed."

They are also the same friends who tend to abhor and oppose the increasing powers of a centralized government. These people, by and large, do not belong to the mainline churches, but they are a growing majority in their individual faiths. These people are the true friends of the Jewish people and of Israel. One couple, Don and Norma Winton, whom we count as among our closest friends, are members of Calvary Chapel of Newport Beach, California. Don is a well-known sculptor and has created some outstanding works of Begin, Herzl, and Jobitinsky, which he donates to organizations in Israel. Don and Norma have visited Israel more than twenty times, and I don't believe any stronger supporters of Israel and the Jewish people exist anywhere. It is time that we recognize who our true friends are, that all Christians are not alike, and that we want to join forces with those friends to bring about our mutually desired results.

Rabbi Lapin's organization, "Toward Tradition," relies heavily on his Christian supporters. He believes strongly that Jewish safety and prosperity in America is due to the fact that America was founded on the Judeo-Christian tradition and that there has never been a single, government-sponsored Christian religion. Jews should be just as sensitive to anti-Christian practices around the world as they are to anti-Jewish deeds.

Is it not time that Jews began to change the criterion by which we distinguish our "friends" from our enemies? The time is past for automatically labeling as enemies those who may have a different position from the Jewish leadership on abortion, gun control, same sex marriage, and all the other "hot button" issues currently in vogue among the Jewish liberals. These issues do not go to the core of what Judaism is all about.

The real tests of friendship should ask who is in favor of restoring morality in this nation; who supports the restoration of the family as the centerpiece of our society; who supports the expansion of individual freedom within those moral limits; who is urging the Arabs to make the concessions they promised to make in the Oslo agreements; who is backing Israel in its retention of its vital territories; who supports bringing competition into the education arena? These are the types of issues that should be used by American Jews in deciding who our real friends are.

It is simply not enough to rely on our prior emotional links to the failed policies of modern liberalism when we pick our political friends. We need to stand back and analyze with fresh eyes which people and policies come closest to our traditional Jewish principles. And even if we find that our "new friends" are among those groups who would previously not have merited a second look from us because of old biases, we must welcome them as allies in our struggle to identify where we should be voting as informed American Jews, who cherish freedom above all values.

LIBERALS, THE JEWISH FAMILY, AND ABORTION

There is little disagreement that the family and its importance to the Jewish tradition are among the strongest elements of Judaism. "God said unto our Jewish patriarchs, Be fruitful and multiply, and replenish the earth, and subdue it..." (Genesis 1:28) The nuclear family, with father, mother, and children, has always been in the Jewish tradition. Why is it then that liberals seem to be on the side of those programs and policies that have as their inevitable result the breakdown and deterioration of the family?

I refer to the high taxes of today which in many cases force mothers to enter the workforce to the detriment of the raising of her children. The advocacy of unlimited abortion at the choice of the woman, regardless of need, has resulted in many divisions within the Jewish family structure. The striving for material well being at the cost of neglecting the spiritual side of family life leads frequently to unhappiness with the present state of affairs. The opposition to freedom of choice for education means that many a Jewish family cannot afford to send their children to Jewish day schools, where the teachings of Jewish tradition and laws would be emphasized. The all-enveloping welfare programs have led to the deterioration of the traditional family and to the massive increase in babies born out of wedlock

The liberal appeal to class envy, and an attack on the wealthy and the entrepreneur—the prime movers of our economy—frequently results in a clash between those people and the groups that could benefit the most from expanded economic activity. All of these and more seem to result in an increasing divorce rate, and the all too often breakup and estrangement of Jewish families from their tradition. These sometimes "well meaning" but ultimately destructive programs are all liberal-sponsored ideas, frequently championed by Jews prominent in politics, religion, and business.

We cannot recreate the past, but from personal experience, the past was frequently more conducive to a stronger family life than is today's more economically advanced society. When my wife and I married, over fifty years ago, out of a salary of $231 a month I netted about $210. There was practically no income tax and very little went to Social Security. Out of that $210, we were able to pay our rent, groceries, and other necessities. My wife took on a part time job for a time, but that ended when I rejoined the navy during the Korean War, and she accompanied me to a tour of duty on Guam. After a brief stint working in the Eisenhower/Nixon campaign of 1952, she did not choose to rejoin the workforce until our children were grown teenagers.

The fact is that taxes then were such a minimum burden that we could use the great majority of my earnings for our own needs. Today, when taxes in all their varieties scoop up almost 40% of the average family's income, it becomes necessary for wives to bring home their share. (I read in the Talmud that one should not give away more than 20% of one's income. I take that as meaning taxes, including tithing, should not exceed 20% of our total income according to Jewish tradition.) In today's business world, with the expansion of the economy, many wives are bringing home half of the total family income.

One would ask, is that all bad? Women today have many careers open to them that were not available back when we were newlyweds. Women are certainly as capable as men to achieve success in many fields, and more power to them. I personally have believed for many years that women were the untapped resource of America. Women are more intuitive in their management skills and can frequently prevent problems from mushrooming. Women are succeeding in the professions to a greater extent than ever thought possible. In my own profession of accounting, I understand that more than one half of new CPAs today are women.

Having said all of that, the point is that today it is no longer a voluntary choice for many families to have the wife and mother work. To live in the style that many people desire, and to pay the onerous amount of taxes—income, payroll, sales, property, etc.—it is a necessity for wives to work. Yet if given their choice, many young women would prefer to stay home and raise their families without the burden of doing double duty by working and doing their household chores. A recent survey showed that over 65% of working married women would prefer to stay at home. So how can that be blamed on the liberals?

Simply this, by advocating and promoting an increasingly powerful federal government to solve the world's problems, both real and invented, this inadvertent or perhaps purposeful philosophy creates a tax and regulatory structure that siphons away too much of our hard-earned income and deprives us of too many of our individual liberties. All of that is against Jewish tradition where women were the family educators, the solid foundation of the Jewish family. Today many women are simply regarded as "equals" to the man of the house with the frequent result being that they do not receive the care and respect and love they are otherwise entitled to. If the Jewish sponsorship of equal rights and pay for women could result in more women being able to stay home and raise their children, that would be wonderful. But for many reasons this is not the result that can be obtained through passing arbitrary laws regarding compensation.

The entire equal rights movement would seem to be contrary to what Jewish laws seek as the role for women. In the notes to Deuteronomy in the Soncino Pentateuch, women are to be the helpmate of man. "A wife is a man's other self…" Only through marriage can man's needs be directed to holy ends. Scripture says, "A man shall leave his father and mother and cleave to his wife," (not the other way) because the woman is the stronger, the ethical and spiritual superior of man. Instead of trying to forcefully equate women with men in the economic world, we should be paying more attention to making it possible for women to fulfill their primary role in life as wives, mothers, and teachers of their children.

When it comes to abortion, and the "right to choose," the major Jewish organizations, including Hadassah, have been prominent advocates for the "pro-choice" abortion rights movement. Where in Jewish tradition does this come from? In the readings that I have done, plus talking to various rabbis, there is nothing in Judaism to support this movement. Although Jewish tradition does not regard abortion as murder, it is a practice that is discouraged and is considered to be a sin. At best, during the first forty days of pregnancy, an argument is made by some Jewish scholars that the soul has not yet entered the body of the fetus, and therefore, an abortion during that period does not carry the same condemnation as those performed at a later period. There is also today some evidence that brain waves and heartbeats do not commence until roughly forty days have passed since inception, which would tend to support the prior statement.

In the *Time* magazine issue of 11 November 2002, there appeared a series of remarkable photographs showing an embryo (or fetus) through its nine-month development to a full-grown baby. The picture of the embryo at forty-two days showed its size at eleven millimeters, with the description that it was now developing a sense of smell, nerve endings, heart, liver, hindbrain, midbrain, and other features. This would seem to fortify our ancient rabbis' theory on the forty-day period when abortion may be tolerated.

An interesting proposal to deal with abortion on a moral basis was put forth by Professor James Q. Wilson, professor at UCLA, in an article written in *Commentary*, January 1994. Professor Wilson' position is that abortion is a moral question, and should not be left to the judges of the Supreme Court to determine our national posture. Instead he urges more voluntary actions based on increased knowledge of what the fetus actually appears to be during the gestation period.

Wilson describes the appearance of the fetus during the first ten weeks of pregnancy, based on actual photographs, and concludes that not until the seventh week, do distinctly human arms and legs become evident. At that time also the eyes and eyelids become visible. In the eighth week, even though the fetus is still only 1 1/2 or 2 inches long, the fingers and the genital organs, unsexed, have appeared. By the tenth week, the fetal face has a clearly human appearance. The photographs in the *Time* article confirm Wilson's statements.

Wilson goes on to propose that before women agree to have an abortion, they should be shown pictures of just what that fetus looks like in their bodies. When one comes face to face with a creature that looks like a tiny creature, the hope is that many abortions would never take place. Probably some of this is done now in certain clinics, but certainly, if more exposure and publicity were given to this approach, progress would be made. All of this could be accomplished without government interference of any kind, but before such changes could really take hold, the Supreme Court's Roe v. Wade decision would have to be reversed.

The problem with that decision is that it overrode all state and local abortion laws, and instead mandated one supreme position for the entire country. That court majority not only prevented any state from restricting abortions during the first trimester, but even during the second trimester, the state could regulate abortions only to protect the mother's health. In the final trimester when the fetus was viable, the state was given the option of regulation unless the mother's health or life was at risk. This latter restriction was soon negated when "health" was defined as "well-being" with the result that only now in year 2000, is the court to decide if states can regulate abortions during the final trimester. The Supreme Court's latest ruling is that the individual states do not have that right, given the supremacy of the Roe v. Wade decision.

Wilson's argument that abortion is a moral question should certainly have provoked discussion on the part of our Jewish establishment. If morality is at the heart of our religion, what subject could have been more ripe for Jewish debate? Yet I have heard more than one Reform rabbi pronounce that Judaism is four square in favor of unlimited abortion, and that is that! No reference to the Torah is given; simply that the woman's right to choose is somehow heavenly ordained.

133

How is it that the entire liberal position, as portrayed in the Jewish supported liberal Democratic Party, is so uniformly in support of unlimited abortion? And to compound the sin, the Democrats criticize the debate that rages within the Republican Party over the correct political position to take on this subject. At least the Republicans have a difference of opinion, whereas the liberal Democrats, led of course by their Jewish component, have no split opinion. If you are a liberal, that's it. You must safeguard this precious "right to choose." But beware, don't be consistent and parlay this right of freedom of choice to the freedom to choose one's school for your children. No, that would be the wrong use of the taxpayers' money, and heaven forbid if that choice of school for your children should result in their attending a school where religious principles were taught. Such hypocrisy is certainly not in the Jewish tradition.

Hadassah, the Jewish women's organization that performs many very worthwhile services throughout the world, and proclaims their strong allegiance to Israel, lists as one of its bedrock positions, the "right of women to choose abortion on demand." I have yet to read in any of their publications any Jewish law or tradition on which they base their position on abortion. The closest they have come is to quote Moses Maimonides to the effect that the fetus should not be supported if it is a danger to the health of the mother. This is a real "stretch" to include this as a Jewish tradition when the great majority of pregnancies do not endanger the health of the mother. It is rather this "unholy freedom" of women to control the functions of their own bodies that seems to serve as the foundation for their policy. The Jewish emphasis on the importance of children seems to be ignored. Here again the Soncino notes are appropriate to quote: "Judaism proclaimed the Biblical view that the child was the highest of human treasures." "O Lord God, what wilt Thou give me, seeing that I go childless?" was Abraham's agonizing cry. "In little children, it was taught, God gives humanity a chance to make good its mistakes. They are 'the Messiahs of mankind,' 'the perennial regenerative force in humanity.'" One would think that of all peoples in this world, Jews should be champions of the right of the unborn to be born.

Abortion is a divisive issue. I have Republican friends who believe it is the most important issue of the day. I don't agree with them. I also don't agree that we can legislate a real solution to the problem. But it should not be the issue of the day. Abortions have been taking place since the beginning of the human experience. Roe v. Wade was a mistake to make this a federal matter whereas previously, it had been a state or local issue. It is a moral decision for women and their mates to make. If more attention were paid to the experience of women who have had abortions and the lasting mental distress they frequently feel, perhaps there would be a drastic reduction in the number of abortions performed in this country.

There is no earthly reason, religious or political, that this should be a Jewish liberal bedrock position. There is plenty of room for honest disagreement. I am sure there are many American Jews who do not agree with unlimited abortion, but they appear to be silent in the face of the almost uniform position of the major Jewish organizations. As the previously quoted Dennis Prager has said with which I agree, he is pro-choice, but anti-abortion.

No one will doubt that the Jews have been among the leaders in America to push for a more expansive welfare program for those in need. One of the main attractions of FDR in the 1930s was his advocacy of all of the New Deal programs. Certainly a case could be made that in the depths of the Depression of the 1930s, there was a need for some type of government help for those out of work and hungry. This was somewhat in the Jewish tradition. But that help was to be of a temporary nature and was preferably the kind that could help the breadwinners attain a marketable skill.

Unfortunately, the nature of government programs is to take on a life of their own. As these programs grow and expand, the waste and excessive overhead costs that accompany those programs expands. The main problem with government (one-size-fits-all) programs is that there are too many individual differences to be solved by one all-encompassing program. There soon develops a corps of government workers whose jobs and careers depend on enlarging and perpetuating those ineffective programs. Lost somewhere in the bowels of those well-meaning statutes is the purpose for which they were created.

Thus there are formed three powerful constituencies: the politicians who appear to be the benefactors of the poor; the bureaucrats who work in implementing and expanding the programs; and of course, the recipients of the benefits. Unseen are those hard-working citizens whose taxes are paying for all of those wondrous programs. Opposition is quickly overcome, and our welfare programs expand and continue without pause. Negligible positive results are glossed over. It is only important that we are doing the "right" thing, and for Jews, we are fulfilling our basic charitable drive.

How have these welfare programs affected the American family, the institution most important to Jewish life? They have been an unmitigated disaster. We have spawned an entire generation of fatherless youths who have grown up largely without a man in the house, and who now must be tamed and civilized by society at large. Does anyone really doubt that the welfare programs—this five trillion dollar monstrosity—has not done serious harm to the structure of our family life? And still the liberal fights tooth and nail to prevent any wind down of those programs.

Prior to the onset of the New Deal, black families were largely two parent families, with few out of wedlock births, as contrasted to today's picture where over 60% of black babies are born out of wedlock. Only after President Clinton's chief advisor, Dick Morris, persuaded him that he would not be reelected in 1996 if he continued to resist, did Clinton sign on to the Republican sponsored Welfare Reform Act, which appears to be working in drastically reducing the numbers of those who had been on welfare in some cases for generations. The latest report shows a 50% reduction in the number of people on welfare since 1996.

The problem with liberals, as Thomas Sowell points out, is they believe that human behavior can be modified by adjusting the underlying social conditions so that people will begin to do the right things and not continue to engage in self-destructive behavior. It is not that easy to change behavior. We simply do not know all the answers. Still the "anointed," as Sowell describes them, believe they do know all the answers, that ordinary people are irrational or immoral, and they need to be led to the good life. Shubert Spero reminds his fellow Jews that the "severest vice was pride, haughtiness or arrogance." It is the arrogance of liberals that they think they know what is best for all, that should alert Jews to the falseness of that philosophy.

The disgraceful actions of the liberals, and their leader President Clinton, in reluctantly supporting the needed reform of our welfare laws, illustrates where the American Jewish majority has been so wrong these past two generations, in their unyielding support of these spirit stiffing, ineffective, government programs. Still the liberals refuse to abandon their positions. One of the few times that the liberal Democrats criticized President Clinton was when he knuckled under to conservative pressures and signed the Welfare Reform Act of 1996.

Yet the liberals fight on, still maintaining that the Reform Act was a mistake, in spite of the fact that the welfare rolls were cut in half by the year 2000. Liberals are great proponents of improving the self-esteem of our children. They seem to ignore the fact that the greatest boost to one's self-esteem is to know how to read and write, to have the ability to think and solve problems, to have a job and become self- supporting. By discouraging the attempts of honest citizens to get off of welfare these past thirty-five years, and by limiting their opportunities to learn a craft or trade, liberals have once again demonstrated the law of unintended consequences. The results have been contrary to what was hoped for and in the process many lives have been destroyed.

If American Jews had been true to their tradition, and remembered that we have always hated welfare dependence, and that one should do almost anything to earn a wage, they would have long ago insisted that the welfare laws be changed. Instead, they meekly succumbed to the blandishments of their liberal leaders that somehow the system would eventually work, which it never did. Has anything been learned by our Jewish leaders from this welfare program disaster? It is doubtful if this example has changed many minds.

One of the traits of liberalism that is so difficult to overcome is their enduring ability to continue battling to achieve their goals. No matter how poor the results from their previous programs, liberals always seem to come up with new angles to justify continuing, and even expanding, their big government programs. Even today, after several years of successful welfare reform, I am sure there are many liberals who are still thinking deep in their hearts, "If only we had given the old programs a few more years, and spent a few more trillion dollars, I know they would have worked." To permanently kill a bad liberal program is tantamount to trying to slay the proverbial dragon. One has to drive a stake through its heart to achieve a meaningful change.

EDUCATION,
THE LIBERAL INFLUENCE
✡

From the time of the mass immigration of Jews to the United States, beginning in the 1880s, there has been a continuous Jewish belief in the wonderful benefits of education. First, it was education to learn the English language by the early arrivals. Then it was the push to educate their children so they could aspire to the higher professions, and finally as the progress of the second and third generations here proved, there was the incontrovertible evidence that it was the public education system that was largely responsible for our success in climbing the rungs of the ladder of economic success. And until around the 1960s, this was true.

When I went to public school in Chicago in the 1940s, we did receive a reasonably sound education in the basics. We were even taught American history in those days, which is a frequently neglected subject today. We respected our teachers, we paid attention in class or else, and we accepted the discipline of our school administrators, few in number in those days, without question. School was where it was at, and for almost all of us, it was the public school. The only exceptions to the public school in those days were those "secret" Catholic schools, which always seemed to turn out tough, competitive athletes. By and large though, we liked our schools, and there was practically non-existent antagonism between the races. There were no sex education classes and the only symptom of sex that emerged was comments about the good-looking girls' gym instructor.

I attended a junior college in Chicago that was two-thirds black, with never a problem. Our basketball team was integrated and our teamwork was excellent. At the school dances, each race danced with others of their own race with scarcely a thought given to doing anything different. Of course this was before the Great Society proclaimed its programs of racial equality. Admittedly, there were problems lurking beneath the surface, but the point is that in those days education was the great equalizer for all those who attended public school. Those who aspired to go on to college took certain courses in high school. Most students in those days had no hope of doing this, and we tended to take those courses that would enable us to get a job. Trade schools flourished and it was no disgrace to attend those schools because this was frequently a ticket to getting a good job.

Then after World War II, came the GI Bill of Rights, perhaps the only government program that truly succeeded in accomplishing the goals it was designed to accomplish. By rewarding those who had served in the military during and after the war, millions of us were given the privilege of attending a college or university of our choice, with the taxpayers of America footing most of the bills. Whether we chose a Catholic school, such as Notre Dame, or a state university like UCLA, or a private college or university, each recipient was given the same benefits, tuition, and $65 per month for expenses. This program resulted in the first truly educated class of citizens in this country that would not have otherwise been able to enjoy a higher education.

In today's world, public education is fighting for its life to retain its privileged system. There is no nefarious scheme afoot to downgrade this once lauded institution. It is simply that like any monopoly, it eventually contains the seeds of its own destruction. A monopoly, by definition, has no competition. This condition is endurable so long as the monopoly produces the results that the public expects. Witness the long tenure of AT&T and the utility industries. Although these companies are now facing the rigors of competition, somewhat surprising to many observers, the results are proving to be beneficial to the public.

With public education, the emergence of powerful teachers' unions seems to coincide with the decline in the success of the public education system. Whether it has been the rise of teachers' unions, or the decline in public morality, or the increase in fatherless children, there are any number of causes that have created a situation in which teachers are afraid to teach and where the test results of our students place them almost in last place among the world's industrialized nations.

William Bennett, the author of *The Book of Virtues*, wrote in 1993, "In 1940, teachers were asked what they regarded as the three major problems in American schools. They identified the three major problems as: Littering, noise, and chewing gum. Teachers last year were asked what the three major problems in American schools were, and they defined them as: Rape, assault, and suicide." This would seem to graphically describe the changes that have taken place in public education during this fifty-year span.

Many writers have analyzed this subject, but what is the bottom line? The bottom line is that changes are needed and not just around the margin. More money is spent today per student than ever before, but still the results are disappointing. The answer appears almost obvious. Competition is what has made this country's economy surge, along with the freedom of citizens to pursue their entrepreneurial instincts. So why won't this approach work in education?

The liberal mentality today is that we need to "mend it" and not "end it." But they stop short of really using competition to "mend it." Instead they cannot seem to come further than to expand the choice of which public school to attend, and to increase slowly the number of charter schools, which have a good record to date of improving the education product. When one suggests giving parents the freedom to use their own tax dollars to send their kids to schools of their choice, be they public or private, the education establishment led by their liberal leaders, and most Jewish organizations, rise up and cry out that this would be the death of public education. If this change would really result in this demise, one could say that they had it coming. If history is any example, however, public education will not die, but will improve because of competition.

As most of America continues to apparently ignore the miserable results of the public education monopoly, logic would dictate that eventually many will advocate a drastic change in our entire system of education for our young people. Why should a system similar to our successful World War II GI Bill of Rights be so opposed for our grammar school kids? One reason is that it would dilute the power of the unions and their political allies in controlling this vital activity. The purpose of teachers' unions today seems to be to protect their members from any penalties for poor performance, and if the children's education suffers, that is a minor factor. Where are our Jewish leaders in this critical fight?

The American Jewish Committee is among the leaders in challenging the right of Florida to begin a very modest "freedom to choose your school" program. In California in 1993, Jewish leaders led the opposition to a modest voucher program for grammar schools. The incredulous aspect of this for Jews is that the record is clear that when Jewish kids attend Jewish day schools, they end up marrying other Jews almost without exception. Besides that, they score well above those attending public schools. While most Jewish leaders moan and groan about the 50% rate of inter-marriage of American Jews, when presented with the opportunity to expand the number and attendance of Jewish day schools because now Jewish parents could afford to send their kids there, these leaders back away, and cover their heads with their blankets of ignorance. They are still living in the past of the 1940s when public schools were doing a fine job of educating us, and when the inter-marriage rate of Jews was negligible.

Professor Jack Wertheimer, in a December 1999, article in *Commentary*, writes of the success of today's Jewish day schools. There are now over 200,000 pupils in 700 Jewish elementary, junior high, and high schools in this country. Mostly Orthodox, there are a growing number of day schools affiliated with other branches of American Judaism. Test scores of day school students are routinely higher than their public school counterparts. Wertheimer writes, "Their alumni are far more likely than others to observe a range of rituals and holidays, to contribute to Jewish causes and institutions, and to maintain a strong attachment to Israel. Most impressive, perhaps, is the finding that graduates of day schools are considerably more inclined to wed other Jews."

The one common problem Jewish day schools have is financial, and here the Jewish leadership is largely absent, and in fact, consistently oppose any form of a "GI Bill" for elementary and high school students. This contrasts with the support that the Catholic Church gives to its extensive system of schools, estimated to exceed five billion dollars annually.

Although a task force of American Jewish leaders did proclaim in 1995 that Jewish day schools were "arguably the most impactful single weapon in our arsenal for educating Jewish children and youth," there has been little follow-through to champion the cause of Jewish day schools by that Jewish leadership.

The main reason that Jewish leaders and rabbis are not leading the fight to expand school choice which will permit more Jewish parents to finance attending Jewish day schools for their kids, is that the current liberal doctrine is dominated by the various teachers' unions, both nationally and in my home state of California. Ironically, many individual teachers would be far ahead of where they are now if there were competition for their services between public and private schools. If the teachers' unions really had the best interests of their members at heart, one would think they would encourage the expansion of additional teaching opportunities. The better teachers would be paid a premium, while the average or inferior teachers would still be able to work, perhaps not at the comfortable wages they now receive due to the coercive power of the union, but still working somewhere. Even those teachers would still have the incentive of improving their abilities so as to advance to the premium levels of compensation. Today's salary structure for teachers in our public schools pays no attention to relative ability, but rather is structured to reward longevity and the number of advanced degrees one has. And of course, there is the dreaded policy of tenure, which makes it practically impossible to terminate incompetent teachers.

Beyond all of this however, is the main point that our children would be receiving far better schooling than they receive today in many school districts under the public school monopoly. The liberal Democrats seek vainly to work around the edges of the existing system, voting more money and smaller classrooms, with little noticeable effect. Until a dramatic change is made in the system to permit and encourage competition, no real long lasting improvements will be achieved. And where are the rabbis, the teachers of our Jewish heritage in this struggle? Not where they should be, at least where I live!

In today's America, it is the political conservatives and libertarians who are championing the right of parents to choose the schools their children will attend. They are joined by those groups who are otherwise Democratic voters—the minority blacks and Hispanics—who also want to send their kids to the best schools they can regardless of where they are located and regardless of whether or not they are religious schools. If there ever were a time for the Jews to unite behind a change in our system to permit and encourage this freedom to choose, it is now! But to do that, they must pierce at least a fragment of their liberal cloak, and open their eyes to the situation that exists today.

One recent answer to the demand for a change in education choice is the Children's Scholarship Fund, started with $100,000,000 donation from Theodore Forstmann, a Jewish Republican, and John Walton, a non-Jewish, non-Republican. In early 1999, the fund had attracted an additional $70,000,000. They then announced that they were offering scholarships to every single low-income family in the United States. These were not full scholarships. The parents with an average annual income of less than $22,000 still had to contribute on average $1,000 every year for four years. And it must be noted that these scholarships were to pay for tuition to send your kid to a grammar school different from the public school now being attended, and that different school included religious and other private schools.

The response was amazing. The fund received requests from 1.25

million families for these partial scholarships. Over 60,000 scholarships have now been awarded, and plans are in place to expand and continue the fund in the future. All of the arguments by the public school advocates were used to oppose the fund. It would destroy the public schools, it would siphon off the best students leaving only the dregs in public school, the poor and minority parents would be incapable of making good decisions when it came to their children's education, etc. Mr. Forstmann replied in the September 1999 issue of *Imprimis* (published by Hillsdale College), that these arguments not only underestimated America's struggling families, but that they ignored the central value that makes America great. That value is freedom and the ability of ordinary citizens to make the best decisions for themselves and their families. Forstmann stressed the point that only through competition will the public schools improve, and only when choice is fully implemented throughout the country will we see a truly uplifted education for these mostly underprivileged children.

Certainly the concept that competition brings out the best for all concerned is not new. In his profound work, *Morality, Halakha and the Jewish Tradition*, Shubert Spero quotes a statement from the Talmud: "Elementary teachers cannot complain that their source of livelihood is being impaired by an influx of teachers from another town, because of the principle that Competition among the scribes increases wisdom." Oh how we wish some of that ancient wisdom could permeate through the thick hides of today's teachers unions!

In the Soncino Press second edition of the Pentateuch and Haftorahs, in the additional Deuteronomy notes, the aim of Jewish education is described. It was to consecrate the Jewish child to Judaism, and was to contain four elements. One was to teach the Jewish religion, the Jewish beliefs about God, the Torah, and Israel. Second was the teaching of the Hebrew language, Israel's historic language, and the key to truly learning the heart of Judaism. Third was the learning of the sacred scriptures, going beyond the Pentateuch. "It is these truths, enshrined not only in

Bible history, but in prophecy, psalm, proverb and moral discourse, that are of transcendent worth to the spiritual development of the child." Fourth was the teaching of Jewish history, the outstanding events and personalities of every age in Jewish history. Only one who learns our history and the contributions Jews have made to the progress of humankind can fully appreciate the value of our religion. Jewish kids are not going to learn this in public schools.

So does it not make sense that our Jewish leaders should champion the ways that more Jewish families could send their children to Jewish schools to absorb this type of learning? Only if families are relieved of at least part of the burden of supporting both the public schools and the private schools of their choice will this come about. Education plays such a prominent part in Jewish tradition that any changes to improve it should take the highest priority with our Jewish leadership. After all, we are the "people of the Book."

In the "Ten Principles For Reform Judaism, a Draft Proposal," as published in *Reform Judaism* Winter 1998, principle 6 reads in part, "Thus we renew our classic devotion to 'chinuch,' to Jewish education, some of us sending our children to Jewish day schools, others to supplementary schools, but all striving to participate actively in our children's Jewish schooling." I don't know whether that draft was finally adapted as the official Reform position, but the concept has certainly not penetrated the Jewish leadership of the powerful teachers unions.

Jewish tradition is based on freedom of choice. The freedom to worship as we choose has been at the heart of our 4,000-year history. The main reason we have endured the persecution from the Christian authorities during those years was because we were not willing to abandon our choice of the "One God," to accept another. The fact that the Jewish leaders and their unions opposed the right of parents to choose the best schools for their children is inconsistent with our Jewish principles and traditions of true justice. To accept the liberal argument that to solve the dilemma of the public schools, we simply need to throw more billions of taxpayer dollars at the problem, almost falls within the definition of insanity. That is when you keep doing the same thing to solve a problem, but expect different results.

Sadly, it is the children of the least privileged that are most adversely impacted from the public school failures. There is a basic inconsistency in Jewish thinking that on the one hand Jews will support any welfare program to help those in financial need, but turn around and oppose a change in education policy that will greatly help the very children of those families receiving that financial support. If conservatives will now mimic liberals in their unwillingness to give up until they achieve victory on a particular issue, then eventually we will see competition enter the education field to the benefit of all children.

Finally in late 2002, the Supreme Court upheld Cleveland, Ohio's school-choice program in its 5 to 4 decision in the *Zelman v. Simmons-Harris* case. The ruling that this program did not violate the dreaded religion/government mix because it gave the vouchers directly to the parents to be used as they decide would seem to open the way for expansion of similar programs in other cities and states.

Another small victory for the educational-choice movement came early in 2004, with Congress's approval of a small 2,000-student voucher program open to low-income students in the District of Columbia. The Milton and Rose D. Friedman Foundation was a prime mover of this proposal. The vote in Congress produced some unusual supporters and opponents. Sen. Arlen Specter of Pennsylvania, a Jewish Republican, voted against it. Sen. Dianne Feinstein of California, a Jewish Democrat who normally votes with liberal Democrats, supported the proposal. Senator Feinstein was also quoted as saying that she had finally reached the stage in her career where she could do the right thing without worrying about the political flak (another example of the "never give up" philosophy?).

JEWISH LIBERALS AND MORALITY

✡

Seldom does one read or hear Jewish leaders and rabbis extol their political liberal positions as somehow being connected with Jewish tradition when it comes to today's morality. Whether the subject is unlimited abortion, promiscuous behavior on the part of our leaders, posting the Ten Commandments in public places, use of TV and movies to depict the worst parts of human behavior, whatever the subject matter, the Jewish liberals are silent about any connection with Jewish tradition and their support for that behavior. Somehow the morality, or lack thereof, does not enter into their thinking. Their key question is whether or not it enhances the freedom of people to do what they want, regardless of how that squares with our traditional beliefs. Self-discipline is an out-moded practice. If it feels good and if it promises to do good so be it. As Judge Bork wrote, "What liberalism has moved away from are the constraints on personal liberty imposed by religion, morality, law, family and community."

During the recent scandal regarding President Clinton and that nice Jewish girl, Monica Lewinsky, I do not recall ever reading any condemnation of Clinton's behavior by any prominent Jewish leader or rabbi. It was as if his behavior was somehow excusable because he was our president, and it was between consenting adults. Since when has this been the measuring stick as to whether behavior is moral or immoral? I had always thought that the Ten Commandments were our God-given guidelines for living a righteous life. Thou shall not commit adultery. Thou shall not lie or steal or worship false Gods.

In *The Essential Talmud*, Adin Steinsaltz writes that no matter how smart or erudite a man may be, if his conduct is contemptible, he should be condemned and despised. The Talmud often stated that if learned people were of dubious character, they were frequently punished, chastised, or excommunicated. Instead of that, our president was able to boast after his non-conviction, that he had really upheld our Constitution by his defense of his actions and by escaping impeachment.

The only voices I heard condemning his behavior were those of the Religious Right, those alleged bigots that the Jews are so fearful will convert our kids. As for the six Jewish members of the House committee investigating the impeachment process, I heard few if any words that described Clinton's behavior as immoral. Senator Joseph Lieberman, the only senator who is an Orthodox Jew, did make one public speech on the Senate floor that made the point that Clinton's conduct had been reprehensible and should be condemned. But that was it. Lieberman never followed through, and his vote not to remove Clinton from office was in line with his fellow Democratic Senators. Politics does indeed make strange bedfellows though. (In light of recent developments in August 2000, it appears that Lieberman's one speech helped him to obtain the vice presidential nomination on the Democratic ticket in the election of November 2000.)

I can hear the defenders of the liberals cry out: "What about the Republican misdeeds?" Certainly Washington, DC is not the city of virtue we would like it to be. I hold no brief for any holder of public office whose behavior is not at least as moral as that of the average citizen. The point is that the American Jews are so one-sided in their approval of anything that their liberal leaders do and are so unanimous in criticizing the actions of Republicans.

The 1993 Senate hearings to confirm Clarence Thomas as a Supreme Court justice are an outstanding example of this. Here the liberals had to walk a fine line. They had to be careful about alienating too many of their black followers, although many blacks did not like Thomas for his conservative views. At the same time they wanted desperately to defeat the nomination put forward by President George Bush. So they dragged

Anita Hill out of obscurity, who had no more thought of attacking her former friend and mentor, Clarence Thomas, for sexual harassment than she had of running for president. Still the liberals managed to "refresh" Ms. Hill's memory sufficiently that she was able to accuse Thomas of saying the most naughty things to her some ten years previously.

No, Mr. Thomas had never done anything physically to her; no, he had not dated her; no, he had not even propositioned her although they had been alone together on many occasions. Yes, he had been kind to her in helping to find her other positions after he had moved on in his career. But still the liberals chewed on every morsel and tidbit of possible scandal to try and block the nomination. Ms. Hill, of course, was duly rewarded for her performance, both financially and career-wise, and became somewhat of an icon for the feminist movement.

Let us recount some of Judge Thomas' testimony before the Senate Judiciary Committee in 1991. "This is a circus. It is a national disgrace … It is a high-tech lynching for uppity blacks who in any way deign to think for themselves, to do for themselves, to have different ideas, and it is a message that, unless you kowtow to an old order, this is what will happen to you, you will be lynched, destroyed, caricatured by a committee of the U.S. Senate, rather than hung from a tree." Considering the long time political affinity between American Jews and American blacks, where were our Jewish Senators in the defense of Judge Thomas? Fortunately, Judge Thomas was narrowly confirmed to the Supreme Court, and is today generally regarded as either the best or second best justice on that court.

Again the question is asked: Where were our Jewish leaders to defend the conduct and reputation of Clarence Thomas? Well of course, he was a Republican, a conservative, and he wasn't one of their black constituents, so they remained silent. Former Senator Warren Rudman of New Hampshire, a Jew, whose name resurfaced during John McCain's campaign for president in year 2000 as one of McCain's advisors, was quoted recently as saying the only reason he voted to confirm Thomas was because he believed Thomas' confirmation was already assured. If he had thought that his vote could defeat Thomas, then he would have so voted. A typical Jewish politician's thinking, even Jewish Republicans?

Compare Thomas' alleged "bad deeds," which were unproven and unsubstantiated, with Clinton's real-life despicable conduct in the White House. Regardless of one's political affiliation, should not the pure morality of what is right and what is wrong lead those in Jewish leadership in this country to have spoken out in condemnation? The prophet Micah said, "It has been told thee oh man, what is good and what the Lord doth require of you, only to do justice and love mercy, and to walk humbly with thy God." It seems we Jews are overdoing the "mercy" part and overlooking the "justice" part when it comes to judging the behavior of Democrats. Shubert Spero defines the principle of Justice in Judaism as "what is right or wrong for one person must be right or wrong for any similar person in similar circumstances." We are to treat all like cases alike. Just imagine how the liberals would have reacted if it had been a President Reagan or Bush who had confessed to doing what Clinton had done?

Are Jewish liberals so afraid of protecting their political positions that they cannot be honest and truthful in stating what they believe to be right and wrong in these United States? Are they so concerned that they will be seen as "holier than thou" if they criticize Democratic politicians as well as Republicans? How can they ignore that most basic concept of our religion of fairly administering justice? Again this appears to be another example of the blind leading the blind; myopic Jewish leadership followed by equally visually impaired Jewish voters.

In the previously quoted "Ten Principles For Reform Judaism," #3 reads in part, "Mindful of our own redemption from Egypt, we commit ourselves to help redeem the new century in modernity, striving to transform it into a realization of Israel's great messianic hope for the establishment of truth and justice, for moral and spiritual discipline, compassion and integrity, and at long last, a world repaired, a world at peace." When it comes to "truth and justice," in judging the conduct of liberal Democrats, our Jewish politicians seem to exhibit a strong case of convenient amnesia.

I received a recent fundraising letter from Mr. Ira Glasser, undoubtedly Jewish, Executive Director of the American Civil Liberties Union (ACLU). I probably received this letter because I am on some Jewish mailing lists, although I certainly have never supported the ACLU. The gist of Mr. Glasser's somewhat hysterical eight-page appeal for funds is that there is a "growing struggle between two competing visions of morality now taking place in America." What are these two competing visions? According to Mr. Glasser, they are "Individual freedom vs. Government authoritarianism." It is so ironic that Mr. Glasser has indeed described the struggle, but his definition of the players and who is on which side is 180 degrees off from reality.

It seems Mr. Glasser and the ACLU are worried that the "New Puritans" want to use the police power of the state to control our actions in our bedrooms; and further, that people like Pat Robertson, Jesse Helms, William Bennett, and Dan Quayle want to measure the nation's morality by old fashioned standards. (What a horrible thought!) That is the "government authoritarianism" segment. What Mr. Glasser fails to mention is that all of these spokesmen happen to be strong, political conservatives whose main drives are to restore morality to America, to reduce the powers of government, and to expand the freedom of the individual citizen to act.

The other vision, the "individual freedom" part that is under attack, is where people are not permitted to do what they choose. The ACLU is concerned that certain "individual" rights are in danger of being abridged. These include the right of schools not being free to omit non-denominational prayer at various ceremonies; of citizens not being allowed the right to burn and trash the American flag; of women not having unlimited abortion rights; and the right of homosexuals to set their own rules of conduct and not be held to the same moral standards as others. Some would describe these actions as "license" and not the typical freedoms from government interference that conservatives are championing. But these are the "freedoms" that the ACLU is worried may somehow be curtailed by the "New Puritans."

Mr. Glasser is worried that the Christian Coalition and "other reactionary groups" are trying to get Congressional action to overrule federal and state court decisions, which have favored many of the ACLU's programs. In his recent book, *Slouching Toward Gomorrah*, Judge Robert Bork writes that one of the major factors in leading this country down the slippery road to immorality and loss of individual freedom has been the decisions of our courts. He believes that the courts in many cases, Roe vs. Wade, being a prime example, have overstepped their authority by taking powers away from the states and the people, and ceding them to the federal government. Mr. Glasser however, apparently welcomes the actions of the courts in achieving his goals, many of which could not have been enacted into law by Congress.

This ACLU letter mentions not a word about the loss of our freedoms through our 40% tax rates, the restrictions on how we can use our property, the invasions of employers' rights via OSHA and the other enforcement agencies, etc. No, these are not the concerns of the ACLU. Their principle worry is that somehow, through the voluntary actions of the groups previously cited, the present trend of a 50% divorce rate and 60% of babies born out of wedlock will be reversed! (I assume Mr. Glasser, et al. will not be satisfied until those rates reach even higher levels.) Nowhere in the literature of the Religious Right or any so-called "reactionary group" is there a call for government controls on peoples' behavior. The only legislative goal of these groups is for a Constitutional Amendment to make abortions illegal. I don't agree with that position and I don't believe that it will ever become national law. The primary political thrust of the Religious Right remains that of reducing the powers of government to interfere in the lives of its citizens and for expanding the individual freedom of its citizens.

To me, the most distressing aspect of Jewish leaders when they comment on political issues is that they make no attempt to relate their positions to their religious heritage. As Shubert Spero writes, "Morality is the essence of Judaism. It is the set of rules which prescribe the way people should behave, and principles which are good or desirable for men." Morality means doing what people instinctively know is the right thing to do. Morality is the chief demand made upon man by God. "Religious theories of morality are related somehow to God, and are based on the Ten Commandments." The last five of those Commandments—thou shall not murder, commit adultery, steal, lie or covet—could have been cited, at least in part, in condemning President Clinton's behavior.

As more books are written and more facts come to light, to reveal the vast amount of lying and cover up that took place within the liberal establishment to protect this president, one would think that finally, some prominent Jewish spokesman would rise up to condemn that behavior. As of this writing, the collective amnesia continues to prevail. Perhaps once a new president is inaugurated, some will find the courage to step forward and fulfill that role.

One spokesperson for upholding morality in one's life is radio talk show host Dr. Laura Schlessinger. For three hours every weekday, Dr. Laura, as she is known, tries to provide moral solutions to listeners' problems that they call in to discuss. The daughter of a Jewish father and a non-Jewish mother, Dr. Laura converted to Judaism many years ago. One of her latest books, *The Ten Commandments: The Significance of God's Laws in Everyday Life,* written in conjunction with Rabbi Stewart Vogel of Temple Aliyah, Woodland Hills, California, discusses each of the Commandments, describes the principles contained therein, and relates them to the everyday decisions we are forced to make in our own lives. It is not difficult to connect the morality she advocates and preaches to political conservatism and not to liberalism. Although Dr. Laura continues to dispense valuable advice to her listeners, in August

2003 she backed away somewhat from living her life as an Orthodox Jew. While still maintaining her Jewishness, she seemed to distance herself from some of her previous beliefs. She has not offered any explanation for this change.

Jews separate themselves from their essential Judaism when they fail to criticize those actions by our political leaders that are truly immoral. As Spero writes, "In Jewish view, morality is the bridge by which man reaches out to God. Values are divine. Morality is the fabric out of which man weaves for himself an ethical self and society achieves its redemptive goal." My hope is that someday this melding of Jewish tradition and political expression will take hold, and then will come about the meaningful change in Jewish voting.

Many American Jewish leaders have been critical of recent Israeli leaders who attempted to draw a hard line when it came to dealing with Palestinian terrorists. There was liberal outcry when it was learned that the Jewish treatment of Palestinian terrorists in jail was not up to our "normal" American standards. On the other hand our leaders have applauded the releasing from prison of hundreds of those same terrorists under the terms of the Oslo Agreement. The fact that Israel is fighting for its very existence, surrounded by hostile forces, seems to cut no ice with our virtuous American Jewish leaders. What is right is right, they proclaim, and if the results lead to disaster, well, at least their intentions were honorable. Such is the state of Jewish leadership and morality in these United States as we enter the new millennium!

JEWS, LIBERALS, AND INDIVIDUAL RESPONSIBILITY

Throughout today's liberal philosophy there weaves the thread that says that the average American citizen does not have the brains, the temperament, or the common sense to make the decisions by which he and his family can live decent lives. Liberals will never come out and boldly make this statement, but behind almost all of their programs, one sees this philosophy. Because this is true, so think the liberals, our citizens must be protected from their mistakes, must be guarded against making foolish decisions, and of course, must be protected from programs that those big, bad conservatives advocate.

Let us concentrate on the three major programs that are under reexamination at the turn of the twenty-first century which illustrate this point. These are budget surpluses, education reform, and Social Security.

The following discussion on budget surpluses at the federal level may now seem irrelevant in light of the huge deficits we now face. At the time of my first writing, who could have anticipated the enormous economic disaster that 9/11/01 created, accompanied by our needed military buildup and our wars to defeat the Islamic terrorists in Afghanistan and Iraq? Also, the unrestrained increases in government spending for domestic programs have added to the problem. This drastic change in our federal monetary picture illustrates the difficulty of making projections far into the future. The two income-tax reductions enacted under Pres. George W. Bush, and attempts to relax job-killing regulations, are certainly steps in the right direction. Hopefully, economic growth and controlled domestic spending will eventually minimize our budget deficits. I believe the discussion on this subject is still relevant to the major point that the principles of Judaism are more closely related to political conservatism than to liberalism.

1. Suddenly, at the end of the 1990s, there was discovered that, unknown to many and not forecast by the most renowned economists, the United States was experiencing surpluses in its federal government budget of many billions of dollars. Not only was this phenomenon occurring in just one year, 1998-9, but the government economists were forecasting surpluses almost as far as the eye could see totaling into the trillions of dollars. How these surpluses came to be is debatable.

Some say it was the Republican Congress, elected in 1994 as the first of its kind in fifty years that held federal spending to small annual increases in the years since 1994. Some say it was the Clinton inspired tax increase of 1993, which triggered the massive increases in federal tax collections. (It is doubtful if any tax increase ever contributes to the growth of an economy.) Many attributed the surpluses to the amazing technological revolution with the computer that improved efficiencies to the extent that more companies than ever earned greater profits, and thus paid more taxes. Some said that it was all due to Allan Greenspan, a libertarian or conservative Jew, who as head of the Federal Reserve System had kept interest rates low, who was really the godfather of our prosperity. Others said it was the growth of the Internet with the spawning of countless new companies with their soaring stock valuations that provided the spark and the increased capital gains taxes paid on the sale of those stocks. But whatever the reasons, we are now challenged with what to do with this excess money being collected by the federal government.

As we enter into the debate of what to do with these surpluses, the liberals, true to their philosophy, argue that we must spend these surpluses by "investing" more dollars for education and other social purposes. The main reason for the current failure of our public education system is primarily that not enough money is being spent, so say the liberals. So if we spend the surpluses for this purpose, we will solve that problem. This of course, ignores the fact that as spending for public education has increased, the test scores of our children have declined.

Then some of that surplus should be spent on more money for the poor and indigent. Five trillion dollars spent on welfare programs has not yet cured the problem, so we must throw some additional trillions at the problem to make it go away. This too, ignores the fact that our massive welfare programs have created a host of social problems of unwed mothers, fatherless youth, and broken families. Only now, beginning with the reformed welfare laws pushed through by the Republican Congress in 1996, and reluctantly signed by President Clinton, have we seen some meaningful reductions in the welfare rolls. But after all, how can more money hurt?

Then of course, there are countless other programs and reasons and good ideas that require the expenditure of most of this "found" money. To liberals, the thought of returning most of this excess to those from whom it was collected is simply not included in their thinking. Once money comes to Washington, DC, it must be spent, and that is all there is to it. This is a golden opportunity for liberals to create more dependent classes by doling out more hard-earned taxpayers money.

The latest scheme conceived by the liberals to avoid returning these surpluses to the taxpayers is to dedicate most of these massive sums to paying down, and eventually paying off, our national debt. This is truly a new idea. For all of these almost seventy years since FDR, the national debt was something that was simply out there, an always-available pot of gold to be tapped and expanded at will. To finance the debt we simply sold U.S. Government bonds of all different varieties, which are now held as secure investments by people and nations worldwide. We pay the interest on those securities without fail, and that interest comprises about 15% of our overall massive national budget, which today exceeds $2 trillion. To pay off the national debt which now exceeds five trillion dollars would take several years, assuming all of the financial projections come true which is highly unlikely, but suddenly the liberals have become fiscally conservative and have nothing but the long-term interests of America at heart. Quite a change of spots for this leopard!

Nowhere are there heard any liberal voices crying out for returning the money to the taxpayers from whence these surpluses have come. Probably if a liberal did advocate this, he would soon lose his standing in the party. No, their attitude is summed up with the previously noted quote from their hero, President Clinton, who said that we cannot trust our citizens to spend their tax refunds for the right things. Those "right things" are the causes that are most dear to liberals' hearts.

So what is wrong with this liberal position as it relates to Jewish law and tradition? Does Judaism proclaim that people are not capable of deciding how to spend their money? Does Judaism say that we must turn over the most important decisions of our lives to others? Does Judaism say that the average person does not possess the common sense to know what is important in his life? To the contrary, throughout the Torah are challenges to the Israelites to either accept or reject God's message, to choose the good or the evil, to live by or reject the Ten Commandments, all choices to be made by the individual, either to his benefit or his detriment.

Nowhere does God say to His people, "I have laid a heavy burden on you to live righteous lives with many difficult decisions to make. If you have a problem in making those individual choices, then I suggest that you elect some super-wise people to make those decisions for you, and thus relieve you of the burden of those decisions. This also takes away your responsibility for any mistakes that may be made, as you can always blame those super-wise representatives for making those mistakes. This will show you just how much I love my people." That is not what God said to his people.

In fact, He said, "I call heaven and earth to witness against you this day, that I have set before thee life and death, the blessing and the curse; therefore choose life, that thou mayest live, thou and thy seed." (Deuteronomy 30:19) In the notes to the Soncino Pentateuch, titled "Free-Will In Judaism," it reads, "Jewish ethics is rooted in the doctrine of human responsibility, that is freedom of the will." It quotes

Maimonides, "Free will is granted to every man. If he desires to incline towards the good way, and be righteous, he has the power to do so; and if he desires to incline towards the unrighteous way, and be a wicked man, he has also the power to do so. Since this power of doing good or evil is in our own hands, and since all the wicked deeds which we have committed have been committed with our full consciousness, it befits us to turn in penitence and forsake our evil deeds; the power of doing so being still in our hands. Now this matter is a very important principle; nay, it is the pillar of the Law and of the commandments."

The Soncino notes go on to say that we are free agents in our choice between good and evil, and that this is an undeniable fact of human nature. It depends on man alone as to what happens to his life, and although he cannot always control his destiny, "God has given the reins of man's conduct altogether into his hands."

When God gave Moses and the Israelites the Ten Commandments that commemorated their redemption from Egypt, His message was that of the God of freedom, and was directed to all the peoples of the world, as individuals. The entire thrust of the Commandments and the other passages of the Torah is that individuals must make their own choices of how they live their lives, and that God has given us guidelines in how to make the most of our earthly existence.

So, back to our opening question on what we should do with our tax surpluses. To be in harmony with our Jewish traditions we, of course, should return those monies to those who paid them in to the federal treasury. The liberals moan that any tax reductions would unduly benefit the "rich." Of course they would benefit those citizens who paid in the most taxes because that is where the surpluses come from. Five percent of American taxpayers are today paying 50% of the individual income taxes. Fifty percent of American taxpayers are paying 96% of the total individual income taxes. This also means that 50% of American taxpayers are paying only 4% of the total individual income taxes. No wonder that public opinion polls show so many citizens don't care about tax reductions.

These excess tax collections should not be given away to those who did not pay them because that violates the doctrine of fairness. If one overpays for a product or service, the Talmud says that the payer must be made whole. Even liberals would agree that we do not get full value from government services for the taxes we pay, so why not at least reduce some of our overpayment. It would be interesting for the liberals to try and equate their positions with some element of Jewish tradition. I doubt if they can make that case, but certainly conservatives can!

2. Education, its failures and successes, is perhaps the most important issue facing the electorate at this time. The poor test results, the inability of almost half of high school graduates to place the Civil War in the correct century, the fact that we are producing generations of illiterates who cannot fill out an employment application on their own, troubles most citizens. When the opposing forces discuss their solutions to the problems, the liberals, true to their beliefs, advocate more money for the public school system, smaller class sizes (which will require more union member teachers), and most recently, improved education and training for the public school teachers. This latter point has just been discovered when it was revealed that a high percentage of teachers could not pass the very tests they were giving to their students. The facts are that as more money has been spent, the results have not been what were expected, and that smaller class sizes are thus far showing negligible benefits. It would help if teachers were schooled in at least the subjects they are going to teach, but apparently we have not quite figured out how to accomplish this.

The opposing forces, the conservatives, say that it does no good to look back on the past successes of public education; the fact is that today that system is failing our children and we need to make drastic changes. We need competition in education, just as we have in all other phases of our society. It is competition that spurs improvement, and it is accountability for results that is the bedrock of successful programs. To bring this about, we need to give parents freedom of choice in how they

162

spend their hard-earned tax dollars for their children's education. Instead of having to pay those taxes to support public schools and then paying again for tuition for some private school, let us give parents something akin to the GI Bill of Rights, allowing them to send their children to any school of their choice: Catholic, Jewish, technical, trade, or whatever.

Gary Becker, winner of the 1992 Nobel Prize for economics, and believed to be Jewish, spoke about competition in a lecture in Chicago given 12 September 1999. When government stifles competition among schools, "locally protected markets enable teachers' unions and government officials to capture the governance of public schools and manage them in their own rather than students' interests," Becker said. And contrary to popular belief, government run schools are not more democratic than private schools. Private schools, Becker said, are "far less segregated by race, income, social background, and every relevant characteristic." What it all boils down to is that competition is "the foundation of the good life and the most precious part of human existence, educational, civil, religious, and cultural as well as economic." Competition is "the most remarkable social contrivance invented during this millennium."

Again, we get to the foundation of Judaism, that of individual choice in making the decisions of how to live one's life and bearing the consequences of those decisions. The liberals say that if we give parents this power that too many of them are simply too dumb to pick the best school for their kids. Liberals say that too many parents simply do not take the time to figure out where the best schools are, that they are too busy with their own pleasures to make educated decisions, and therefore, the public school system is the only alternative for these folk.

Although liberals don't come right out and say it, they really are referring to black and Hispanic parents, living in the inner cities, who will be taken advantage of by charlatans who will offer private schools that will do an even worse job than the miserable public schools in those inner cities are now doing. It is not those "smart" white folk in the suburbs who liberals are worried about making bad decisions; it is really those "others" who cannot be relied on to do what is best for their kids. Isn't this hypocrisy at its worst, because this is the same part of the electorate that the liberals depend upon to keep their busybodies in office, election after election? The Democrats are not shy about boasting that their core constituency includes blacks and Hispanics.

The irony of this is that these inner-city parents are overwhelmingly in favor of school choice for their kids. It is these "dumb" parents that instinctively know that it is the current public school system that is failing their kids, and that parental choice of schools results in uplifted grades for the pupils in those schools. No matter how the teachers' unions try to downgrade this alternative approach to public schools, or try to offer a partial alternative in the form of charter schools, both common wisdom and actual results dictate that we must undergo a radical reform of our educational system via competition in order to achieve the results those children deserve.

Gary Rosen, associate editor of *Commentary*, writes in his February 2000 article, "Are School Vouchers Un-American?" that today's voucher experiments are in response to the failing record of the public school system. Mr. Rosen writes that thus far, every study of existing voucher programs shows that the parents of the children involved are "vastly more satisfied with the quality of their children's education" than they were when their children were going to public schools. This satisfaction is due to several reasons including better classroom discipline and more rigorous homework assignments. Contrary to the liberals' thinking, these low-income parents are vitally interested in their children's academic progress, and "school choice is above all a way to save their children's minds…"

Another result of the fledgling voucher programs is that the public schools in the local areas frequently respond to the new competition by making substantial improvements after many years of complacency. In New York, Florida, and Milwaukee, Wisconsin there have been meaningful improvements in some of the public schools competing with voucher programs in their areas. Mr. Rosen predicts that based on these results, if school choice were implemented on a broad national basis, this could generate a meaningful turnaround in the public schools in the inner cities which today frequently resemble battlefields more than schools.

Again the Jewish position should be that of giving the power and responsibility of education to the parents and the families of their children. In the Soncino notes to Deuteronomy is written, "Jewish law and custom ordained the provision of elementary instruction to all the children of the community, rich and poor alike. Be ye heedful of the children of the poor, for from them does the Torah go forth, was the warning of the rabbis."

The question is why? Why is the Jewish liberal leader not in the forefront of the movement to expand parental choice? From the Biblical references quoted above, they are not reading their own liturgy. They are also being held captive, for whatever reasons, by the politically powerful teachers' unions, whose sole purpose seems to be maintaining the perks and privileges of their members, and to hell with the educational results of those they are paid to teach. In California, the lobby that spends the most money to influence state legislation consists of the teachers' unions. They are the ones who have thus far successfully fought off any expansion of parental choice. If Jewish leaders could somehow gather their imposing wits about them and see the light on this subject, they could provide the catalyst that would ignite the profound changes needed to improve the education system both in California and throughout these United States.

3. The third prominent subject under discussion, once called the "third rail" of politics, is the Social Security system. Originally designed to provide a minimum retirement payment of $30 a month if one lived to be sixty-five, when the average age at death was sixty-three, the Social Security system has grown to be the elephant of American redistribution schemes. Politicians of both parties came to realize these past sixty years

that by raising benefits they could not only get reelected easily, but the costs could be passed on to the next generation of taxpayers and elected officials. What a deal: Look good to your public, inflict higher costs only gradually, and hope and pray that somehow all would come out okay somewhere in the distant future. As with all Ponzi schemes, the Social Security mess has finally broken through the surface and is now perhaps the most talked about domestic political issue as we enter the twenty-first century. (Ponzi scheme: Collect money from Peter to pay Paul, and then hope Peter dies before his turn comes to collect benefits.)

The alternative solutions proposed include raising taxes, increasing the retirement age, somehow improving the rate of return on monies collected, and variations thereof. The liberal position here does not differ from conservatives in the first alternative. No one wants to increase taxes, which already are at a combined 15+%. We have already decreed that the retirement age will increase by 2022 to sixty-seven from sixty-five, and there appears to be a reluctance to increase that age further, although with the increased lifespan of most seniors, it is still a possibility that this alternative will be exercised. The majority of the discussion seems to center around how to invest the enormous sums that are collected annually, and are not yet being paid out in benefits to the current recipients. Should we continue to increase the IOUs that represent those surpluses or should some new way of investment be considered?

The liberal position is that we continue to let government accumulate those funds, invest them in low interest bearing government bonds, and exclude the participants from having any decision making role on what to do with those funds. Again the theory is that our citizens, who are brilliant enough to continue electing liberals to Congress, the presidency, etc., are still too stupid to control and invest any of their own monies that will later form their Social Security benefits. Liberals answer the question as to how to maintain the solvency of the system by saying that we will be prudent enough in future Congresses to not spend those surpluses foolishly, but will secure them by reducing the national debt, thereby freeing up sufficient funds in the future to pay the recipients their guaranteed benefits. This answer requires a great leap of faith that somehow the Democrats will be precluded from ever controlling Congress again, because surely once they reacquire control, those surpluses would somehow vanish for new "investments" in public education, welfare, the environment, etc. (Even the Republicans, unless given a strong majority, are not immune from freely spending this "free money.")

The contrary position, and what should be the Jewish position, is to be consistent with the principle that the individual is capable and must be responsible for his own actions. If we permit the individual taxpayer to invest his own money in higher yielding investments, the future Social Security deficits will not only be manageable, but the retirement benefits will be far greater for the individual than under the current system. The historical record of the stock market shows that over each ten-year cycle, dating back over one hundred years, the average annual return is 9%, far higher than the 2-3 % yield currently being credited to the Social Security fund. There is an element of risk of course. With higher potential reward there must go some higher potential risk. However, even if those funds are invested in higher yielding government bonds, the returns to the participants will be far greater than they are under the present system.

There is another major difference between the two approaches, liberal and conservative, to the Social Security issue. The liberal position is that it is too risky to permit citizens to convert some of their contributions to privately held accounts. It is only government that can safely invest those monies. What they do not say is that Social Security is not an insurance program, that the American citizens have no property right in their theoretical Social Security benefits, and that Congress could if it so decided, drastically reduce those benefits sometime in the future.

The truly risky position is to continue the program as it is. There needs to be fundamental changes if Social Security is to survive past this generation. The conservatives' position of permitting some portion of the payments to be invested privately creates an actual property right to those funds, which then become part of one's estate. This can be passed on to one's heirs, or otherwise invested at retirement age. If I pay in to Social Security all of my life, and then die at age sixty-five with no wife and no minor children, what happens to all of the money my employers and I have paid in for fifty years? That money reverts to the government. If any private insurance company tried to sell an insurance policy like this, their executives would land in jail. Yet this is what our current program really is.

As the Supreme Court has ruled in two cases, Helvering v. Davis and Flemming v. Nestor, Social Security conveys no property rights to the participants, and it is in reality a welfare program that can be changed and altered at the whim of Congress. The fact is there is no Social Security fund out of which future benefits are to be paid. Future benefits will be paid by the taxes that workers in the future will pay. If at least a portion of future payments is invested in mutual funds, bonds, or treasury bills, as those amounts compound through the years, they will become a part of that person's estate, and will relieve the future liability of the fund to pay that portion of the benefits.

It is the principle here that is critical. Do we, in this free country of ours, have the brains and common sense to guide our own destinies? Or do we need Big Brother to watch over us to keep us from falling prey to our own mistakes? The Jewish position should always err on the side of individual responsibility, because that is what God decreed when He gave us His Commandments to live by. They were His rules, and we could either accept them or reject them to our sorrow. We grow by overcoming adversity, and we grow by making mistakes and accepting the consequences thereof.

On a personal note, the stock market crash of October 1987 caught me in an exposed margin position. The fall that fateful Monday of over 500 Dow Jones points, or over 20%, was so swift that it prevented us margin investors from selling out with some portion of our previous holdings. We could not withstand the furious force of that declining market, and because we were on margin, we were obligated to liquidate our positions at a fraction of their previous worth. If I could have held on beyond that day, I would have eventually recovered my original position, and even have seen it grow in the months to come. But the margin problem prevented my holding on and forced the liquidation resulting in heavy losses.

That day's experience was both humbling and humiliating. Not only did it decimate our net worth, but it also exposed me as a somewhat careless investor (speculator). I had not provided our account with enough cushion of equity. Fortunately, it did not lead my family to seek welfare. We picked up the pieces and have survived nicely since then. The point of the story is that this experience was both humbling and enlightening. Never again would I expose myself to the wonders of margin trading, and never again would I take lightly the wonderful day to day delights that one experiences in his normal existence. I achieved, I believe, an increased awareness of the blessings I enjoy from my family, from my work, and from my religion.

We rise or fall in this life pretty much on our own. We learn by our mistakes and, as we age, we should make better and better decisions. It is a hopeless task to try and shield people from the consequences of their own actions through some form of government intervention. This never achieves the aims sought and inevitably leads to more restrictions on individual freedom.

All of these three major subjects—taxation, education, Social Security—when placed under the glass and observed through a Jewish magnifying lens, must lead an objective observer to believe that current liberal positions are antithetical to Judaism and Jewish tradition. The liberal positions are probably all taken with the best of intentions, but as Daniel Webster said, "Good intentions will always be pleaded for any assumption of power. The Constitution was made to guard the people against the dangers of good intentions. There are men in all ages who mean to govern well, but they mean to govern. They promise to be good masters, but they mean to be masters." And let us not forget that "the road to Hell is paved with good intentions."

AFFIRMATIVE ACTION (RACE PREFERENCE)

Words are powerful things. If we were to label affirmative action today as a system of quotas and discrimination, it is doubtful that system would exist. It would be particularly noxious to Jews, because we have been kept out of many professions and opportunities throughout our history simply because the powers that be did not want too many of us in that occupation, school, club, or industry. We were the "killers of the Messiah" and as such did not deserve our rightful places to be earned by merit. Thus it has been an ultra sensitive point to most Jews that we, as well as all others, be given equal opportunity to pursue our goals in whatever career we chose, regardless of our race, color, or religion.

It is this strongly held belief that was behind the Jews marching alongside black Americans during the civil rights struggles of the 1950s and 1960s. We did not believe that blacks should be denied those rights open to other Americans. The right to vote, to eat where you choose, to ride whatever buses you wanted, to attend the school of your choice cannot be denied to any American. Jews in general were not advocating special privileges for black Americans. No, they simply wanted equal opportunity for all, the same struggle Jews have been engaged in for thousands of years.

Senator Hubert Humphrey, the noted Democrat liberal of that time, assured the Senate at the time of debating the civil rights laws in the 1960s, that these laws were not intended to favor one people over another. They were intended to level the playing field for all so that no person would be given favorable or unfavorable treatment simply because of the color of his skin. Thus was launched, with the best of motives, the laws that have resulted in our affirmative action programs.

One could easily argue that all of this was in harmony with Jewish tradition. We believed in fair and equal treatment for all. Even our slaves were to be released in the seventh or jubilee year.

The Civil Rights Act of 1964 authorized courts to take affirmative action to remove racially discriminatory practices and it also said that race preference was forbidden. Thus affirmative action and race preference are entirely different. It was race preference that was to be eliminated. The "affirmative action" part meant to proactively go after and eliminate from our society those practices that were in fact race based.

The problem is that the entire thrust of the civil rights laws was turned upside down by the courts and the bureaucrats who implemented and enforced these laws. Instead of carrying out Humphrey's pledge that no person was to be favored over another for a job or an education because of the color of his skin, the reverse came into being. People were favored over others simply because of their skin color. There arose throughout the government, business, and educational communities an entire body of rules that tended to mandate favorable treatment for minorities. If you were non-white, you were given priority in getting contracts, gaining admission to certain schools, or in the rate of advancement to higher positions. For an entire generation, little opposition was voiced to these policies and programs.

In the late 1990s, the Supreme Court revisited some of its earlier decisions. There appeared to be a trend toward slowly getting back to the original purpose of civil rights laws to make them more neutral in their implementation. As more politically conservative judges are appointed to the Supreme Court, further progress can be made in restoring the original purpose of these laws.

Unfortunately, the Supreme Court seemed to regress in their recent University of Michigan cases, where they ruled that the race of an applicant can be used as a criterion for admission. Although the court in the case of *Gratz v. Bollinger* ruled that the undergraduate school could not automatically add twenty points to an applicant's score because of race, it did not disaffirm the concept that race can be a factor in the admissions policy of the university. In *Grutter v. Bollinger,* the court welcomed the law school's use of race to admit applicants in order to achieve a "more diverse student body," with its accompanying "advantages." Those advantages were never documented by the court but were simply assumed to exist.

After all in the original 1954 case of Brown v. Board of Education which established the concept of bussing, (a forerunner to the civil rights law), Thurgood Marshall then executive director of the NAACP, wrote that "Distinctions by race are so evil, so arbitrary and invidious that a state bound to defend the equal protection of the laws must not invoke them in any public sphere." In his 1978 Bakke decision, Justice Lewis Powell wrote, "The guarantee of equal protection cannot mean one thing when applied to one individual and something else when applied to a person of another color. If both are not accorded the same protection, then it is not equal."

The March 1998 issue of *Commentary* conducted a symposium on the question, "Is Affirmative Action on the Way Out? Should It Be?" Some interesting thoughts were expressed in answer. Author Joseph Epstein wrote that affirmative action produces the same devious conduct when people are trying to do good as when they are out to do evil. He refers to the cheating that has been going on in the admissions policies of universities and law schools to permit more minority students to attend than what was warranted by their qualifications and test scores. Epstein predicted that we shall struggle along for several years with various compromises without finding the correct solution, because despite the best of efforts, we live in "an intractably unjust world, and all artificial attempts to make it just, seem chiefly to have the effect of creating new, subtler, but often no less real injustices—sometimes even, sadly, for those they set out to help."

Leslie Lenkowsky, professor of philanthropic studies at Indiana

University-Purdue University, wrote, "A sound affirmative action policy would seek to ensure that members of minority and other disadvantaged groups had the opportunity (and if necessary, some help) to pursue success in whatever directions they desired. But it would not insist, as we have been doing, that by the end of the race, every group should have a proportionately equal share of the prizes."

Norman Podhoretz, senior fellow at the Hudson Institute, and an original backer of affirmative action, now writes, "I am therefore an unqualified and unapologetic abolitionist with respect to affirmative action, and I hope (though I doubt) that the people who think it is finally on the way out are right. If it were abolished, we would be obeying the injunction laid upon doctors when they are told, 'First do no harm.' Nor do we need a new social-engineering gimmick ready to hand as a substitute."

Lino A. Graglia, professor of law at the University of Texas, Austin, sums it up most graphically. "It is a prescription for racial consciousness and conflict inconsistent with the maintenance of a viable multiracial society; it means abandoning hope for an integrated society and accepting the inevitability of separatism. For most people, it is simply morally wrong for government to treat people on the basis of race."

It would seem that whatever holds true for "race" must of course hold true for religion, and this is the connection I believe, of affirmative action, to Judaism, and where Jews should stand on this subject. As we have struggled these thousands of years for the right to be treated the same as other peoples, and not be discriminated against because of our religion, and as we have succeeded in that endeavor in these United States, so should we be fighting the good fight against any other form of discrimination based on being a member of a particular class. But where have our Jewish leaders been this past generation on the subject? Not very visible in protesting how affirmative action was being implemented, I'm afraid.

Even the learned thinkers participating in *Commentary's* symposium did not make any connection to Judaism as it relates to government-sponsored actions. Perhaps they thought it was so obvious that Jews should be against affirmative action as it evolved, that it needed no reference. I believe it does need that reference, and it should be shouted loud and clear from every Jewish rooftop. As Jews we must oppose all forms of government-controlled favoritism for any group or class, because we know from our history that what is favored today, may well be reversed into drastic negative actions against a particular group or class tomorrow. Freedom is still what it is all about!

The relationship of Democratic liberals to affirmative action is well known. Both Bill Clinton and Al Gore have stressed that these programs are simply intended to give a hand up to those who need it. This is the usual spin that liberals use to justify their government programs. What it ignores, of course, are those invisible persons who are harmed by these actions and will lose out because they are not part of the favored class.

It reminds me of Henry Hazlitt's famous example of the window that is broken by a vandal in his classic book, *Economics in One Lesson*. The broken window provides new business for the glazier, and thus the incident seems to have generated new business activity. To update Hazlitt's version with all due respect, what is visible is that in today's world, the insurance company will reimburse the store owner for that damage, the window repair people will enjoy additional business, the store owner is not out any money, and everyone will be better off for that window breaking. The effect not seen is that the insurance company has to use its funds to fix something that did not previously require repairs, and thus there was a net loss to the community. And what is not seen at the time is that probably insurance premiums for property coverage will increase for everyone at renewal time. If breaking windows made for economic progress, what a simple and wonderful world this would be.

Speaking of simplicity, Mr. Hazlitt once summed up the whole of economics in a single sentence that is almost totally ignored today by our teachers and politicians. He wrote, "The art of economics consists in looking not merely at the immediate but at the longer effects of any act or policy; it consists in tracing the consequences of that policy not merely for one group but for all groups."

And so it is with affirmative action programs. Those few who are actually helped are visible. What is not seen are those who are denied either jobs, promotions, or access to schooling to which they otherwise would be entitled to without the workings of affirmative action. As Judge Bork writes, affirmative action began as an outreach program, but then was turned into a quota program. This has led to greater group antagonisms and increased racial acrimony. He quotes the well-known personality, Ms. Susan Estrich, 1988 presidential campaign manager for Democrat Michael Dukakis, as saying that affirmative action was never intended to be permanent, and it is now time to move on to another approach. This is quite a stretch for Ms. Estrich, as she can normally be counted on to toe the liberal line on almost all issues. What this seems to indicate is wide agreement that affirmative action, as implemented, was not consistent with the original purposes of the law as promised by Senator Humphrey and his supporters.

Judaism stresses the development of the individual to be the best he can be with whatever talents the Good Lord has bestowed upon him. The act of becoming consists of the act of overcoming. When Jews came to this country, penniless, not knowing the language, but imbued with a fierce desire to better themselves and to prepare a better life for their children, there was no affirmative action. If anything, there was the opposite. Many occupations and professions were closed to Jews at the beginning, so Jews gravitated to those occupations and professions that were not closed.

One wonders that if our ancestors could have availed themselves of some type of government action to smooth their way, would we all be better off today? I doubt it. All we Jews have wanted throughout our history is to be able to play in the game of life on an even footing with everyone else. No special favors, but no big handicaps are what we wanted. For Jews to now support race preference, which is what today's affirmative action really is, represents a departure from our core beliefs and our traditions. It is time for American Jews, and especially their leaders, to revert back to our ancient Jewish traditions, and oppose all forms of quotas and preferences given to groups consisting of a particular gender, race, religion, color, nationality, or sexual orientation.

I do have one brief comment on this last category of sexual orientation. Personally, I have known and worked with homosexuals at various times in my career. They were, for the most part, excellent workers who kept their sexual preference to themselves without flaunting it. In today's America, I believe it is this "flaunting" aspect, with the wild parades and public displays of same-sex affection, that turn most people off. The insistence of many gay and lesbian leaders to obtain special preferences in employment and industry for their "class" is also negative.The drive to educate our children that homosexuality is simply an alternative lifestyle is opposed by most parents. And the notion that certain of our clergy now sanction same sex marriage is to my mind completely contrary to Jewish law and tradition. This is another example of members of a particular group wanting to be treated not as individuals, but as a special class.

In early 2004, the subject of same-sex marriage thrust itself onto the front pages of our newspapers and onto our television sets, as same-sex wedding ceremonies were performed at locales ranging from Massachusetts to California. Some observers believe that this drive was really about forcing the public to accept the homosexual life style as simply a reasonable alternative to the traditional family. Whether Americans will eventually accept this drastic change in the definition of the age-old traditional meaning of marriage remains to be seen. As to how Jews should react, if they hearken to Leviticus 18, there would be no doubt. The Soncino's notes to this chapter emphasize the seriousness of marriage "as a Divine institution, under whose shadow alone there can be true reverence for the mystery, dignity, and sacredness of life." They continue, "Marriage is a primary religious duty. He who has no wife—say the Rabbis—lives without comfort, help, joy, blessing, atonement (true religious communication with God)." It will be interesting to chronicle how the various shades of Judaism respond to this latest challenge to our traditions.

When God chose the Jewish people to be His own treasure, out of all the peoples of the earth, He did not choose them because they were more or fewer in number, but because the Lord loved them, and wanted to keep the oath He had sworn to Abraham, Isaac, and Jacob. (Deuteronomy 7:6-8) The relevant point here is there was no affirmative action then, and there is thus no precedent in our traditions for Jews to now be such avid supporters of this pernicious policy.

LIBERALS, GUNS, AND JEWS

The latest cause célèbre of the liberals is the gun control issue. Suddenly after two hundred years of Americans having the right to own guns, as authorized by the Second Amendment of the Bill of Rights, and brought on by a rash of shootings in various public schools, liberals have fingered guns as the basic problem. Eliminate the guns, and by definition, we will eliminate this cause of so much misery and sadness in this country. No matter that it takes some human being to get the gun, load the gun, take the gun to whatever location the gun holder wishes, and then actually aim and fire the gun with the intent to maim or kill, liberals still reason that it is the gun that is the problem. All we have to do is construct some new rules to make it more difficult for the average citizen to buy a gun, to own it, and then to use it, and somehow this cause of killings will vanish.

The fact that the number of fatal gun accidents is at its lowest level since statistics were first kept in 1903 is incidental. A fact given by Dave Kopel in *National Review*, that people with adult criminal records or who had criminal convictions as juveniles commit most murders is also incidental. Liberals seldom let the facts get in their way of proclaiming some holy virtue. Government must take drastic action to bring about their desired results regardless of the means to be used.

Conservatives and libertarians, not just the National Rifle Association, argue that there are already sufficient laws on the books that, if properly enforced, would cure the more outrageous uses of guns. Criminals will always manage to obtain guns. Even though there are an estimated 250 million weapons that are stashed away somewhere in the closets and garages of Americans today, the number of actual crimes, killings, and accidents involving those weapons is a statistically insignificant number. One article estimated that one half of all the families in America now possess some type of gun.

To purchase a gun in today's America, one must go through a process of delay, depending on the individual state's laws, that can take a week or more to complete the transaction. Some states require the buyer to take an instruction course; some states require a waiting period of several days; gun shows have the same requirements as gun stores. All states prohibit the purchase of guns by felons, children, or mentally handicapped people. Thus, there are plenty of state laws that already make it somewhat difficult to simply walk in and purchase a gun over the counter.

There is also a substantial body of evidence as accumulated by Dr. John Lott in his book, *More Guns, Less Crime*, that the use of guns by citizens in their defense has saved far more lives than guns have taken when used by the attackers. Just the presence of guns in a household, and the showing of them by people in their homes, have prevented many robberies, assaults, rapes, and other crimes. Those states that have concealed weapons laws, permitting gun holders to carry guns on their persons or in their cars, have experienced noticeable drops in reported crimes. When a potential mugger or rapist or robber is unsure if his potential victim may be armed, it is natural for him to think again about following through with his attempted predatory action.

Thus on balance, it is questionable whether the widespread distribution of guns of various sorts really is the problem that the liberals are championing. The height of absurdity is the move by states to hold gun manufacturers liable for damages and injuries caused by the users of those guns as if the gun manufacturers had any control over their use once in the hands of the buyers. The threat of legal action by states has already caused one of the old-line companies, Colt Manufacturing Company, maker of the original American handgun, to discontinue the production of civilian handguns in America. Colt, seller of more than thirty million firearms since 1836, announced in October 1999, that it would quit making almost all of its civilian handguns. Colt had become a casualty of threatened anti-gun lawsuits. The liberals rejoiced over this action. It was another step in their crusade to relieve the individual of responsibility for any of his actions. Somehow, liberals believe if we can remove all temptation and means for doing evil acts, we will achieve the ideal society.

We ignore, at our peril, what our founders thought and wrote on this subject. Thomas Jefferson wrote, "The strongest reason for the people to retain the right to bear arms is, as a last resort, to protect themselves against tyranny in government." It may be difficult for today's Americans to understand that when Jefferson wrote these words, there was a real fear that a strong centrally controlled government could someday come into peoples' homes and deny them their liberties. In those days, citizens did not have to worry that much about burglars and other civilian predators as we do today. It was the unrestrained force of government that most concerned them, as is true today in many parts of the world.

Does any of this relate to Judaism, Jewish law, and tradition? Are the liberals in sync with our tradition in their advocacy of eliminating guns and weapons from our society? And let no one be confused about their ultimate aims. As early as 1976, the leader of the group Handgun Control, Pete Shields, explained their long-term strategy. First, they want to slow down the number of handguns being produced and sold. They then wanted handguns to be registered. And finally, they wanted to make the possession of all handguns and ammunition, except for the military, police, and certain groups, totally illegal, and thus subject to confiscation. Although unstated in such clear terms by today's liberals, it is undoubtedly what they are striving to accomplish.

Although the Torah was written well before the era of guns, one can get a general impression from what God instructed our Jewish ancestors on the use of weapons of the day. In Deuteronomy 7:2, when God was bringing his chosen people into the Promised Land. He said, "Thou shalt smite them; then thou shalt utterly destroy them, nor show mercy unto them." He did not specify the weapons to be used, so one must assume that Jews were to use whatever weapons were at their disposal. In Deuteronomy 20:13, when the Jews were going forth to battle against their enemies, if they made no peace with the Jews, "thou shalt smite every male thereof with the edge of the sword." So we were authorized by the Lord to use the weapons of the day to achieve the victory. These would be considered to be rather harsh commands for our society today, but they were God's commandments to the "civilian" Jewish armies of that time.

All of this may seem far afield from the question of eliminating guns from our possession, but the point is that to the Jews in particular, considering our sad history of persecution and exile, one wonders if history would read differently if the Jews had possessed and used the weapons of their day to defend themselves from their attackers. If they had, perhaps they would not have been forced to continue to wander around the globe for all of those centuries.

In the twentieth century, imagine if the Jews of Germany, Poland, Austria, and all those countries where they were evacuated to the death camps, had possessed guns that could have been used in their defense. Those innocent people, believing themselves to be secure in their homes and an integral part of society, had willingly given up their weapons when instructed to do so by their governments. By 1937, German Jews had surrendered their weapons by order of the Hitler-dominated government. If they had disobeyed that order, perhaps they would not have been such helpless victims when the swaggering Nazi storm troopers burst through the front doors of their homes and shops to carry them away to concentration camps, torture, and death. They did not have our Second Amendment to guarantee their lawful possession of guns to defend themselves.

As a persecuted and frequently hated minority, Jews should always be wary of the forces of government that may suddenly be used against them, for whatever reason. Rather than worrying about whether the Religious Right is somehow going to woo away our young people from Judaism, we should be more concerned about whether an all-powerful government is going to some day storm into our homes and offices on some pretense and really convert us, not to another religion, but into another world.

In April 2000, Americans and the world witnessed the naked use of force by the American federal government. The case of the Cuban child, Elian Gonzales, found floating in an inner tube in the waters between Cuba and Florida, rescued and brought to Miami, Florida, held the attention of this country for several months. Elian's mother drowned in her effort to bring six-year-old Elian to America to live in freedom, and escape from Cuban dictator, Fidel Castro. Elian was then placed in the custody of his father's relatives in Miami to await the decision as to his future. His father, a worker for Fidel Castro's dictatorship in Cuba, took almost five months to make his way to the United States. Finally he arrived and, backed by the Clinton administration, asked to be reunited with his son, whom he had not seen for some time having been divorced from Elian's mother for three years, and then return to Cuba with Elian.

The United States Justice Department then engaged in negotiations with Elian's family in Florida to relinquish their custody so that the father and child could be reunited. The family believed that it would be in the best interests of the child for the family and the father to meet and jointly arrange for the custody transfer. They believed that after five months of nurturing the child and providing a surrogate mother for him, that some healing period was necessary.

Just as negotiations between the family in Florida and the United States Justice Department led by Attorney General Janet Reno in Washington, DC, were nearing an agreement on a meeting place to effect the custody transfer, all hell broke loose. On early Saturday morning, the day before Easter Sunday, the Justice Department and the United States Immigration Service, sent in armed swat teams to literally snatch Elian from the arms of the fisherman who had saved him and hustle Elian to Washington, DC, into the waiting arms of his father.

Using overwhelming force, in just under three minutes, the front door of the family's house was knocked down and amidst shouts of warning to stay still or be shot, the "rescue" was completed. The American public would have had only the report of their government to go by except for one intrepid Associated Press photographer. He managed to get into the house during the raid and produced an unforgettable picture of an armed agent pointing his machine gun at the fisherman and Elian before grabbing the child to remove him from the house. That one picture, truly an historic one, should have sent chills up and down the spine of all Americans, and particularly, American Jews.

Aside from the custody question, aside from whether the government's action was legal, and aside from the political fallout of this action, this one picture showed the true nature of the naked force that can be used by government against its citizens. Of course, Attorney General Janet Reno pointed out that the machine gun in the picture had its safety switch on and that the gun was not really pointed at the child, but was only pointed in his general direction. And of course, she said she had no other alternative to ordering this action, because negotiations had broken down, which was contradicted by her appointed negotiators who were on the scene in Miami. Regardless of what the final legal outcome of this episode turns out to be, the picture for Jews should be clear.

This is what can happen even in this God-blessed nation of America, the land of the free and the home of the brave, if the people running this government take it upon themselves to read the law in a particular way, or in this case perhaps to even break the law. Individual rights vanish, and we are left only with a faint hope of defending ourselves, or having our supporters help to defend us. Oh yes, the Justice Department used the excuse for using such overwhelming force that there were rumors there were weapons in the house. So even if there were guns, and there were none, an attempt was made by the government in this case to associate the violence used by them with the possibility that legal guns owned by American citizens were at the core of the problem.

The entire history of the Jews is filled with similar incidents. Most of them were perpetrated against us simply because we were the outcasts, the Jews of that society, and as such we did not possess the rights of other citizens of those countries. Most of us living all of our lives here in America have never experienced such humiliations. One has only to read the history of anti-Semitism however, to understand what our ancestors have experienced. We Jews should be the foremost champions of the right to bear arms and to defend ourselves in our homes against intruders, both civilian and government. In the Gonzales case, even the distinguished Alan Dershowitz (the same who commented that the Religious Right is our enemy), wrote that the government had no right to do what they did and that the naked use of force was a sad day for this nation. Although he did not publicly relate his comments to his Jewish heritage, one can sense that this connection must have been uppermost in his mind.

Once again, it would appear that liberals are on the side of an issue that is not in harmony with Jewish law, tradition, and experience. President Clinton continued to play on the emotions of Americans that guns are the problem, without paying much attention to the fact that we are not enforcing our current laws as stringently as they should be enforced. Our legal system which takes decades to punish murderers and which allows interminable appeals to those criminals, must bear some responsibility for the outbreak of major crime in recent years. My and my wife's personal chiropractors, Dr. and Mrs. Douglas Ryan, were murdered in their home in Chino, California, over seventeen years ago. Their convicted killer is still alive in prison, continuing to wage more appeals. Justice delayed is justice denied.

To blame guns for recent tragic shootings of children is similar to blaming automobiles for the 50,000 highway deaths that occur annually. Autos and trucks do not drive themselves. It is people, their values, their habits, and their actions that are the root cause of deaths, either by gun or via autos. Judaism tries to set people on the right paths in life and gives them the proper guidelines to live those lives. What happens from then on is up to us, both individually and as a nation.

THE POLITICS OF
CLASS WARFARE

Liberals love to quote statistics on the great differences in income of the different classes. The disparity between those Americans who are "making it" in our society and those who are struggling seems to be growing. The number of workers who remain below the poverty level does not seem to shrink much, in spite of the enormous public funds spent to relieve that situation. The fact that over a period of sixteen years, from 1975 to 1991, only 5.1% of those who were formerly in the bottom 20% of the income table, remained at the bottom, and that almost one third of the poor families in 1975 had moved to the top brackets in 1991 (Federal Reserve Bank of Dallas report), does not seem to dent the liberals' constant complaint that our system does not seem to work for too many people. Therefore, we must continue to shovel out massive sums of money and other benefits to assist those unfortunates in getting off that bottom rung of the income ladder.

Thomas Sowell in *The Vision of the Anointed* points out another argument used by liberals to emphasize class differences. There is a class of people, the "benighted," that require the superior wisdom of the "anointed" to carry on with their lives. Whatever their problems may be—poverty, irresponsible sex, crime, inability to rise above their inborn status—are all caused by society and therefore must be remedied by society, and not through individual efforts. There is increasing recognition among thinking and perceptive black Americans, such as Sowell, that one of the results of all of the myriad of welfare programs has been to create a "dependent class" that is easy prey for those politicians regarded as the benevolent grantors of government's largess.

Judge Robert Bork writes that modern liberals think in terms of groups, not individuals. A free society such as America will always produce disparities in success and achievement, but liberals appeal more to class envy, rather than truly encouraging individual effort. Yet the "chattering classes," as Bork calls them, the intellectuals who dominate the media, always deny that as a group they are liberals, but 91% of reporters acknowledged recently that they voted Democrat in a recent national election.

In making their case, liberals, either purposely or not, attempt with some success to pit class against class in this country. By grouping people into classes, such as black, Hispanic, gay, poor, or females, liberals seek to create an antagonism for one group against all others who seem to be doing better than they are. Bork writes that envy shapes our political culture, and the thrust of the liberals is to bring down the more fortunate instead of encouraging those below to rise to higher levels.

Liberals, who on the one hand are great defenders of individual liberty when it comes to satisfying any personal desires, seem to forget that we as individuals are members of a group only by someone's definition. There are good and bad within any group. One of the big mistakes in trying to solve problems through government action is that people are not treated as individuals, but rather, are included as members of a group whether they like it or not. The result is that because there are such great differences between people, one cannot apply the same remedy to all and expect successful outcomes.

Judaism recognizes that there are differences in people, in their status in life and their incomes, but stresses that they all must be treated with equal justice. "Ye shall do no unrighteousness in judgment; thou shalt not respect the person of the poor, nor favour the person of the mighty; but in righteousness shalt thou judge thy neighbor." (Leviticus 19:15) The notes to Soncino Pentateuch make the point that even though Judaism gives great consideration to the poor, who when in need is to be helped ungrudgingly, still justice requires he be given no special favors when he is in the wrong. By the same token, the rich shall not be given special favors. "Judge every man in the scale of merit; refuse to condemn by appearances, but put the best construction on the deeds of your fellowmen." [(Talmud) As quoted in Soncino's notes to Leviticus 19:15]

Certainly the implication of this is that each case must be considered on its own merits, each person as an individual, regardless of his status in life. Justice requires no less than this. No mention is made of classifying people in groups, other than to describe them in general, but there is to be no special treatment for them because of their being so described. The notion that members of one class owe something to those of another class is so contrary to Judaism that it is amazing that the idea has not been more strongly challenged by our Jewish leaders.

Although Judaism is described frequently as a "community" religion—that is, we are each of us responsible for our brother—there exists a plethora of laws that command treatment be administered to Jews as individuals. "The fathers shall not be put to death for the children, neither shall the children be put to death for the fathers; every man shall be put to death for his own sin." (Deuteronomy 24:16) The Ten Commandments are directed to us as individuals, not as classes or groups. Class envy can grow into coveting your neighbor's possessions, which is expressly forbidden by the Tenth Commandment. We are to adhere to these Commandments on our own, regardless of what others may do.

Moses' final peroration in Deuteronomy 30:19-20, "(T)hat I have set before thee life and death, the blessing and the curse; therefore, choose life, that thou mayest live, thou and thy seed; to love the Lord thy God, to hearken to His voice, and to cleave unto Him; for that is thy life, and the length of thy days," seems to sum it all up. We are each responsible for our individual actions, and we prosper or despair accordingly.

To pit one class or group against another is contrary to Jewish law and should be strongly condemned by our Jewish leaders. When Hitler selected Jews as the supreme evil that must be destroyed, he did not evaluate each Jew as an individual, but instead, he took anyone who had the least amount of Jewish blood to be his victim. Jews as a group had to be extinguished. He succeeded with terminating the lives of two-thirds of European Jews, and if he had won the war, would probably have reached his goal. Of all people, Jews should reject any hint of judging individuals according to their class, whether it is economic, racial, religious, color, or any other type of grouping. At the same time, trying to pit one class against another is to violate the concept of loving one's neighbor as thyself that is stressed throughout Judaism.

The complaint by the liberals that the "rich are getting richer, and the poor are getting poorer" should be answered by Jews, not with a nodding head, but with some affirmative statements. We should be replying that to solve this problem, if indeed it is a problem, we need to improve our educational system by giving parents choice of schools; expand our system of trade schools; improve our family structure; improve the ease of starting a business of your own; and remove those governmental restrictions that inhibit the formation and expansion of new businesses. These are the types of positive changes that are needed to solve the income disparity issues. In the end, each of us must fight his own battles. It would be hoped that those who are burdened from birth with handicaps would receive help from charitable institutions and from individuals, with very limited support from governmental agencies. Such help must always be granted on an individual basis and not by any group or class status.

The very call to action by class, as used by liberals, should be an affront to Jews. As a group that has been so abused throughout history because we were classified as members of an undesirable group, our hair should stand on end and our skin should tingle when such actions are advocated. Judaism preaches unity, brotherhood of all men, and waits for the day when all peoples will accept and worship the one God. The notes to Deuteronomy of the Soncino Pentateuch emphasize this. "The belief in the unity of the Human Race is the natural corollary of the Unity of God, since the One God must be the God of the whole of humanity . . . Through Hebrew monotheism alone was it possible to teach the

Brotherhood of Man; and it was Hebrew monotheism which first declared, Thou shalt love thy neighbour as thyself." The very words of the Shema, "Hear, O Israel, the Lord is our God, the Lord is One," in addition to being the central principle of Jewish religious thought, is a call for the unity of all mankind. To divide people on the basis of their individual differences for political gain to achieve political power is simply not in keeping with our Jewish traditions and should be soundly rejected by American Jews.

The latest example of using class warfare for attempted political gain was most graphically demonstrated by the 2000 presidential campaign's Democrat candidate for president, Al Gore. Mr. Gore, apparently shedding his cloak of being a "New Democrat," openly appealed to the voters' class envy instincts by proclaiming himself as the champion of "working families" against the "powerful." While not completely defining who qualified as a "working family," he made it clear whom the "powerful" were: Big Oil, Big Drug Companies, and apparently any "Big" enterprise that he could identify. Whether that appeal for votes on this basis attracted or repelled voters is questionable. The fact is, however, that the common sense of American voters apparently rejected this unwholesome appeal to the lowest common denominator among us, as the Gore/Lieberman ticket lost by a whisker.

Thomas Cahill, an Irish author, in his book, *Gift Of The Jews*, claimed that the Jews gave two gifts to mankind. The Jews were the first in human history to claim individual freedom, that human beings are not destined to stay in their same class forever, and that they could make the future better than the past. Cahill also wrote, "There is a direct link between the ancient Jews and the American Declaration of Independence." It is that Declaration of course, which proclaims our individual right to life, liberty, and the pursuit of happiness, not as any form of class or group, but as individuals. Judaism has always stressed the importance of the individual, and we should lead the way in rejecting any form of class warfare.

LIBERALS AND UNIVERSAL HEALTHCARE

✡

Shortly after William Clinton was elected President of the United States in 1992, along with his "co-president," Hillary Clinton, both embarked on an ambitious program to reform our healthcare system. Clinton declared that one of his first major projects was to "fix" our healthcare system, because it was badly broken. His wife, Hillary, although not an elected official in her own right, was given the power to assemble a mighty task force to construct a new policy. Some critics charged this assignment was payback for Hillary's standing by Bill amidst all of his amorous wanderings and scandals. In any event, Mrs. Clinton, along with her chief aid, Mr. Ira Magaziner, a Jew, proceeded to work with that task force to produce a new healthcare system.

What resulted from months of effort with meetings held for the most part in secrecy, and the spending of several million dollars, was a mind-numbing 1,342-page report on how we should change our existing health system into one that would provide wonderful healthcare for all, at a minimum cost, with a benevolent government watching over all.

This report recommended a system where 14% of our American economy, which represents the healthcare industry, would have come under the power and control of federal bureaucrats. In its effort to create security for the American public, their system would have controlled the activities of the medical profession to a degree that could have been duplicated only by that of the most dictatorial nation. Doctors would have been jailed if they did not adhere to certain rules about how many patients they should treat and how they should treat them. Charges for services would have been strictly controlled and our citizens would have been forced to choose services that fit closely into proscribed formulas.

Choice of doctors would be denied and certain wise men, appointed to their positions by the president, would rule over the entire system with few avenues open for appeal of their decisions. It was the old story of "we know what's best for the people."

In spite of 60% initial public support for a new plan, of nonstop campaigning by Hillary Clinton, and of a Democrat-controlled Congress, once enough details of the plan were given, people figured out that our current system was not that bad in comparison. Hillary's project came crashing down to ignominious defeat. Even many of her fellow Democrats ran away screaming from the proposal. After being promised a simple plan, this one turned out to be a disaster in the making. The major mistake made by Hillary and Ira was to continue to believe in the old "command and control" way of accomplishing things. If only enough brilliant people could be gathered together—and there were at one time over 500 of them working on this project—then certainly a correspondingly brilliant plan could be devised. It almost reminds one of the jest that if you assemble enough monkeys, laboring for a long enough time, and give them enough typewriters, they would eventually produce the Declaration of Independence.

Instead of concentrating their extensive efforts in the direction of freeing up the medical system to permit more individual freedom of choice, while still maintaining some security for the poor, and insuring against major medical expenses, the task force tried to impose its will from the top through its 1,342-page plan. Studies have shown that 80% of Americans spend less than $1,000 per year for medical services. It is really those major medical problems that require insuring against. Instead Hillary and her group refused to consider any approach other than one that involved government as the ultimate controlling authority, rather than the patient.

I personally wrote a letter to Mrs. Clinton in February 1993, in which I urged her to enlarge the workings of the free market to help solve the problems in our healthcare system. In particular, I recommended that we expand the use of medical savings accounts via an IRA-type of savings account to pay for minor expenses, in addition to establishing catastrophic insurance coverage for those serious illnesses costing more than a certain amount. I wanted to have the FDA encourage the use of vitamins and herbs instead of placing roadblocks in their use. I suggested that wherever possible, the FDA should reduce the time needed for approving new drugs for public use, and even to consider permitting doctors and their patients to try new drugs without FDA approval. I never did receive a reply.

There are problems with our current healthcare system. The main one is that we as the patients are not directly responsible for paying our own bills, or even caring much about how much the services cost, because they are being paid by third parties, either insurance companies or in the case of Medicare and Medicaid, the government. A Rand Corporation study in the early 1990s showed that people who paid for their own healthcare spend 33% less than those who have the so-called "free care." The "fix" for this problem, as such astute observers as Michael Rothschild, president of the Bionomics Institute of San Francisco, and author of *Bionomics*, has written, is to introduce that old liberal bugaboo—competition—into the fray.

Rothschild wrote in the magazine *Upside*, that if we had allowed Darwinian innovation (another term for competition) over the past thirty years, medical costs would be one-third less than what they are now, and would thus be much more available to the masses. The alternatives now to our current third party insurance system include such ideas as medical savings plans to permit people to monitor and pay the smaller medical expenses, while still providing insurance to pay for the major medical bills, along with some type of subsidized vouchers for the poor. These changes would stimulate more creative capitalism, but this would also allow more freedom of choice, which the liberals, as exemplified by Hillary and Ira, are dead set against. So we are still saddled with our third party system, still in need of constructive changes, and still fighting the liberal drive to socialize the entire system.

One may now ask, how does this particular subject relate to Judaism? When I look up the word "health" in the index in the Soncino Pentateuch, I am directed to Leviticus 11, which describes the dietary laws that Jews are to observe. Only those beasts that parteth the hoof, who are wholly cloven-footed, and cheweth the cud, may we eat. Only those creatures of the seas that hath fins and scales are eligible for our consumption. Only those winged swarming things that go upon all fours, which have jointed legs above their feet, pass the test, which includes locusts, crickets, and grasshoppers. Chickens, turkeys, and the like seem to be permitted by omitting their description from all those fowls that are described as forbidden to eat, such as the vulture, the falcon, the eagle, the ostrich, etc. Thus we are given strong commands as to what to eat and what not to eat, which if closely followed will surely guide us to maintaining good health, and in today's vernacular, avoid those high medical costs and even alleviate the need for costly medical insurance.

But this is not where I believe the real conflict is between the liberal position on the control over medical practice and Jewish tradition and laws. It again revolves around the Jewish call for individual responsibility, as contrasted with the liberal's view that we must look elsewhere for our cover, and that we should not be held responsible for our own lives. Even in a matter so vital as creating the most responsive health system for Americans, liberals prefer to resort to government rules, regulations, penalties, and complicated administration rather than relying upon the common sense of our citizens to choose wisely among the alternatives offered.

In the Soncino notes to Ezekiel 37, in describing Ezekiel, as at "once priest and prophet, preacher and writer, inspirer of the nation and pastor of individual souls," it adds "a characteristic feature of his teaching is his insistence on individual responsibility." Ezekiel preached that no matter how wicked one becomes, when he turns away from that wickedness, and does what is right and lawful, that he can save his soul. Again the message of Judaism is that we must be responsible for our own actions, to cleanse our own souls of wickedness, so as to be able to live a just and rewarding life. I fail to find that message extant in any liberal position, even when it pertains to a subject as apparently neutral as healthcare.

Even though our health system is in need of change, it is still here that people from other countries in need of the finest care come with their ailments. The frequently touted healthcare system of Canada, with its cheaper drug prices, also has huge waiting lists for patients that need certain medical care. The reason their drug prices are cheaper is that Canada simply takes the drugs created and produced in America and sells them for less because their Canadian companies have not had to spend the billions in research and development that the United States companies have spent.

One reason our drug prices are so high is that it takes up to fifteen years for a new drug to go through all of the testing that our Food and Drug Administration requires. If we would simplify that process and give doctors and their patients the freedom to try for themselves new, experimental drugs at their own risk, we would see a faster time to market for many life-saving drugs, and also lower the cost of them once they came to market. The FDA is another example of the "government knows best" mentality that liberals have succeeded in establishing as the gospel in this country, which frequently works to the disadvantage of our citizens.

IMPORTANCE OF JEWS CHANGING THEIR POLITICAL POSITIONS

Before going on to discuss other political issues that illustrate the difference between the liberal position and Jewish tradition, it is now appropriate to spell out why this writer believes it is so important that this change occur now. It is not a matter of favoring one political party over another because one side contains more honorable people than the other. It is primarily because the principles supported by one party are so much closer to Jewish tradition and Judaism that is the deciding and determining factor. We have the history of the past seventy years to see what the slavish support by American Jews of liberalism has resulted in, and now a change is required.

The Jewish population in America is shrinking. As detailed in Elliot Abrams 1997 book, *Faith Or Fear*, Jews now are 2% of the population in America, down from 3.7%. The majority of Jews marrying since 1985 have married non-Jews. In the late 1980s, there were approximately 5.7 million Jews in America, but the prediction is that given current trends, that number will decline to 4.7 million by 2020.

The current Jewish leadership position against encouraging Jewish education through expanding Jewish day schools via some type of voucher program, works to continue the trend to marry outside of the Jewish religion. The division of opinion on the Oslo peace process in Israel has tended to soften and dilute that once strong, unified position that seemed to bring American Jews together in support of that tiny land, and to keep enthusiasm for Judaism alive. The great Jewish novelist, Herman Wouk, in his latest book, *The Will To Live* On, expresses his hope that the resurgence of American Jewish life for the long future is in "a massive return to our sources in faith, literature, and history." I get the feeling in reading this book that if we would all become Orthodox, observe the Sabbath and the Commandments, and live our lives as truly observant Jews, our future would be secured.

Unfortunately, that is probably not going to happen. Almost 80% of American Jews are Reform and Conservative, about evenly divided between these two branches, with just 8% Orthodox and 13% unaffiliated. There are too many distractions in our lives along with the lack of interest and required commitment that keep us as Jews of various varieties, but certainly, not very observant. We can only hope that soon Jewish education for our children in religious schools via various voucher programs will be expanded so that they will grow up and marry other Jews, remain more dedicated to our religion, and bring up their children accordingly. I personally believe that this is the most hopeful prospect on our horizon today, along with the preservation of the State of Israel in its present form, to stop and reverse the shrinking of our American Jewish population.

My secondary hope and a primary reason for this writing, is that if we can persuade a significant number of non-Orthodox Jews to change their political beliefs, and turn from being liberals to becoming conservative or libertarians, this in itself could help bring about at least a minor renaissance in the lives of the American Jewish population. If American Jews can be made to see that their individual interests plus their desire to improve the world are better served through changing, and equally important, if they can see that in so changing, they are actually coming closer to Jewish tradition so that Judaism becomes more meaningful in their own lives, we will kill two birds with one stone.

When one considers the importance in so many fields of activity that Jews are prominent in, if such a change should occur, the repercussions of that change would be tremendous. In the major media alone, Jews are prominent in all phases—newspapers, radio, television, cable, the movies, the theatre, and now the Internet economy. Almost without exception these Jews are liberals who promote and distribute the liberal political messages. If there should be a change here with, at the minimum, neutrality between the two major ideologies, this would be very meaningful. Most people are getting their news from television. If equal time were given to reporting the non-liberal positions, there would be a gradual recognition of the values that conservatives are trying to espouse.

Instead of looking to government for answers to our social problems, the emphasis would turn to what the private sector could do and what people acting alone and through their organizations could accomplish, as was the case before the 1930s. Most Americans today, according to recent newspaper reports, believe that it is the private sector and not government that has been responsible for and should be given credit for the great economic boom of the 1990s. Thus there is already a drift away from the liberal notion that we owe all good things to the actions of government.

For too long American Jews have voted their emotions, rather than using their intellect and their knowledge of Jewish tradition to guide them. Just as the Information Age has now overtaken the Machine Age and changed the way we do things, so now is it time for Jews to change their political thinking. Paul Johnson writes that the growth of United States Jewry in the late nineteenth and twentieth centuries was as important in Jewish history as the creation of the State of Israel. It gave Jews a role in shaping policies here, a role that we have not enjoyed at any other time. We need to use our influence now to help promulgate those Jewish values such as honesty, morality, and individual responsibility for the benefit of all Americans.

American Jews cannot decide the destiny of Israel. We can only support those forces there that we believe will act wisely in the best interests of preserving that precious state. Here in America however, we do have more direct power to influence events, even though we are less than 3% of the population. As Hans Kung writes, quantitatively, the Jews are negligible, but as a religion, they are a great power. We can also be a great power though our influence in the media and its effect on public opinion. We thus have a responsibility to lead this country back to its moral and spiritual roots, and this is not where modern liberalism is taking us.

Once Jews become convinced that their own religion contains many of the answers needed to solve our most pressing social and political problems, then perhaps their interest in Judaism and the desire to practice it more traditionally would take hold. In one sense, this approach may be tackling the problem of assimilation through the back door, but so what? If this political change would arouse in the minds of today's non-observant, politically liberal Jews, an interest in studying the Torah and the Talmud, to find out for themselves the link between Judaism and conservatism or libertarianism (and not to liberalism), then in this case, the ends justify the means. Emerson said the end pre-exists within the means. Here, the means used for this desirable end are definitely within the bounds of honorable, good intentions.

Important changes have occurred more than once in Jewish history. The coming of Reform Judaism in America, as exemplified by the Pittsburgh platform in 1885, was just such a change. Johnson writes that Reform rejected the old rules on diet, purity, denied return to Zion, and changed messianism to a struggle for truth, justice, and righteousness. Some of those changes are now being modified and even reversed, but the point is that significant changes are not new to Judaism. On an individual basis, our first Jewish Supreme Court justice, Louis Brandeis (1856-1941), evolved or changed from being a nonobservant Jew, to believing and saying that to be a good American, Jews must become better Jews, and then become Zionists.

In order to bring about this change in political thinking, I believe there must be a full airing of what liberalism is as it exists today, and as to why that dominant philosophy is truly not in harmony with Jewish tradition and law. More examples beyond what are contained in this brief writing must be developed. There are a meaningful number of politically conservative Jewish writers who can, I am sure, add weight and substance to this effort to relate how Judaism and political conservatism are truly linked.

I have quoted extensively from Dennis Prager, Rabbi Daniel Lapin, and Elliott Abrams. I have read Michael Medved, Mona Charen, Norman Podhoretz, Bruce Herschensohn, and Don Feder to name a few whom I would hope expand their own writings on this particular subject. It is worth repeating that Lipset and Raab had reported in their book, *Jews And The New American Scene*, it has been the Orthodox writers who have emphasized the close relationship of conservatism between religious matters and politics. What is needed now is to enlarge the circle of writers who will also echo this theme.

Beyond these notable personalities, who else will be the logical conveyors of this thinking? It is going to have to be the Jewish leaders in each community who first become convinced that political change is needed and then embark on a crusade to spread their knowledge to the circles of people they can influence. I am hopeful many Reform and Conservative rabbis will be involved, but I do not hold out much hope that they will be in the vanguard. I believe rather, that the early advocates could well be the leaders of Jewish federations, Jews who are active politically, and perhaps some media personalities. To accomplish this the word must go forth that this is truly an important undertaking, deserving of a substantial contribution of time and effort by those involved.

At the core of Judaism as I understand it, is this undying, unquenchable, undefeatable, indefatigable thirst for individual freedom: The freedom to worship, to live, to carry on with our lives as we as individuals choose, guided always by the Commandments given to us by our God. This is what our 4,000-year history says to me. We have often strayed from the path that leads to God's desired results. I believe that Jews following the political liberal philosophy here in America these past two generations represents such a straying from the desired path, to the detriment of our religion and our nation.

Now is the time to wrench ourselves back on the right path to fulfill God's Commandments that we be a light unto all the people of the world, and to once again bring God's message of ethical monotheism and individual freedom to our fellow Americans. By doing this, we will save this blessed land from the creeping collectivism that is slowly and steadily enfolding us, and at the same time spark a renewal and resurgence in our interest and love for our own Jewish religion. God does not ask that we succeed, only that we try. What more noble cause could one pursue?

OTHER ISSUES

At this point we have detailed more than a dozen significant reasons why American Jews should cast off their politically liberal cloaks and begin to vote other than liberal. Whatever Jews want to accomplish politically—helping the less fortunate, keeping their kids from being converted to other religions or to no religion at all, universal peace and freedom, universal healthcare to all—this writing attempts to show them that these desirable ends can only be brought about through a change in their political thinking. Being liberal and voting for liberals simply is not going to cut it!

The question may now be asked, are there some current issues where the liberal position is somehow in harmony with Jewish law and tradition? Let us try to answer this question by briefly discussing an area that liberals have made one of their top priorities when it comes to passing new and expanding existing laws. This is the area of keeping our air clean, our water pure, our endangered species alive, and the preservation of as many of our irreplaceable national parks and forests as possible. Toward that end there has been enacted a host of federal laws, all endowed with noteworthy titles: The Clean Air Act; The Clean Water Act; The Tidelands Act; The Endangered Species Act. These laws, which are intended to regulate and punish certain behavior on the part of American citizens and businesses, have undoubtedly made some progress in achieving their goals. Whether on balance they have done more good than harm, and whether their restrictions on individual freedoms are leading to more and more control over our ability to live our lives as we choose, is left open for future debate. The question remains, are these laws in harmony with Jewish law and tradition or do they fall outside of that structure?

WHY JEWS SHOULD NOT BE LIBERALS

There is also the new scary specter of global warming that warns us that if we do not somehow reduce the amount of carbon hydrates released into the atmosphere, in less than a century the ice caps will melt and we will be inundated with rising oceans of water that will surge beyond their present banks. Do all of these forecasted doom and gloom scenarios mean that we must use the fearsome powers of government to restrict human activity and human freedom from those actions which are deemed harmful and which are allegedly bringing about those unpleasant results?

I doubt that at the time of this writing, even our wisest of men have definitive answers to those questions. There is great disagreement among the most prominent of scientists the world over as to what are the causes for global warming, how permanent are the changes affecting it, and even whether or not the warming will be good or bad for our civilization. There is too much we do not know about our universe and the many elements that affect our environment for we as citizens of this country or any country to pass laws and use the force of government to pick a definite direction upon which to embark.

For example, if one wishes to see how inaccurate predictions of future disaster can be, I refer to *The Resourceful Earth* written by the late Julian Simon and the late Herman Kahn in 1984. In 500+ pages these two men, both Jews, along with about two dozen expert contributors, analyzed the Global 2000 Report to the President, published in 1980, and determined that almost without exception, the conclusions reached in that weighty report were wrong, based on the evidence known at that time. And now that we have reached and passed year 2000, Simon and Kahn are proven even more correct than they were when they wrote their book in 1984. I hope that somewhere in the spirit world these two mental giants are having great laughs to see how far off those "other experts" were when they predicted doom and gloom.

In their executive summary, Simon and Kahn highlighted their differences. The Global 2000 report, prepared by the best experts, both government and non-government, that then President Jimmy Carter could assemble, was given wide circulation, high priority by the administration, and undoubtedly influenced the thinking of legislators in the passing of additional restrictive legislation.

In brief, Global 2000, as summarized in *The Resourceful Earth* stated: "If present trends continue, the world in 2000 will be more crowded, more polluted, less stable ecologically, and more vulnerable to disruption than the world we live in now. Serious stresses involving population, resources, and environment are clearly visible ahead. Despite greater material output, the world's people will be poorer in many ways than they are today. For hundreds of millions of the desperately poor, the outlook for food and other necessities of life will be no better. For many it will be worse. Barring revolutionary advances in technology, life for most people on earth will be more precarious in 2000 than it is now—unless the nations of the world act decisively to alter current trends." If this is not "gloom and doom" I don't know what is.

Simon and Kahn, and their experts, in analyzing Global 2000, arrived at completely different conclusions. They used the same sentence structure as Global 2000, but changed some key words and phrases: "If present trends continue, the world in 2000 will be less crowded (though more populated), less polluted, more stable ecologically, and less vulnerable to resource supply disruption than the world we live in now. Stresses involving population, resources, and environment will be less in the future than now... The world's people will be richer in most ways than they are today... The outlook for food and other necessities of life will be better... Life for most people on earth will be less precarious economically than it is now."

An abbreviated summary of the main points cited by Simon and Kahn to support their conclusions included:

1. Life expectancy has been rising rapidly throughout the world, a sign of demographic, scientific, and economic success.

2. The birth rate in less developed countries has been falling substantially during the past two decades.

3. Many people are still hungry, but the food supply has been improving since at least World War II.

4. Trends in world forests are not worrying.

5. There is no statistical evidence for rapid loss of species in the next two decades.

6. Water does not pose a problem of physical scarcity or disappearance.

7. The climate does not show signs of unusual and threatening changes.

Simon and Kahn found that the main assumption for the gloomy Global 2000 predictions was that there would be a declining growth in the rate of increase in per person productivity. Apparently the government experts gave little thought to the coming explosion in productivity brought on by the computer revolution, which was visible in 1980. As recently as June 2000, Federal Reserve Chairman Alan Greenspan somewhat reluctantly concluded that the productivity improvements brought about by the computer age are real and permanent.

As for the predicted species loss, which is at the foundation for our endangered species laws, Simon and Kahn make the point that the idea of saving every species, regardless of cost, is unreasonable. By preserving certain species, we prevent the incubation of new species, a renewal cycle that has been happening since the beginning of time. There have been a number of incredible decisions to save certain species that negatively impact business expansion and the creation of new jobs.

The story of the Delhi Sands Flower-Loving Fly is worth telling. This is a fly, about an inch long, with a half-inch long proboscis for sipping nectar. This insect appears for only a few weeks every August. For the rest of its two-year lifespan, it lives as a larva in the sand. At present it lives exclusively within an eight-mile radius in Southern California. It became listed as an endangered species in 1993, just as San Bernardino County broke ground for a $487 million dollar hospital. The county agreed to move its site to preserve the sandy habitat, but federal officials insisted that there needed to be a "100 foot-wide fly corridor" in case the fly wanted to cruise into new territory.

The county, various organizations, and homebuilders sued to prevent the federal government from maintaining these restrictive rules. They argued that the fly is not an article in interstate commerce and has nothing to do with interstate commerce. The Clinton administration replied that the fly does play a role in the nation's commerce, because it has been the subject of interstate trade among insect collectors. Sad to report is that the court of appeals upheld the federal position, because endangered species in total affect interstate commerce, and even though this fly was in only one state, Congress still had the power to take control of them. The last I heard this decision was on appeal to the Supreme Court, but it is doubtful if it will be heard there.

As it stands, the fly has triumphed over a new hospital with all of the benefits and economic growth that would have accompanied its building. "And God created man in His own image" and gave man "dominion over the fish of the sea, and over the fowl of the air, and over every living thing that creepeth upon the earth." (Genesis 1:27-28)

The latest update on the Delhi Sands Flower-Loving Fly is that it continues to cast a giant shadow over pending developments in Riverside and San Bernardino counties. Although San Bernardino did finally negotiate a land-swap deal to permit the building of the Arrowhead Regional Medical Center, the county was forced to set aside ten acres for a "fly" zone. This set-aside now prevents the county from actively promoting the building of medical offices, pharmacies, and related businesses as additions to the hospital. Other projects, including a sports park and industrial parks, are either on hold or have been shuffled off to less desirable locations. However, all is not lost. The federal fish and wildlife agency has assured the county that the fly will be removed from the endangered list as soon as the population—the fly population, that is—reaches a sustainable level, hopefully by the 2020s.

Is this not a perfect example of the craziness that has infected the body politic on this subject?

As we now have lived through the year 2000, we can all agree that the predictions and conclusions of Simon and Kahn are far closer to reality today, than were the dire predictions of Global 2000. Today, we are debating the pros and cons of joining the world in agreeing to scale back our use of energy, so as to limit the amount of carbon dioxide in the air, and thus prevent further "warming" of the globe. Again, if we look at the Simon and Kahn analysis compared to the government report, we must think again about restricting our economic activity, and reducing our standard of living to bring about a result which may well be contrary to what we desire. Some experts predict that if this country were to implement the Kyota treaty, which would mandate a substantial decrease in energy production in the United States, the results would be catastrophic to our economy by scaling back much of our recent economic growth. Yet the prior liberal administration continued to push for this dangerous treaty's acceptance.

Jewish tradition calls for the preservation of our natural resources to the best of our ability, while at the same time, honoring the law that people have the right to use their own property as they choose, subject only to certain community restrictions. Those restrictions were only those that were deemed paramount to the well-being of the community, and were limited to a select few. One could conclude that this entire area of preserving the environment, the wetlands, the endangered species, et al., should not be considered as another "exclusively" liberal position, nor can it be viewed as either a Jewish or conservative one. It is simply a subject that must be given the fullest exposure to debate of informed differences of opinion.

Due consideration must be given to the rights of property owners and the economic fall-out from any restrictions placed on the use of that property. The weight of government power should be carefully husbanded and restricted to the most elementary and basic items. We need to be wary of those liberal environmentalists who claim a privileged position because of their alleged special knowledge or ability to foresee the future. No political party or philosophy has a monopoly on wanting the best environment for our citizens, but the methods of attaining those goals are open to honest differences.

In the fall of year 2000, the unwelcome news appeared on the American scene that we were in some sort of energy crisis. Oil prices rose upward dramatically and this was reflected in gasoline prices at the pump of almost $2.00 per gallon. The liberals immediately pointed their accusing fingers at the giant oil companies, who they claimed were suddenly making obscene profits. (Profits naturally increased but this was a by-product of the increased cost as determined by the producers.) They also bewailed the fact that our "friends" in the Arab dominated Organization of Petroleum Exporting Countries (OPEC) were not increasing their production sufficiently to reduce prices. At the same time, liberals continued to oppose expanding drilling for oil and gas in our own domestic territory. They would rather preserve our pristine environment for future unborn generations and suffer the consequences of depending on foreign oil, which could endanger our own security. Such is the mentality of liberals today.

The facts are that this thinking does endanger the security of this country, as well as tending to harden world opinion against Israel. If we are so dependent on oil from the Middle East, then we must tread lightly in our dealings with those oil-producing countries, including many that remain Israel's enemies.

It has been the actions of the liberal environmentalists during the past dozen years that have prevented the building of any new refineries, which are badly needed to increase the flow of gas and heating oil to consumers. They have also won the fight against building new nuclear

211

plants, which have proven to be the safest source of energy throughout the world. The result of their actions is that in the past eight years, the Clinton years, the percentage of foreign oil that satisfies our domestic needs has increased from 40% to 60%, and the end is nowhere in sight.

This entire argument that preserving the environment takes precedence over the needs and security of our citizens is completely contrary to Jewish tradition. "And God said: Let us make man in our image, after our likeness; and let them have dominion over the fish of the sea, and over the fowl of the air, and over the cattle, and over all the earth, and over every creeping thing that creepeth upon the earth." (Genesis 1:26) There has to be a balance between preserving worthwhile portions of our natural environment and the needs of our people. I would rather disturb the migration patterns of some caribou in the Alaskan Wild Life Refuge and drill for oil there, as compared to groveling before the Arab sheiks to plead for additional production of their oil. In the process we jeopardize the security of Israel because of our dependence on staying in the good graces of the Arab potentates. I would also prefer to see a few more oil rigs in the ocean off of the California shore, which have turned out to be rather picturesque and are fine breeding areas for fish, than be dependent on foreign oil.

The bottom line to all of this is that life consists of making choices. There is seldom a perfect answer. Judaism always stresses choosing the life of its people over any other alternative. In this important matter, it is hoped that American Jews will reconsider their support of restricting the expansion of our domestic sources of oil and gas. The security of both our country and of Israel may well depend on the decisions that we make.

SOCIALISM, LIBERALISM, AND AMERICAN JEWS

Recently my wife, Ellie, and I were discussing current politics with a younger, fairly close relative and her husband. Not only were they diehard liberals, but also together they joyfully proclaimed themselves to be socialists. Their solution to the world's hunger problems was to force Bill Gates to divest himself of his entire multi-billion dollar fortune and distribute his money to the poor and hungry of the world. When we responded that even if this could be accomplished, after a few days of feeding, or even a couple of months, then what would save the poor and hungry of the world from their miserable existence. Their only answer was to then take the next few billionaires in America and do the same to them, until we ran out of billionaires. Thus, in a couple of magic strokes these two liberals would solve the age-old problem of hunger in this world. It is so easy to be a utopianist; it requires so little thinking and it's so liberal.

Perhaps if they knew more about the historic link between socialism and anti-Semitism, being good Jews they might want to reconsider their position. We did not have time to tell that story then, but it is certainly worthy of reciting now.

The link between Jews and socialism in modern times can be traced to the mass exodus that took place from Eastern Europe to the United States, beginning in 1881. Jews fleeing the tyranny of the czar followed the liberal cause, which was to liberate them from the ghettos. Liberal was a heroic term in Europe, and to break the czar's rule, socialism was the doctrine most often preached as the way to a better life. Probably most Jews accepting socialism really were not aware of the dictionary definition: "Control by the state of all means of production and economic activity." They knew only that anything was better than living under the czar, and socialism, with its veneer of brotherhood and charity and sharing, was appealing.

When these Eastern European Jews came to this country, many joined the Socialist Party of America, along with organizations such as the Workers Circle. Many related socialism to the Talmudic tradition of communal provisions, ignoring the difference between voluntary sharing and giving under Judaism, and forced giving, sharing, and control under socialism. So perhaps at that time, around the turn of the twentieth century, it was understandable that there was a certain appeal to socialism. Socialism as a distinct party slowly faded away as the twentieth century progressed, reaching its high point under Norman Thomas. Thomas himself eventually ceased running for President of the United States in 1948, saying that the Democratic Party had now adopted all of his most important issues, so there was no longer a reason for a separate Socialist Party.

What was apparently little known or publicized here during this period was the growth of anti-Semitism in Europe and its connection to socialism. Dr. Tyler Cowen, professor of economics at George Mason University, writing in *Freeman* in a January 1997, article titled, "The Socialist Roots of Modern anti-Semitism," traces this development. Cowen writes, "The socialist origins of modern anti-Semitism illustrate the link between statism and the persecution of minorities. Anti-Semitism as a formal, intellectual movement arose in the middle of the nineteenth century, when Jewish conspiracy theories grew in popularity. German writers picked up on earlier anti-Enlightenment theories of a Judeo-Masonic conspiracy to rule the world." Eventually the Masonic side was dropped, and the focus was on the Jews. (This was around the time that the "Protocols of the Elders of Zion" was revived.)

In 1879, the German writer Wilhelm Marr, is credited with coining the term "anti-Semitic." Marr expanded on the medieval attacks on Jewish traders and usurers and could not accept the economic success of

Jews. Adolf Stocker's Christian Social Party (1878-1885) joined Marr by combining Marr's religious approach with socialist economics. Jews were evil because of their religion (Christ killers) plus they were mostly capitalists, which was opposed to socialism. Georg Ritter von Schonerer followed in Austria with a similar anti-Semitic, anti-capitalistic platform in the 1880s. Schonerer became a hero to Adolph Hitler, who it is said, hung Schonerer's slogans over his bed.

Professor Cowen writes, "The initial link between socialism and anti-Semitism arose through intellectual affinity." Because European Jews, the Rothschilds in particular, were such prominent capitalists, "Many socialists considered anti-Semitism to be a way station on the path toward a more consistent socialist viewpoint." Karl Marx, a Jew by birth, continued the anti-Semitic attack with his writings. Marx and his followers believed that if the public could be persuaded to hate Jewish capitalists, they would eventually come to hate all capitalists. Elie Kedourie in his book, *The Jewish World*, wrote that Karl Marx thought the Jewish problem would disappear when capitalism disappeared since the Jew is the most striking version of a capitalist. Paul Johnson wrote in *History of the Jews*, "Socialism became the anti-Semitism of the intellectuals."

Socialism has also had a profound influence on the State of Israel. In 1920, David Ben-Gurion believed Palestine, as it was then called, must be socialistic. He believed that the Jewish question could not be solved within a capitalistic framework. Ben-Gurion stated he had three principles: Jews return to the land; the language must be Hebrew; and the country must be socialistic. (Two out of three isn't bad.) It has only been the past twenty-five years, since Menachem Begin was elected prime minister and the Likud Party assumed control in 1977, that Israel has slowly but steadily, begun the difficult process of casting off the shackles of a socialistic economy, and adapting the free market concept. There still remains much to change, but with the tremendous growth of the Israeli economy in recent years, there appears to be little desire to go back to the old government controlled system.

Socialism seemed to progress by pretending to be a liberal, revolutionary movement, freeing up the lives of its supporters, when in reality its basic doctrine is more state control over peoples' lives. The Nazi Party was known as the National Socialist Party. Communism in Russia was identified as the International Socialist Movement. It was no coincidence that the word "socialist" appears prominently in both of these totalitarian regimes, which together, practically decimated European Jewry. Still, there is little doubt that socialism continues to cast its enticing spell over many of our intellectuals today, some of whom have influential teaching positions in our leading universities.

The irony of it all is as Kedourie writes, American Jews have long believed anti-Semitism was encouraged by the political right in America, with the right's alleged ignoring of the social problems of poverty, prejudice, and its alleged practice of discrimination against Jews in business. Only recently are American Jews discovering that many of our problems emanate from the left with its affluence, permissiveness, wishful thinking, and its substitute of secular liberalism for their own Jewish religion.

What American Jews must always remember is that totalitarian regimes come to power by promising everything to everybody, and then remain in power through force and intimidation. And when things eventually go bad for them, there is always the need for a scapegoat, and who else fits that role but the Jew. Sidney Hook, a liberal for much of his life is quoted as saying, "I was guilty of judging capitalism by its operations and socialism by its hopes and aspirations; capitalism by its works and socialism by its literature." Winston Churchill wrote, "The inherent vice of capitalism is the unequal sharing of the blessings. The inherent blessing of socialism is the equal sharing of misery."

I don't know whether our young relatives will eventually see the error of their thinking, or if they will ever read this writing. I hope they represent only a tiny minority of their generation of American Jews. Based on the beliefs of our own two adult children, who are strong conservative or libertarians, I tend to believe that the socialist theory of life is not making that much headway among the baby boomers in America. Certainly if one leans toward Judaism in practically any way, and if one does any studying of the history of socialism and its links to present day liberalism, one would have to reject following socialism in any of its forms.

Beyond all of this there must be the realization that socialism, and its twin liberalism, by granting more and more power to the state, by looking to the state to solve all of our social, economic, and even personal problems, in effect makes the state the "God" whom all should worship. By elevating the state to this supreme position, socialism or liberalism by definition, does thereby demote the eternal and One God, to an inferior position. In so doing these philosophies defy the Second Commandment, when God thundered to Moses and the Israelites on Mt. Sinai, "Thou shalt have no other gods before me."

THE 80/20 PRINCIPLE
AND POLITICS

✡

After plowing through the preceding chapters which seem to paint conservatives as completely good, moral, and upright citizens, and liberals as arrogant, uninformed, and less than moral citizens, I do not wish to leave the reader with the impression that I believe the above to be 100% true and accurate in all cases. There are many exceptions to the general rule, and this certainly holds true for politics. As the Torah says, we are all a mixture of good and evil. The key is to accentuate the good and eliminate as much as possible the evil.

President Ronald Reagan was fond of saying that if you were with him on 80% of his positions that was good enough for him. The 80/20 principle was perhaps first discovered by the 16th century economist, Pareto, who determined that in any body of data, it is usually 20% of that data which produces 80% of the results. In many companies' sales staffs, it is frequently 20% of that staff that produces results comparable to that of the other 80%. Many businesses are now learning with the help of new computer programs, that 20% of their customer base is responsible for 80% of their sales, and so on. The point is that I do not expect any conservative to be 100% consistent with the conservative philosophy, and similarly I do not look for liberals to be 100% with their philosophy. (They may be on the right side of issues 20% of the time.)

A current example of this that has just made the headlines as I complete this writing is the selection of Senator Joseph Lieberman of Connecticut as the vice presidential running mate of Al Gore. This is the first time in the history of America that a Jew has been selected as a candidate for one of the top two elected positions in our government. I had referred to the senator in earlier pages as the one prominent Jewish politician who had at least stepped forward to condemn President Clinton's immoral behavior. I also noted, however, that when it came time to cast his vote to remove Clinton from office for lying under oath and obstructing justice, Lieberman backed off and voted against conviction.

In addition to this inconsistency, Senator Lieberman's voting record in the United States Senate reveals that on several issues, he supports the conservative position, rather than the liberal one. He has supported school vouchers, welfare reform, privatizing Social Security, and supporting the Gulf War in 1991, which most of his fellow Democrats opposed. There are other issues where Lieberman has voted against the majority liberal position, which illustrates I believe, the 80/20 principle. (Although Lieberman's selection as his running mate did somewhat clear Al Gore of his close association with the tainted Clinton, it was insufficient to provide the winning margin.)

During the recently completed Republican convention, hardly a word was heard about cutting back the overgrown, wasteful, federal bureaucracy, which now spends $2.4 trillion annually. Instead the Republican nominee, George W., Bush, a self-described conservative, proposed increased spending for education, teachers' training, and various other federal programs. The only program to increase individual freedom was that of reducing individual income taxes. Was this just reaching out for the independent voters, or was it another example of politicians being less than 100% in support of their proclaimed political philosophy? The 80/20 principle again?

In my own case, there are parts of capitalism that I do not like. I abhor the actions of certain major corporations who terminate the employment of long-term employees when they near their retirement age in order to avoid paying out full retirement benefits. I have a friend who was recently laid off by a major aerospace company after twenty-four years of faithful service. He was simply called in one Friday and told that he was no longer needed because the man upstairs had ordered a cutback.

There was nothing told him about what benefits he had coming, only that he might be recalled some day. Fortunately, after almost one year had passed by, he was recalled, but in the interim he suffered much stress. I am hopeful that in this enlightened age, such examples are diminishing.

There is no question that there are many injustices that occur in the marketplace under capitalism, but when one searches for a better alternative system, we have yet to find one. (Remember Churchill's quote.) We pass certain laws that help protect the individual rights of people, no employee discrimination because of age, sex, religion, etc., and these are effective so long as they do not become the plaything of attorneys wielding their "class action" swords. As imperfect human beings, any political and economic system we live under will always have its share of injustices. One difference between conservatives and liberals is that conservatives expect these imperfections and try to minimize them, whereas liberals seem to believe that human conduct is somehow perfectible in this earthly existence, and we only need more government programs to completely eliminate any and all injustices.

The less than 100% allegiance to a given philosophy occurs right within the Sternberg household. My wife Ellie, who is usually more consistent that I am in adhering to the conservative or libertarian creed, is a strong supporter of eliminating smoking from public restaurants by decree of government. She believes that tobacco smoke is deadly wherever it occurs, and as such should be outlawed because it is a health hazard. She believes that even though the air within a private establishment is theoretically "private," still the danger of tobacco smoke to everyone is sufficient to warrant the ban on smoking in restaurants.

Although I agree with her that it is pleasant not to have to worry about smelling tobacco fumes when eating because smoking in restaurants in California is now illegal, should not this preference be left to the marketplace to decide? We all have a choice as to where to eat, and if we don't like a certain place because of its tobacco odors, we do not have to patronize it. Also I have read that the public health reports on the dangers of secondhand tobacco smoke were vastly overstated. Over Ellie's strenuous objections, I still feel that she departs from her basic libertarian philosophy in continuing to hold to her position, thus making this her 80/20 example.

In my own case, I depart from my basics in that I believe we should have universal military training for our young men. If we would take every youth at the age of eighteen, and insert him into a branch of our armed forces for one to two years, we would have a much healthier nation. At age eighteen, most kids do not know what they want to do. Many lack discipline and are already developing bad habits. The experience of serving in our military even for that brief time, would give most of them a new outlook on life, and result in reducing the amount of crime and dissipation that is currently associated with that age group. I believe that my own service in the navy for over four years, first as an enlisted man and then as an officer, made me a better person.

I have read where the marines can take a group of kids coming from the worst of our neighborhoods and in just thirteen weeks of basic training, completely change their attitudes and lives for the better. Yes, this is an example of using the force of government to bring about some good in this country, and I plead guilty to advocating the use of such force for this purpose. So this is my 80/20 example.

To sum up this 80/20 section, as one of our recent presidents was wont to say, let me be perfectly clear on this issue. All conservatives are not good and all liberals are not bad. There are inconsistencies and exceptions on both sides. Liberalism says vote for them, even though they don't believe you have the brains and common sense to live your lives in your own best interests, and that you need the "wise men" of government to lead you and to protect you from your mistakes. Conservatism says we must keep government out of our lives to the maximum, but continues to advocate a Constitutional amendment to prohibit abortion, and refuses to even consider moderating our draconian illicit drug use laws, which result in flooding our jails and prisons with nonviolent offenders.

As Jews, however, I would hope that the decision as to which philosophy is closest to our own religion and traditions has been made clear in this writing. Judaism and conservatism are an almost perfect match. Judaism and liberalism, like oil and water, are an impossible match.

THE POSSIBLE DOWNSIDE OF A POLITICAL CHANGE

When making any sort of a major change in one's life, such as is advocated in this writing from liberal to conservative, one must take into consideration the possible downsides to making such a change. We need to worry about how this change will affect our mental processes, our physical health, our relations with our friends and loved ones, our business contacts and career, and in a broader sense, how this change will influence current happenings in our country and the world. Wow! No wonder such changes occur infrequently and usually only after some cataclysmic event. Well, I cannot say that reading and agreeing with this book fits the description of such a happening, but let us briefly think about the possible repercussions of a massive switch taking place among American Jews from being the sheep-like liberals of today, to the free thinking, independent, rugged, self-disciplined conservatives of tomorrow.

First, to address worry, somewhere in my vast readings I came across the formula on how to handle worry. It seems that on the average, 95% of the things we worry about in our daily lives never come to pass. All our everyday worries (dying in an airplane accident, passing tomorrow's test, our spouse cheating on us, making next month's mortgage payment, the stock market crashing, etc.) either never happen or if they do, they end up being merely a ripple in one's life stream. Of course, each one of us is an individual so different events will affect us in different ways. As I think about almost all of my own nighttime fears and worries, except for the possible exception of not selling my stock portfolio in September 1987, as I dreamed I should have, I really cannot remember anything of consequence that I worried about that became an actual problem.

Taking away 95% of the 100% leaves just 5% of our worries to deal with. Of the remaining 5%, again on the average, 4% of that 5% are problems or challenges that we handle more or less successfully. In other words these are real items that one way or the other, we solve and go on with our lives. As to the final 1%, these are the worries that probably remain with us for an extended period of time. Is my career progressing satisfactorily? Am I in the right profession or job? Will I find the right person to spend my life with? Will our kids find their proper life's companions? Will the citizens of this country use their common sense and make the right political decisions that will safeguard the freedoms of our people? And so on. This remaining 1% we struggle with and hopefully either eventually resolve to everyone's benefit, or simply live with the results.

The bottom line of all of this is that in considering the possible effects of Jews' political change, we need discuss and worry about only the most important of the possible consequences that may occur to the reader as he or she contemplates this momentous change. The following are the questions that I believe are worthy of asking and answering.

1. Will I have to find a new spouse? No, not if both of you will become enlightened together; or at worse, if one of you absorbs the message, and the other one remains at the minimum, neutral. Otherwise, if only one of you sees the light, and depending on the importance of this issue in your particular household, you may need to revise your *katubah*, the Jewish marriage document.

2. Will I need to find new friends to associate with? No, not if you can use your powers of persuasion and eloquence and give them a copy of this book to assist them in making this change in their thinking. You need convert only a few of your closest friends to enjoy your new philosophy. Otherwise, I suggest that you begin to attend seminars led

by noted conservatives in order to make new friends more in keeping with your new ideology. I suggest subscribing to the publications of the Foundation for Economic Education (FEE) as a worthy beginning.

3. Will I need to change temples and find a new rabbi? Probably yes. Unfortunately, until the ideas expressed herein attain wider circulation and acceptance among our learned clergy, and until Hebrew Union University begins to graduate men and women who are at least politically neutral, this problem will persist. As noted earlier in this writing, I still have not yet found a rabbi with whom I can feel politically good about, except for Rabbi Daniel Lapin of Seattle, Washington, and that is a long way to travel for Friday and Saturday services.

4. Will this change make me want to stop watching, listening, and reading the major media? Definitely yes. With your newly opened mind and eyes, you will soon come to realize that there is an unwritten rule among the major media people that liberalism is good and conservatism is bad, and that they slant and report the news accordingly. You will either have to live with no TV blasting in your house, or find the relatively few channels where the news is as least reported in a more neutral fashion. You will also probably find yourself listening more and more to talk radio, where many of your newly discovered political principles are being used by most of the talk show hosts as they explain and interpret the news. You will also quickly abandon the liberal newspaper you are now reading, saving perhaps only the sports section, and begin to subscribe to the authentic conservative and libertarian magazines that are available.

5. Will this change affect the future of this country? I

certainly hope so. If we could witness the present 80-90% of American Jews who vote liberal today, change to 80-90% conservative, the results would be breathtaking. Key states such as California, New York, and Florida would switch permanently into the Republican column with a corresponding decrease in the size and powers of government, and the accompanying increase in personal freedoms. The entire thrust of politics would change to how quickly we can roll back the intrusive powers of government in our lives, and make it more possible for individual citizens to make their own decisions on how to spend their own hard-earned money without Big Brother controlling our every move. With the support of the influential Jewish community, perhaps the current Republican Party will once again have the fortitude to strongly proclaim their basic conservative philosophy, without having to fear broadsides from the liberal media

6. Will this change affect my feeling about my religion, and could it somehow help me to become a "better Jew"? Again, I hope so. Rabbi Lapin has written that American Jews have come to substitute secular liberalism to replace their Judaism. If this is true, and I agree that it is for many Jews, then it must follow that if Jews abandon their secular liberalism for conservatism more in harmony with traditional Judaism, they will become "better Jews." How much better will they become, who knows?

At a minimum, if they will begin to relate their Judaism to their political positions, this will be a major step forward. If they will begin to rethink the positives about Judaism, and I don't necessarily mean the ritual part, this will enhance the meaningfulness of their change. We need to reemphasize some of those positives: the importance of the family and

Jewish education; the spirit that God had endowed us with to choose good over evil, life over death; the importance of having been granted the freedom of moral will that permits us to make the proper decisions in life; the value of observing and living by the Commandments; and that it is incumbent upon all Jews to continue to strive for and defend the freedom that we have struggled for throughout our 4,000-year history. If some of this accompanies political change, then yes, "better Jews" will result.

And that is the bottom line for this discussion of possible downsides of change. The answer to the question of whether there are any downsides is "There are no downsides." Political change of American Jews, I believe, will result in a better and freer America, a more politically enlightened group of Jews, and hopefully, a Jewish citizenry that rediscovers some basic truths about their religion with its links to what we identify today as political conservatism.

CONCLUSION

Now the reader may well ask, is this writer trying to make the case that if I am a Jew, then I cannot be a political liberal because the two are antithetical to each other? That is a pretty harsh conclusion to draw. And if liberalism is so bad, then can I safely turn to becoming a political conservative, or even a libertarian, and still hope to accomplish my Jewish social goals? The answer to these questions, after reviewing all that has been written here, is **yes**. Liberalism in its modern form holds to positions that are contrary to Jewish law and tradition, and modern conservatism's positions are very much in tune with Jewish law and tradition. It seems to me that no matter how a liberal may twist or turn or obfuscate, there is no way out from concluding that liberalism and Judaism are like oil and water, they just do not mix!

Remember one of the main reasons a rabbi wrote me that he was a liberal was that only liberalism could bring about the needed help to those who could not manage for themselves. Two generations of activity have proven that massive government programs do not accomplish what they aim to and that they are contrary to the welfare tradition of Judaism. Welfare in Judaism is to be of a temporary nature only. One should accept even the lowliest of tasks rather than accept the community's help. The highest form of charity is to teach a man a skill or craft or profession so he can earn his own keep. By keeping people dependent upon government assistance, the Jewish principle that we are each responsible for our own actions is diluted and ignored.

For those concerned that by abandoning their liberalism they will somehow be entering a new, cruel world of conservative meanness, your fears are groundless. Just as the Jewish free market included many acts of charity and mutual assistance, there is little question that today's conservatism also includes the spirit of cooperation and honesty. Our free market economy is built upon voluntary actions between the producers and the consumers of products and services, and produces so much wealth that charitable donations in America are reaching the $200 billion mark annually. Our system appears to be similar to that described by Tamari when he wrote that the pronounced entrepreneurial spirit and the voluntary assumption of the financial burden of Jewish communal welfare are what characterized the Jewish free market economy.

We are here schooled for life eternal, as the Reverend Edmund Opitz used to say at FEE sponsored seminars. If we are not encouraged to fight our own battles, to overcome obstacles, we may never achieve what our grand destiny is. Political conservatism, with all its faults, preaches this message as consistently as it can, given the exigencies of modern politics. At the same time, there is now general acceptance of the concept of society providing an economic floor for those people who simply cannot make it on their own. Again Tamari writes that kindness and morality were part of the Jewish market mechanism, with the apparent recognition that the free market was a necessary tool to produce the surpluses that could be given to those in need.

The fear of anti-Semitism and its alleged connection to the political right is what keeps many Jews in the liberal camp. They continue to overlook the fact that real anti-Semitism can take root only when the powers of government are concentrated in the hands of the few. He who ignores history remains ignorant. Today's liberal doctrine seeks to add more and more powers to government. No matter what the problem is, real or concocted, liberals want to solve it by granting some new or expanded power to government. Are oil prices too high? Do drugs cost too much? Are the schools not teaching their students to read and write? The answer per the liberals is to take some type of government action as the cure. To turn for answers to the marketplace, or to the privatization of previously controlled activities, or in some cases to merely let nature take its course, simply escapes the liberal mind. Government, with all of its "wise men," has to be the answer. This approach again is completely contrary to Jewish law and tradition.

It is the coercive force of governments of all shapes and varieties that has driven the Jewish people to wander the globe in search of freedom. Finally, they found that freedom here in the United States of America, and Jews should make as their first priority the preservation of that individual freedom. Remember the old story of how to boil a frog. You don't throw it into boiling water, because the frog would immediately jump out. Instead, you put it in tepid water, and gradually turn up the heat until the frog is unaware that it is now a boiled frog. The story is the same regarding the lose of our individual freedom here. It is not lost all at once, but slowly, given the liberal programs to expand the powers of government, we may one day wake up and find out that we have become completely dependent for our daily existence on the good graces of government and the "benevolent" people running it.

The words of Alexis de Tocqueville from his writing *Democracy in America* are to the point. "The will of man is not shattered, but softened, bent and guided; men are seldom forced by it to act, but they are constantly restrained from acting. Such a power does not destroy, but it prevents existence; it does not tyrannize, but it compresses, enervates, extinguishes and stupefies a people, till each nation is reduced to nothing better than a flock of timid and industrious animals, of which the government is the shepherd." This was written in the 1840s, and one can almost sense De Tocqueville looking down on us today and saying, "See, I told you so."

Jews must be the "canary in the coal mine" and serve as the warning signal to the American people, that our freedoms are being eroded. Only by changing their political stance, can American Jews carry out this responsibility. We owe it to our fellow citizens, almost in gratitude for our free existence here, to perform this necessary function. Instead, we are too often serving as the "attack dog" in advocating and pursuing new powers for government.

The liberals' drive to eliminate almost all traces of religion in our public life is again opposed to Jewish tradition. Our entire religion is based on observing the Commandments and the laws in our daily lives. As Jews we must try to live as close to those principles as we can. In our zeal to prevent an overwhelming Christian presence, we go overboard the other way and seek to make this country a religion-free society. As Rabbi Lapin has put it, Jews have substituted secular liberalism for their religion in an effort to escape the religious rules of Judaism. The word "secular" is used so often these days that perhaps we forget what its definition is. Secularism is "a system of political or social philosophy that rejects all forms of religious faith and worship." I have a suggestion to make. If American Jews want to be "secular" then at least let them be "secular conservatives." That way they will preserve at a minimum, some vestiges of their Jewish religion, because conservatism is so much more in harmony with Judaism than is liberalism. Jews have survived by being true to their heritage and conserving and transmitting the eternal principles of their religion. Thus it has always been and thus it will always be.

Hans Kung in his book, *Judaism*, quotes a paragraph from Abraham Joshua Heschel's *God in Search of Man*: "(T)he spirit of Judaism is not the spirit of conformity to American secular society, but above all is the spirit of protest, embodied in the great prophets, against a confusion of the true God with the many earthly, false idols of this society. Also the protest must be made on matters of religion and law. To be a Jew is to renounce allegiance to false gods, to remain free of infatuation with worldly triumphs, and never to succumb to splendour."

Whatever the subject may be—education, healthcare, taxes, abortion, guns, affirmative action, you name it—the liberals are on the wrong side when it comes to aligning their positions with Jewish law and tradition. I'm sure I am not the only one who notices that American Jews when propounding their liberal positions invariably fail to make any connection to our religion as a foundation for their thinking. Or if they do try and make such a link, as with charity or welfare, they fail to give the traditional Jewish principle, that such help is meant to be temporary, and is to be given only if all other attempts by the recipients at making a living have been in vain.

Even with the selection of Orthodox Jew Senator Joseph Lieberman as the vice presidential candidate on the Democratic ticket, the good senator seemed to take particular pains to avoid associating his religious beliefs with his political positions. Oh yes, he is for affirmative action, refusing to call that activity by its correct name, which is "racial preference" or quotas, which Jews have always fought against. School choice for parents is a position that the senator has expressed on occasion previously, but now as the VP candidate to liberal Al Gore, he seemed to be backing away from that stance. For Lieberman to qualify as an authentic liberal, which he does, there has to be a major disconnect between his Orthodox religion and his politics. That is unfortunate, because if a Jew had been named as a VP candidate on the Republican side, we would have undoubtedly seen some real connection between political conservatism and traditional Judaism.

Now the reader may ask, after all these years of Jews being liberals and considering all of the brilliant Jewish writers who have discoursed on this subject, how come you, an unknown semi-retired CPA, should now proclaim himself an expert on the subject and attempt to persuade Jews they must change their political thinking? My answer is, I really do not have an answer. I only know that someone, somehow, must have the passion and the interest to present in one writing as many of the reasons as possible why Jews have become liberals, and as many reasons as possible why they should not be liberals. Fortunately in this blessed nation, we have the freedom as individuals to follow our own instincts in attempting to meet this challenge. Albert Einstein in 1950 wrote, "Everything that is really great and inspiring is created by the individual who can labor in freedom."

To sum it all up then the question remains, are you really saying that as Jews we must abandon our long-held emotional links to liberalism and move over to the other side of this political divide? This is my answer.

Regardless of what kind of Jew you are, Orthodox, secular, Conservative, Reform, Reconstructionist, or any other variety; whether you believe that Judaism is an individual or a communal religion; whether you believe we were or were not chosen as God's messenger to the rest of this world; whether you believe property rights are secondary to human rights; whether you observe or do not observe most of our rituals; whatever you believe, if you have a modicum of Jewish blood in your veins, either by heritage or through conversion, or by osmosis, you must believe that after our belief in the One and Only God, for Jews, freedom is the most important value of all, and that government exists to protect that freedom and to interfere as little as possible in our lives.

Therefore you must cast off your emotional, familial, or any other historical ties to liberalism, and join those of us Jews who have already freed ourselves from that secular and foreboding philosophy to become enlightened, self-interested, self-disciplined, and motivated voluntarists, or in the current political vernacular, conservative or libertarian or Republictarian.

During the battle for Jerusalem in 70 CE, as reported in Josephus *The Jewish War*, translated by G.A. Williamson, there was a struggle within the Jewish ranks inside the city. (As usual, the Jews were divided among themselves.) The Zealots were running rampant, taking the law into their own hands, and generally terrorizing the general populace. The balance of the citizens looked for leadership from their high priests. The oldest of the high priests, Ananus, spoke to the people to rally them against the Zealots within, and against the Romans led by Titus outside the walls of Jerusalem.

Josephus reports the speech of Ananus. In part he says to his fellow Jews, "You are plundered without protest, beaten without a murmur, witnesses of murder, without one audible groan... They have seized the strongest place in the City... Will you really wait for the Romans to recover our holy places? Have you really lost the most honorable and deep rooted of our instincts, the longing for **freedom**? Are we in love with slavery and devoted to our masters as if our fathers had taught us to be doormats... Again and again they fought to the bitter end for independence, defying the might of both Egypt and Persia, rather than take orders from anyone."

It is this freedom, this most honorable and deep-rooted of our instincts in the words of Ananus, that is at risk here in America. Only by containing the growth of government powers may we as Jews be protected from any force that seeks to again make us the sacrificial lamb for society's problems. To those who may say it cannot happen here, I hope and pray it will not, but we can ensure it will never happen through our eternal vigilance. And as a plus to changing our political allegiance is the fact that we will be moving closer to aligning our political positions with traditional Judaism.

To the non-Jews who have always wondered why we Jews have persisted in following the liberal line these past two generations, I hope that this writing sheds some light on the answer. You can help mightily to bring about this political change by continuing to support Israel with the same devotion that many of you presently do, and to be patient with this "stiff-necked" people whilst this change germinates and eventually blooms.

To those Jews with minds open enough to explore at least the essence of this writing, my hope is that this will lead to further thinking and discovery on your part so you may eventually shed your liberal cloak. To those Jews who are already sympathetic to the views contained herein, I congratulate you and urge you to expand your efforts to carry this message to your own inner circles of family, friends, and associates. To those Jews who are dedicated liberals, and see no reason to change, my condolences to you. Perhaps someday the light will dawn and you will be able to connect your Judaism to your political beliefs. To all others, my thanks for reading these words, and for helping me to fulfill a lifelong journey.

POST SCRIPT—
15 DECEMBER 2000

Although the theme of this book is somewhat timeless, the historic presidential election of 7 November 2000 merits some special comments. This was an election that was the closest in over a century, and whose final results were in doubt for thirty-five days. The election exposed some real problems in the election machinery of counting votes, registering, and qualifying voters, and even the design of the election ballot, all matters which receive little attention between elections. I hope there will be some constructive and meaningful changes made before 2004, so that the chance for error and confusion will have been reduced, if not eliminated, and the word "chad" will revert to being just a man's name or a country in Africa.

The relevance of the election to this writing in my opinion is that: it was the first time that a Jew was a candidate for either president or vice president on a major party ticket; Jews continue to vote liberal or Democrat by a huge majority; and there may be some hopeful, still obscure signs, that perhaps American Jews may be beginning to open their minds to changing their political allegiance.

As noted previously in several chapters, Senator Joseph Lieberman of Connecticut was chosen by Al Gore to be the vice presidential candidate on the Democratic ticket. Prior to his selection, the senator had earned a favorable reputation from most observers as a man of conviction and integrity. They respected him for living by his Orthodox Jewish principles without hiding or evading them. Even so tough a critic on politicians as nationally syndicated radio talk show host, Don Imus, would fairly gush with praise whenever Senator Lieberman appeared on Imus' morning program. Imus frequently would praise Lieberman as one of the few honest politicians that he knew. Although Lieberman prior to his VP selection was known as somewhat of a maverick among liberal Democrat circles, still he had compiled an 81% favorable voting record according to Democrat standards and was thus part of the liberal establishment.

Al Gore, the Democratic presidential nominee, had personally disapproved of President Bill Clinton's sexual misbehavior. Gore had enjoyed a long, successful marriage with his wife, Tipper, and wanted to be recognized as a solid family man, in contrast to the reputation of Clinton. He knew that he needed to somehow obscure any connection that voters may have between Gore and Clinton, at least in the area of personal morality and behavior. If Gore now chose as his partner the one senator who had gained national attention with his denouncement of Clinton's personal behavior, this would serve as a significant message to the voting public to disassociate Gore from Clinton. (Gore went so far in this separation from Clinton that he restricted Clinton's participation in the campaign to making "cameo" appearances on rare occasions.)

Gore also was aware that among the key, "battleground" states that would decide the election, he could capture Florida with its sizable, retired Jewish population, with the right running mate. With a Jew, and a liberal Jew at that, beside him, this would have to make a positive impact on the Jews of Florida, as well as many Jews in the major cities of America. Any possible downside for selecting Lieberman, such as potential backlash from fringe anti-Semitic groups, was discounted. One Democratic strategist commented that any voters who would turn on Gore because he had a Jew for a running mate would probably never have voted for Gore in the first place.

Thus it can be assumed that these were among the primary reasons Gore selected Lieberman as his running mate. As it turned out, this was a strategically sound decision. Although there are no reliable statistics to prove the point that Lieberman was a "net plus" for Gore, there appeared to be no backlash from any group (black voters sometimes accused of being anti-Semitic voted 93% for Gore), and the amazingly close Florida vote had to be attributed at least in part to Lieberman's presence on the ticket. On a personal basis, I had more than one Jewish friend, previously undecided, who decided to vote for Gore because of Lieberman.

Lieberman proved to be a stout campaigner, and soon swung into line behind Gore on all the major issues. The senator faithfully echoed Gore in the latter's promises to solve all of the nation's problems by simply spending more and more money, and creating more and more government rules and regulations. Lieberman had no hesitation in joining Gore in trashing George Bush's "risky" tax scheme to return part of our tax overpayment back to those who had paid in those excess taxes. To be fair, Lieberman did on occasion attempt to expound on his moral positions, in particular, that our Constitution did not intend to eliminate religion and God from our lives, but was intended only to prevent government from imposing any religion on the people. For this the American Civil Liberties Union (ACLU) immediately condemned him, and thereafter he seemed to soften those remarks. As a candidate for vice president (in addition to running for re-election as Senator from Connecticut), part of the price Lieberman apparently had to pay for this honor, was to recant all of his previously held, somewhat conservative positions (opposition to affirmative action, approval of school vouchers, changing Social Security, etc.). This led to the disapproval of Lieberman by many of his previous supporters (Imus among them). Still as 7 November 2000 approached the race was too close to call.

As the results came in that night there were some unexpected results. Gore lost his home state of Tennessee, as well as Clinton's home state of Arkansas. Bush failed to win two of the three most important "battleground" states, Michigan and Pennsylvania. As the night wore on, all attention became focused on the state of Florida, with its twenty-five electoral votes, and whose governor was Jeb Bush, brother of George W. Bush, the Republican presidential nominee. If one were to have written a script for this election, he could not have done a more suspenseful job.

First, based on exit interviews with voters, the major media stations called Florida, and in effect the election, for Gore. This tended to discourage many voters in Florida and in the West from voting, Republicans claimed. Hours later the major stations reversed their call and placed it in the undecided column. Then in what seemed to be their final call, they awarded it to Bush, and with that, the election. Just before Gore was about to call Bush to concede, the votes began to pour in from Democrat precincts, and finally late in the evening, the count ended with Florida as too close to call. In the early morning of 8 November, the final machine count left Bush with a narrow lead of less then 1,800 votes out of almost six million votes cast. This close margin necessitated an automatic machine recount, which a few days later still left Bush in the lead by less than 1,000 votes.

What proceeded then need not be detailed here. Continuous legal maneuvering, judges' decisions, judges overruled, armies of attorneys battling, with ultimately the United States Supreme Court rendering, on a five to four decision, the final verdict that Bush's narrow margin of a few hundred votes must be sustained, kept the American public on edge for five weeks. Thus after this historic election, George W. Bush became our forty-third president, and Joseph Lieberman returned to his Senate job, as he had wisely run for both positions in November. So what does this all mean for the political future of American Jews and their voting patterns?

The fact that a Jew was chosen as a nominee for one of the two top political positions in the country should be viewed as a plus. It should prove the point that to be a Jew, and particularly an Orthodox Jew, is no barrier in these United States to becoming a prominent voice in our national life. That old shibboleth that we must not raise our heads up too high as Jews because we may bring down on our heads the wrath of the Christian majority has definitely been demolished. For this we have Al Gore and Joe Lieberman to thank. It is just too bad that our first Jewish nominee had to be a liberal. Perhaps the next time around we will get a Jewish nominee whose views are more in line with the theme of this writing.

In one sense the fact that roughly 20% of Jews voted for the Republican Bush is encouraging. With a Jew on the Democrat ticket, and with the normal emotional tie between Jews and the Democratic Party, one would have thought that perhaps 90 to 95% of Jews would have voted for Gore. That would have matched the percentage of American black voters, many of whom apparently were so convinced by Jesse Jackson that their rights were going to be taken away from them by Bush, that they surmounted their previous majority for Democrats by voting 93% for Gore!

That there were still 20% of Jews who resisted the siren song of the Democrats in 2000, may be considered as a base to build on for the future. The votes of senior citizens in Florida, as distinguished by their age and not their religion, appeared to be almost evenly split between Gore and Bush. This may reflect the attractiveness of Bush's campaign pledge to lower income taxes for all and to permit younger citizens to choose to make their own decisions on how to invest their Social Security taxes. After all, many of us grandparents want our grandchildren to get more out of the Social Security program when they retire, than many of us now realize from this program.

Another hopeful sign for the future was reported in an exit poll conducted in the greater Philadelphia area among Jewish voters, ages 18-29. Almost 60% voted for George W. Bush. My hope is that this writing will lend further encouragement to young Jews to continue this change in their political affiliation from liberal to conservative.

The closeness of the popular vote with a margin of less than one-half of one percent separating the two candidates, out of over 105,000,000 cast, can be taken as an indication that if Jews will eventually see the light as presented in this writing, they could become a decisive force for enhancing political and economic freedom in this blessed land. One would have thought that with all the Democrats had going for them in this election, peace and great prosperity, a sitting vice president with twenty-four years of federal service as their candidate, and a relatively amateurish Texas governor as the opponent, this should have been a slam dunk Democrat win.

That it was not a Democrat win means to me that there is perhaps a growing belief among the American electorate that big government has its limitations, and that possibly it is time to try some new approaches to solving our most pressing domestic problems. Certainly there must be a number of Jews who are among this group but who are still too emotionally tied to their Democratic backgrounds to make the definitive split. My message to these Jews is to open your minds to new thoughts, to take another look at the disconnect between your Jewish religion and today's liberalism, and to not be afraid of taking the plunge to change your voting pattern.

So we begin 2001 with a Republican president and with Republicans in control of both houses of Congress for the first time in fifty years. How much they will be able to accomplish to improve the lives of our citizens is unknown at this time. I can only hope and pray that their actions will bring credit to themselves, their families, and this country, and that the cause of freedom for all will be advanced.

We close this writing as we began, with the premise that the highest political goal for Jews must be **freedom**. Freedom for Jews to live our lives as we choose, to worship our God without restraint, to recognize that to help others we must strengthen and enhance our divinely inspired system of free enterprise, and to ensure the continuation of our role as God's "chosen people" through a renewal of faith in our Jewish religion and traditions. Only by discarding the outworn and obsolete liberalism, which has served as an unwelcome surrogate for Judaism these past two generations, and still entraps too many American Jews, in this writer's opinion, can these goals be achieved. I hope that in a small way this book will provide assistance and encouragement to those who are open to making this critical change.

POST SCRIPT— 21 OCTOBER 2004

The most important election in my lifetime, perhaps, is just twelve days hence, and I am feeling some concern about the probable results. I simply cannot visualize or tolerate the thought that the anti-American, (progressive) liberal senator from Massachusetts, John F. Kerry, may actually become our president for the next four years and his running mate, the North Carolina politician masquerading as a compassionate trial attorney, Sen. John Edwards, may become our vice-president. Both of them stand in such contrast to our patriotic, red-blooded candidates, George W. Bush and Dick Cheney, that one would think the contest should be a landslide instead of too close to call.

The thought that keeps resurfacing in my mind, however, is can it be possible that Bush lost the campaign based on the first debate against Kerry, held on 30 September 2004? This is the one that was supposed to favor Bush, as the subject was foreign affairs, his specialty. Instead, Bush appeared tired, whereas Kerry, with his resonant voice, looked quite presidential. Bush did not get into Kerry's terrible voting record on defense issues but devoted much of his time to simply saying it is "hard work" to try and democratize Iraq after twenty years of dictatorship.

The results were that Kerry was adjudged the winner of the debate by a large margin. His poll numbers leaped upwards, reducing his losing margin to Bush from eight points to a slim two. Was this another case, I wondered, where the Republican candidate, debating against a Democratic senator from Massachusetts with the initials of JFK, would lose the election based on that debate?

After all, let us remember that in 1960, an incumbent vice-president, Richard Nixon, in the lead at the time, debated against a first-time

Catholic candidate, a Democratic senator from Massachusetts, with those same initials of JFK. That JFK, of course, was John Fitzgerald Kennedy, who went on to defeat Nixon in a very close election, aided by the "theft" of Illinois and Texas, courtesy of his father, Joe Kennedy, reportedly in collaboration with the Mafia.

That decisive debate, when Nixon appeared tired on TV, in contrast to a healthy-looking John Kennedy, seemed to turn the tide in favor of Kennedy. Ironically, the voting public did not know at that time that Kennedy was loaded with serious physical problems. In contrast to the TV image, on the radio Nixon seemed strong and more positive than Kennedy during this debate. Most observers believed that Nixon won the debate on radio but lost it badly on TV. The Kennedy victory in that debate proved to be an important element in his close win. I kept asking myself after the Bush/Kerry debate, was history going to repeat itself some forty-four years later? The Nixon/Kennedy contest was held before the massive American involvement in the Vietnam War, which commenced in 1964 under the Lyndon Johnson administration, and in one sense the election was not as important as the current one, where we are now engaged in a war against the fascist, murderous Islamic terrorists. So was this going to be a repeat?

Without waiting for the final results to come in twelve days, I write now and predict that this time it will be different. This JFK is no John F. Kennedy. This JFK lacks the character, the charisma, the principles, and, yes, the patriotism of the old JFK. This Republican, George W. Bush, although not quite qualifying as a true conservative, still possesses the strength, character, and steadfastness of purpose that Nixon lacked in his campaign. This president has "balls," faith, and the wisdom to correct errors and misjudgments before they lead him in the wrong direction. This Republican, George W. Bush, will win the election for president and by more than a small margin, as the Lord God has ordained it to be.

I shall now place the matter in the Lord's hands and trust in His Divine intervention, as needed, some twelve days from this date.

Flash Forward to 2 November 2004.

As I was driving home from work in the early evening of Tuesday, 2 November 2004, election day, I was listening to my favorite talk show on KABC in Los Angeles. The moderator is an outstanding, articulate conservative named Al Rantel. Al and his associates on the program, including the Republictarian, the great Larry Elder, were reviewing the early "exit" polling reports that had come in from the important swing states of Wisconsin, Ohio, Pennsylvania, Florida, and other Eastern and Southern states.

Almost without exception, these early reports reflected amazingly strong showings by the contender John F. Kerry. Even some of Bush's Southern states demonstrated close contests. One of the radio guests predicted that, based on these reports, the election would be a landslide for Kerry. Al and Larry could do little other than to try to pinpoint the reasons for this apparent Republican defeat. They and their guests agreed that, of course, Bush's lousy first debate against Kerry had turned the election on its head and assured him a loss. Why oh why, they moaned, had Bush not prepared himself better for that tussle, and why oh why had he looked so drawn? If only Bush had appeared his normal confident, positive self—why, he would have blown away the dour-looking Kerry and made this election a sure Republican victory.

For most of my sixty-minute drive home, listening to these two politically conservative commentators whom I greatly respected, I reconciled myself to the thought that history was repeating itself and I would have to get used to the idea of a "President Kerry." I switched off the radio. Even though I had placed the matter in the Lord's hands some twelve days previously, with perfect faith that He would see that the American voters would render the right decision, for the remainder of my commute, my hope was lost.

Four years earlier, in the Bush/Gore contest, I had arrived home about seven o'clock in the evening to be greeted by my wife with the bad news that apparently Bush had lost. At the time, considering the nation was at peace, with no big problems facing us, I was rather calm. I had thought that a Bush win was a long shot, so this was no big deal. Then, as the evening progressed and the networks changed their call on Florida, I became more excited and went to bed somewhat confident that we had triumphed. This time, in 2004, with our nation at war and the result more important to our country's future, I was truly depressed as I hit our front door.

Surprise, surprise! My wife smiled as she greeted me and said that, based on the actual results pouring in, it looked as though President Bush was going to win—not by much, but by enough. I could hardly believe my ears. What about those early exit polls? It seems they had either been manipulated to make it appear that Kerry was leading or the samples had been inaccurate, or the networks had magnified the tentative findings, or whatever. No matter the reason, they were all proving to have been totally, and I mean totally, wrong. Not only was Bush winning Florida handily, but he was leading in Ohio and close in the other swing states of Michigan and Pennsylvania. Aha, I breathed—the Lord was still on the job, making sure that His blessed United States of America would not chart the wrong course and wind up in the wrong port.

History was not repeating itself. The debate was not the determining factor, although admittedly it had tightened the race. The majority of the American voters had apparently retained sufficient smarts and wisdom to plow through all the gobbledygook generated by the liberal media and all the scurrilous attacks launched against Bush by the liberal monied people, and they had weighed in on the side of righteousness, morality, strength, and patriotism, by reelecting George W. Bush as president. And for the first time since 1988, the winner had received more than 50% of the popular vote. It was 51%, to be exact—more than 60 million votes.

Not only did the president receive a resounding vote of confidence, but the Republicans gained four Senate seats and a like number of House seats. Was this a real mandate to the Republicans to make some meaningful changes and reverse the enormous growth of government?

With the war in Iraq against the radical Islamic terrorists still far from over, it would be difficult to reduce defense expenditures. But given the enormous size of the federal budget, perhaps there was room to make changes in our tax, education, and welfare systems and many of the ineffective programs that consume our tax dollars without giving value in return.

And what about the reported swing to the Republican ticket by American Jews? A swing it was not, but it was still a modest improvement. Exit polls showed a possible 25% of Jews voting Republican, as contrasted with just 19% in 2000 and a very weak 11% in 1992. So there was some progress, particularly among under-forty and Orthodox Jews, in seeing the political light. It remains a challenge to continue to strive to turn on that political light for more Jews, to help them connect the dots between the principles of their religion and political conservatism.

What will happen next, no one knows. I hope for the best. In the meantime, I will continue my personal mission of trying to politically convert American Jews from their godless liberalism to a more God-centered conservatism, for the benefit of not only this nation but American Judaism itself.

SELECTED BIBLIOGRAPHY

As the author, I have chosen to list here the writings that I have found useful in the writing of this book. This bibliography is by no means a complete record of all the works or sources that I have consulted. It indicates the substance and range of reading upon which I have formed my ideas. It is intended to serve as a convenience for those wishing to pursue their own inquiry deeper into the subject of this book.

Books.

Abrams, Elliott. *Faith or Fear.* New York: The Free Press, 1997.

Adler, Morris. *The World of the Talmud.* New York: Schocken Books, 1963.

Birmingham, Stephen. *Our Crowd.* New York: Dell, 1967.

Bork, Judge Robert. *Slouching Towards Gomorrah.* New York: Regan Books, 1996.

Cahill, Thomas. *The Gifts of the Jews.* New York: Nan A Talose, 1998.

de Sola Pool, Rabbi David. *Why I Am A Jew?* New York: Nelson, 1957.

de Tocqueville, Alexis. *Democracy in America.* New York: Alfred A. Knopf, 1987.

Dershowitz, Alan. *Chutzpah.* New York: Simon & Shuster, 1991.

Dosick, Rabbi Wayne. *Living Judaism: The Complete Guide to Jewish Belief, Tradition, and Practice.* New York: HarperCollins, 1995.

Johnson, Paul. *History of the Jews.* New York: Harper & Row, 1987.

Kedouri, Elie. Editor. *The Jewish World.* New York: Harry N. Abrams, 1979.

Kirk, Russell. *The Conservative Mind.* New York: Gateway Edition, Ltd., 1978.

Kristol, Irving. *Two Cheers for Capitalism.* New York: Basic Books, 1978.

Kung, Hans. *Judaism.* New York: Crossroad, 1992.

Kushner, Rabbi Harold. *Who Needs God?* New York: Summit Books, 1983.

Lapin, Rabbi Daniel. *America's Real War.* Sisters, Oregon: Multinonah Pub., 1999.

Lipset, Seymour Martin and Earl Raab. *Jews And The New American Scene.* New York: Harvard College Press, 1994.

Lott, Dr. John. *More Guns, Less Crime*. Chicago: University of Chicago Press, 1998.

Mayo, Bernard. *Jefferson Himself*. Charlottesville, Virginia: PUBLISHER, 1942.

Murray, Charles. *Losing Ground*. New York: Basic Books, 1984.

Podhoretz, Norman. *The Prophets: Who They Were, What They Are*. New York: The Free Press, 2002.

Rivkin, Ellis. *The Shaping of Jewish History*. Charles Scribners, 1971.

Rothschild, Michael. *Bionomics*. New York: Henry Holt & Co., 1990.

Schlessinger, Dr. Laura. *The Ten Commandements*. New York: Harper Trade, 1998.

Schwarz, Dr. Fred. *Beating the Unbeatable Foe*. Washington, DC: Regnery Pub., 1996.

Simon, Julian and Herman Kahn. *The Resourceful Earth*. New York: B. Blackwell, 1984.

Sombart, Werner. *The Jews and Modern Capitalism*. New York: The Free Press, 1913.

Sowell, Thomas. *Visions of the Anointed*. New York: Basic Books, 1995.

Spero, Shubert. *Morality, Halakha and the Jewish Tradition*. New York: Yeshiva University Press, 1983.

Steinsaltz, Rabbi Adin. *The Essential Talmud*. New York: Basic Books, 1976.

Tamari, Dr. Meir. *With All Your Possessions: Jewish Ethics and Economic Life*. New York: The Free Press, 1987.

Hertz, Dr. J.H. ed. *The Pentateuch and Haftorahs*. London: Soncino Press, 1973.

Van den Haag, Ernest. *The Jewish Mystique*.New York: Stein & Day, 1969.

Weyl, Nathaniel. *The Jew In American Politics*. New Rochelle, New York: Arlington House, 1968.

Williamson, G.A. The Jewish War/Josephus. New York: Penguin Press, 1981.

Wouk, Herman. *The Will to Live On*. New York: Cliff Street Books, 2000.

Lecture.

Wyschogrod, Michael. Lecture at the Symposium "Conservative Trends in American Jewish Life." Spring 1964.

Periodicals.

Prager Perspective
Commentary
Judaism
Moment
Outpost
Reform Judaism
Freeman
Imprimis
National Review
Upside